ECOLOGICAL PERSPECTIVES IN BEHAVIOR ANALYSIS

ECOLOGICAL PERSPECTIVES IN BEHAVIOR ANALYSIS

Edited by

Ann Rogers-Warren, Ph.D.
Research Associate
Bureau of Child Research
University of Kansas

and

Steven F. Warren, Ph.D.
Research Associate
Department of Special
    Education
University of Kansas

University Park Press
Baltimore · London · Tokyo

UNIVERSITY PARK PRESS
International Publishers in Science and Medicine
Chamber of Commerce Building
Baltimore, Maryland 21202

Proceedings of the Kansas Conference on Ecology and Behavior Analysis,
held at the University of Kansas, Lawrence, Kansas, in October, 1976.

Library of Congress Cataloging in Publication Data

Kansas Conference on Ecology and Behavior Analysis,
University of Kansas, 1976.
Ecological perspectives in behavior analysis.

1. Behavior modification—Congresses.
2. Environmental psychology—Congresses. I. Rogers-
Warren, Ann. II. Warren, Steven F. III. Title.
[DNLM: 1. Environment—Congresses. 2. Social
behavior—Congresses. HM291 Kl6e 1976]
BF637.B4K36 1976   301.31   77-8329
ISBN 0-8391-1148-7

Contents

vi   Contents

Contributors

Donald M. Baer, Ph.D.
Department of Human Development
132 Haworth
University of Kansas
Lawrence, Kansas 66045

Robert M. Berland, Ph.D.
Child Behavior Institute
Department of Psychology
University of Tennessee
1720 Lake Avenue
Knoxville, Tennessee 37916

David E. Campbell, Ph.D.
Department of Psychology
421 Fraser
University of Kansas
Lawrence, Kansas 66045

Thomas D. Coe, Ph.D.
Child Behavior Institute
Department of Psychology
University of Tennessee
1720 Lake Avenue
Knoxville, Tennessee 37916

Donna M. Gelfand, Ph.D.
Department of Psychology
University of Utah
Salt Lake City, Utah 84112

Paul V. Gump, Ph.D.
Department of Psychology
418 Fraser
University of Kansas
Lawrence, Kansas 66045

Emily Herbert-Jackson, Ph.D.
Lawrence Day Care Program at
  Meadowbrook
313AA Bristol Terrace
Lawrence, Kansas 66044

Jacqueline Holman, Ph.D.
Education Department
Mitchell College of Advanced
  Education
Bathurst, N.S.W. 2795
Australia

David Krantz, Ph.D.
Psychology Department
Lake Forest College
Lake Forest, Illinois 60045

George Leske, M.A.
Child Behavior Institute
Department of Psychology
University of Tennessee
1720 Lake Avenue
Knoxville, Tennessee 37916

Todd R. Risley, Ph.D.
Department of Human Development
127 Haworth
University of Kansas
Lawrence, Kansas, 66045

Ann Rogers-Warren, Ph.D.
Bureau of Child Research
Language Project Preschool
1318 Louisiana
Lawrence, Kansas 66044

Robert G. Wahler, Ph.D.
Child Behavior Institute
Department of Psychology
University of Tennessee
1720 Lake Avenue
Knoxville, Tennessee 37916

Steven F. Warren, Ph.D.
Department of Special Education
308 Carruth O'Leary Hall
University of Kansas
Lawrence, Kansas 66045

Edwin P. Willems, Ph.D.
Department of Psychology
University of Houston
Cullen Boulevard
Houston, Texas 77004

Preface

Some time ago, we were involved in several discussions with Don Baer and Jackie Holman about the merits of Ed Willems' arguments for an expanded environmental awareness in the application of behavior change strategies. Jackie was finishing her review and critique of Willems' arguments (see Chapter 4), and we were conducting some ecologically relevant research related to teaching language to young children. We would have continued our nondirected, but interesting, discussion with few consequences, if Don Baer had not suggested that the arguments were timely ones that might be of interest to others in the field of psychology. Instead, following Don's suggestion, we planned a conference that would be a forum for the discussion of these issues.

The participants were invited, the conference convened, the papers read, and, to our delight, everyone participating was very excited about this new exploration of the intersection of behavioral and ecological concerns. Frankly, we were surprised. Even the most interesting research and theory often is lost in oral presentations at a conference. It is certainly an unusual circumstance when every participant actually is interested in the arguments of the other participants. The conference was a first, purposeful meeting of ecologists and behavior analysts, and the occasion represented the recognition of a common critical term: environment. Both groups had previously spoken out for the importance of environments in relation to human behavior, but they had focused on their own diverse concerns. In this meeting, the focus was on defining commonalities and shared interests as a means of developing an ecological perspective in behavior analysis.

The marriage metaphor cited in several of the chapters seems to be an appropriate description of the sudden coming together of ecologists and behavior analysts. The "marriage" may have been one of necessity, rather than the culmination of a long, romantic courtship. Behavior analysts admittedly were having difficulties with the environmental aspects of behavior change procedures, and were becoming increasingly aware of the need to consider both the target subject and the setting when formulating interventions. A behavioral ecology was imminent with, or without, a formal union.

The conference was a shotgun wedding, of sorts, but as Don Baer pointed out, even shotgun weddings can be fun. Willems' previous invitation to behavior analysts to embrace some ecological methods and concerns was accepted, at least tentatively, and the wedding was on. The behavior analysts set forth to specify a marriage contract that would be congruent with their therapeutic objectives and empirical methods. The ecologists, while willing to contribute to the behavioral technology, rightfully demanded recognition for their contribution as describers of natural ecologies and behavior. There were numerous problems of role definition, determining responsibilities for both partners, and selecting a new name (ecobehavioral) to represent the interests of both parties. And of course, there were objections to such a hasty union (see the concluding Overview for David Krantz's final comments).

In spite of it all, the wedding came off, culminating in a free exchange of ideas and the discovery that ecologists and behavior analysts have much more in common than was apparent at the start. The in-laws seemed to enjoy each other, and both sides indicated that they were pleased at the prospects for the new union.

Most weddings are fun, but relatively few marriages are as enjoyable. It remains to be seen how the ecobehavioral union will fare. There are numerous issues yet to be resolved. Many of those issues will become apparent only as the two factions interact across time and through applications of the new perspective. Todd Risley's observation, that behavior analysts will adopt an ecological perspective as quickly as the research opportunities arise, is likely to be a realistic one. If so, tests of the ecobehavioral union will be frequent, varied, and validated through empirical observation. It may be some years before the success of the marriage can be assessed accurately.

Regardless of the eventual outcome, the conference and this volume represented for us a rare opportunity to participate in the development of an intellectually exciting and potentially useful aspect of behavioral psychology. The graciousness and thoroughness of the contributors made convening the conference and assembling this book most reinforcing tasks.

A final note: Although the considerable influence of Ed Willems' initial charge to behavior analysts will be apparent throughout this volume, we wish to recognize it here as well. Behavior analysts might very well have recognized and dealt with ecological concerns as they arose; however, Willems provided an important prompt toward a new direction in behavioral research. Not only is Ed Willems a good ecological psychologist, he's a fine behavior shaper as well. He prompted us to deal with ecological problems, and by his continued interest and support, he thoroughly reinforces approximations to the target behavior. His prompts and reinforcement were critical to the current exchange of ideas between ecologists and behavior analysts.

Acknowledgments

For her invaluable help in preparing the manuscript, in all its many phases, the editors wish to thank Patsy Horner. For their input and advice throughout the course of this project, particularly in its early stages, special thanks go to Dr. Donald M. Baer and Dr. Joseph E. Spradlin. Finally, we wish to thank Dr. Richard L. Schiefelbusch, Director of the Bureau of Child Research at the University of Kansas, for arranging financial support for the Kansas Conference on Ecological Perspectives in Behavior Analysis, held in October 1976, and for his knowledgeable advice at all stages of this project.

This book is for Ruth, J. V., and Loretta, who provided the appropriate ecologies during our earliest years.

ECOLOGICAL PERSPECTIVES IN BEHAVIOR ANALYSIS

PART I
INTRODUCTION

1

The Developing Ecobehavioral Psychology

Ann Rogers-Warren and Steven F. Warren

For many years ecologists and behavior analysts have peacefully coexisted, each group paying little, if any, attention to the work of the other. In 1974, the silence was broken by Edwin Willems. In his paper "Behavioral technology and behavioral ecology," published in the *Journal of Applied Behavior Analysis* and reprinted in this volume (Chapter 2), Willems brought behavior analysts to task for not monitoring and attending to possible unintended effects of behavioral interventions. Willems argued from an ecological viewpoint that behavior does not exist in vacuuo, but is part of a delicate system. When a single behavior is changed, there are likely to be other concomitant changes. He charged that behavior analysts have a responsibility to monitor these "side effects" when conducting behavioral interventions because these effects may cause greater harm than the difficulty that the intervention was designed to alleviate. In essence, Willems demanded that behavior analysts extend their focus beyond the single target behavior and its contingencies to the broader ecosystem in which the behavior occurred, and he suggested that failure to do this would indicate irresponsibility on the part of the intervener.

The initial reply from the behavior analysts (Baer, 1974; reprinted in this volume, Chapter 3) was polite, succinct, and behavioral: if such side effects do occur, what can we do about them? Baer stated that it was necessary to know how often such effects occurred, how serious they were, and how they might be remediated before behaviorists could follow Willems' suggestions.

The new exchange between ecologists and behavior analysts did not end with Baer's remarks. Perhaps because of Willems' and Baer's articulate statements of their positions, or perhaps because Willems' comments were particularly timely and behavior analysis was rapidly coming in contact with some of the side effects and ecological considerations he had pointed out, the initial exchange has opened new channels of communication between the two groups. Integration of behavioral and ecological issues seems to be a topic whose time has come.

In October 1976, a small group of behavior analysts and ecological psychologists gathered to discuss the evolving ecological perspective in behavior analysis. This volume contains the papers presented at that conference with formal replies and comments directed toward those papers. The ecological perspective discussed at the conference and in this volume is one strongly influenced by behavioral methods and interests. It is ecological in many senses, but it is a focused form of ecology with strong ties to behavioral intervention tactics and purposes.

Ecology is a term shared by psychologists, sociologists, and educators (cf. Auerswald, 1969; Barker, 1963; Michaels, 1974; Wahler, 1972), yet there is little agreement concerning its precise definition. The meaning of ecology is still evolving, and the reported state of its evolution varies with the reporter's purpose and perspective. At least two "ecologies" are discussed in this volume. One use of the term refers to the system of intrapersonal behavior. (See the chapters in this volume by Willems, Baer, Holman, Wahler, and Warren.) The subject is viewed as demonstrating a complex of interrelated behaviors, and changes in one behavior may result in changes in other behaviors. The behavior change might be either positive or negative. For example, if a child is punished for noncompliance, other behaviors, such as physical aggression and verbal abuse, might increase. A positive behavior correlation might indicate that positive verbal and non-verbal interactions increase when sharing is reinforced in a preschool child. A second ecological perspective focuses on the subject within the physical and contingency milieu. Here it is argued that the arrangement of the setting influences the subject's behavior. The second definition is more closely aligned with the environmental ecologists' viewpoint (see Barker, 1963); however, it is definitively behavioral in its perspective. That is, although the environment is viewed as influential, it is considered a potential intervention base (see the chapters by Rogers-Warren and Risley). Environmental rearrangement is suggested to support behavior change by working in conjunction with contingency-based interventions. Using ecological information as a basis for an intervention strategy has not been traditional among ecologists, whose work has been primarily descriptive.

While these two views of ecology are somewhat divergent in definition, they share a common base: both are person-centered analyses of behavior. Thus, the term ecobehavioral has been used to distinguish current ecological issues from those that speak to broader non-person-centered concerns. For example, the work done by Barker, Wright, and their colleagues (cf. Barker, 1963; Gump, 1969; Wright, 1969), is setting-centered. The behavior of persons in the setting is of interest only as it reflects the effects of the setting dimensions. It is implicitly assumed that all persons in the setting will behave in much the same way as a result of the setting variables. Descriptions of the setting are not oriented toward any sort of therapeutic goal—the role of the ecologist is that of describer.

Ecobehavioral analysis may share the methods of ecology, but it does not share its goals. Whether viewing the intrapersonal ecosystem or the broader setting system, the analyst looks toward better, more thorough means of changing behaviors of particular persons. This is an important and difficult distinction: important because it typifies the direction of this new ecological perspective; difficult because the difference in ends (one descriptive, one change-oriented) makes the translation from ecological to behavioral methods tedious. Persons with such nearly opposing goals make uncomfortable, although enlightening, bedfellows.

The current volume does not resolve the differences between behavior analysts and ecologists, nor was it intended to. The papers presented here do not even display the full range of possible ecological perspectives. Rather, some of the currently prominent issues in ecological application in behavior change have been presented. Several papers are extensions of arguments made previously, although all of the papers (with exception of the 1974 articles by Willems and Baer) were developed for this volume.

The book contains four major sections and a concluding comment (Overview). Part I is an introduction to the issues discussed in the remainder of the book. The 1974 paper by Willems and Baer's rejoinder are reprinted here to provide the reader with additional perspective on the issues discussed in the subsequent chapters.

Part II extends the discussion of unplanned effects from the comments made in the 1974 papers. Willems offers further suggestions for integrating ecological concerns and methods into behavior analysis. He outlines four specific changes in method that will ideally provide insight into the complexity of human behavior systems. His emphasis is, as it was in 1974, on detecting the possibility of unplanned effects before they occur, and he repeatedly asks the question, "Where are the scientists ahead-of-time?" Holman approaches the issue of ecological perspectives from another viewpoint. She finds the ecological challenge to behavior modification a disturbing one, and decides it cannot be lightly discarded. Nevertheless, while retaining considerable sympathy for the viewpoint expressed by Willems, her thesis is essentially a negative one: to cease behavioral programming (and thus maintain the status quo, and eliminate the possibility of new, undesirable side effects) would be unethical, and for behavior modifiers to satisfy the ecological perspective would be a pragmatic (and theoretical) impossibility. However, she does suggest an alternative means for detecting unplanned and troublesome effects—the extended use of consumer satisfaction measures. Baer again takes up the issue of side effects and proposes a logical series of questions to be asked when and if such effects are encountered. This series of questions represents a behavior analytic approach to the problem. Baer proposes that under certain conditions the behavior analyst may be able to deal with the effects, in fact learn more about behavior by encountering them, but that in other instances, consistent, negative, difficult to control effects may signal withdrawal of behavior modification tactics from the particular problem at hand. Baer concludes that it may be necessary for the behavior analyst to learn a fine discrimination between circumstances in which side effects signal that it is not appropriate to intervene and those circumstances that signal the need for further or more thorough behavior modification. The section concludes with a summary comment by Gelfand.

In Part III, an ecologist and a behavior analyst report their views of the current state of ecological perspectives in behavior analysis. Surprisingly, their views are quite similar. Gump proposes that an ecological perspective is not only necessary, but that it is already present in behavior analysis. The only unsettled issue is whether or not behavior analysts will begin the scientific pursuit of ecological issues they encounter. Gump cites three types of relationships that ecologists currently consider and that behavior analysts must recognize as part of the evolving ecological perspective: behavior-behavior relationships (such as the side effects issues discussed in Part II), behavior-environment relationships, and environment-environment relationships. In overviewing behavioral research, he concludes that some work is already being done in each of these areas and that behavior analysts may already know more about environmental importance than they readily report.

The chapter by Risley supports Gump's conclusions to a certain extent. Risley reviews his recent work as examples of ecological concern already apparent in applied behavior analysis. Behavior analysts are, he contends, adopting an ecological perspective as quickly as the opportunities for application arise. However, implicit in the developing ecological application is an insistence on experimental analyses of environmental variables rather than descriptive data. It is at this point that the ecologists' and behaviorists' methods diverge, although they may continue to share similar perspectives on the importance of environmental variables. A brief overview and comment by Campbell concludes this section.

Part IV contains three prescriptions for applying an ecological perspective in behavioral research, the last of which is accompanied by a report of a research program that integrates both behavioral and ecological concerns. Warren proposes that a useful ecobehavioral orientation for behavior analysis can be derived from some already existing criteria of successful behavioral interventions. The criteria emphasize the durability, generality, and appropriate rate and form of a therapeutic intervention, as well as consumer satisfaction with it. They are meant to measure the outcome of a behavioral intervention. Warren argues that if the intervention is successful by these criteria, it is acceptable to the environment, and, if the intervention fails by one or more of these criteria, the intervener must change something in the treatment to make it acceptable to the surround.

The chapter by Rogers-Warren presents guidelines for application before intervening into a setting. These guidelines are intended to measure the potential support a setting offers for changing a specific behavior. She suggests that many of these guidelines may already be used by successful researchers in the process of designing interventions, and, if they are being used, they may represent an implicit ecobehavioral assessment strategy ongoing in behavior analysis. The information gained from ecobehavioral assessment may indicate not only whether or not it is possible to successfully change a target behavior in a particular setting, but it also may give some indication about what specific strategies will be most likely to succeed.

Wahler and his colleagues argue for a more broadly based systems analysis model as an alternative to the current "reeducation" model of behavior change. While the reeducation model assumes that a reprogramming of stimulus contingencies in social environments can be accomplished by teaching persons in the target subject environment the principles of operant conditioning, the systems analysis model suggests that the intervener must deal with the subject as he/she exists within a network of social systems (the family, peers, the school, the community, are a few examples of such systems). The subject is seen as a system of covarying behaviors, as are the other units of social analysis. The system of behaviors is the context in which behavior change occurs, and must be a foremost consideration in planning an intervention strategy.

Part IV concludes with two brief comments. The first, by Herbert-Jackson, is a response to the proposed tactics for implementing an ecological perspective outlined in the chapters by Warren, Rogers-Warren, and

Wahler et al. The second comment, by Krantz, speaks to the more general focus of all the chapters. Krantz suggests that there may be greater theoretical differences between ecologists and behavior analysts than first meets the eye, and he cautions both parties to proceed slowly, because joining forces could be potentially harmful for both schools of thought.

Finally, a closing comment and caution to the reader: these papers should not be taken as a complete or final definition of the possible interaction between ecology and applied behavior analysis. It is hoped that this volume reports only the beginning of a long and dynamic relationship. The definition of ecobehavioral psychology will be a complex one. Certainly, it is not yet clearly defined. There are many signs of growing pains. As Krantz points out, the terms of the wedding contract must be carefully considered before either party enters into such a potentially wonderful and troublesome agreement. Perhaps no wedding will occur, but only a long-term friendship based on shared interests and accomplishments.

It is hoped that this volume will be read in the spirit in which it was compiled: not as a search for simple answers, but as an exploration of a developing segment of the science of human behavior.

LITERATURE CITED

Auerswald, E. H. 1969. Interdisciplinary versus ecological approach. In W. Gray, F. J. Duhl, and N. D. Rizzo (eds.), General Systems Theory and Psychiatry, pp. 375–386. Little, Brown and Co., Boston.

Barker, R. G. 1963. The Stream of Behavior. Appleton-Century-Crofts, New York.

Gump, P. V. 1969. Intra-setting analysis: The third grade classroom as a special but instructive case. In E. P. Willems and H. L. Rausch (eds.), Naturalistic Viewpoints in Psychological Research. Holt, Rinehart, and Winston, New York.

Michaels, J. W. 1974. On the relation between human ecology and behavioral social psychology. Social Forces 57: 313–321.

Wahler, R. G. 1972. Some ecological problems in child modification. In S. W. Bijou and E. Ribes-Inesta (eds.), Behavior Modification: Issues and Extensions, pp. 7–18. Academic Press, New York.

Wright, H. F. 1969. Children's behavior in communities differing in size. Parts 1, 2, 3, Supplement. Department of Psychology, University of Kansas, Lawrence, Kan.

2

Behavioral Technology and Behavioral Ecology

Edwin P. Willems

Technology is the systematic application of tested scientific principles to pragmatic, real-life tasks and problems. On these terms, applied behavior analysis, or behavior modification, is a behavioral technology *par excellence*. In fact, the basic research paradigm is also the basic treatment paradigm, and the basic research manipulation—contingency management—is also the treatment manipulation. This close coordination of the treatment model to the research process surrounds applied behavior analysis with an enviable degree of explicitness, rigor, and precision.

Once developed, technologies are usually used, and the tendency to use them increases in proportion to the precision with which they can be applied. Thus, we can anticipate phenomenal growth in the array of behavior problems, settings, age groups, and diagnostic groups to which behavior modification will be applied, partly because its precision and specificity will continue to increase, and partly because its developers and users display an unusual amount of zeal and optimism about their work. The purpose of this paper is to raise some troubling questions about this expansionist approach by outlining a larger ecological framework within which the enthusiastic proliferation of simple strategies of behavior change should be evaluated and planned. "With each decade, scientific findings translated into technology radically reshape the way we live. Technical capacity has been the ruling imperative, with no reckoning of cost, either

Reprinted by permission from *Journal of Applied Behavior Analysis,* 1974, 7:151–165.

Work on this paper was supported in part by Research and Training Center No. 4 (RT–4), Baylor College of Medicine, funded by Social and Rehabilitation Services, USDHEW.

ecological or personal. If it could be done, it has been done. Foresight has lagged far behind craftsmanship. At long last we are beginning to ask, not *can* it be done, but *should* it be done? The challenge is to our ability to anticipate second- and third-order consequences of interventions in the ecosystem before the event, not merely to rue them afterward" (Eisenberg, 1972, p. 123).

Even though its major principles are just now being formulated, the ecological perspective on behavior should offer the behavior technologist grounds for deep concern about his work. To set the stage for these arguments, a word is in order regarding behavioral ecology, some of its general implications, and some of its commonalities with applied behavior analysis.

AN ECOLOGICAL PERSPECTIVE

Complex interrelationships and interdependencies within organism-behavior-environment systems and the behavioral, adaptive dependencies between organism and habitat are among the central interests of the ecological perspective on behavior. These are challenging issues, because full understanding of such interdependencies requires attention to complexity of a kind for which psychology is hardly prepared. These issues can be illustrated by examples and analogies, some of which fall outside of psychology.

Macro-Ecology

We know now that large-scale attempts to rid whole areas of insect-borne diseases and to release crops from the ravages of insects have created very unpleasant but unanticipated results, also on a large scale. Some 20 years ago, with the noblest and most humane intentions, the world-wide use of insecticide technology began. Many results of this world-wide experiment are now in, and we have observed: (1) new, larger outbreaks of insect pests due to the killing, by the insecticides, of their natural predators, (2) explosive emergence of insect strains that are resistant to even the most advanced insecticides, and (3) the accumulation of high concentrations of insecticides sufficient to do great harm to and threaten the survival of many top carnivores, such as birds of prey and, perhaps, even man.

The second example comes from the Aswan Dam on the Nile River (Murdoch and Connell, 1970). The reasons for building were humane and respectable—to supply water for irrigation, to prevent floods, and to manufacture electrical power. However, two sets of unpleasant and unanticipated effects resulted from the dam. One was the reduction in the sardine harvest in the Mediterranean Sea, from 18,000 tons to about 500 tons per year because the dam disrupted the cycle involving silt-nutrient seeding, plankton, and fish. A second effect has been a profound increase in both the incidence and virulence of schistosomiasis among the people of the Nile, because quiet waters (behind the dam) harbor snails that carry more virulent blood flukes than running water (the old river) and because the new stable bodies of water have attracted large numbers of people.

It is clear that our humane efforts to apply proven technology and to alleviate human suffering on a large scale can go awry in the most vexing ways. More importantly, (1) we simply do not have enough basic understanding of environmental systems, and (2) there is something pervasively wrong with our available understanding of environment-inhabitant systems and the impact of singular intrusions into those systems. In the insecticide and Aswan Dam cases, we are now quite sure that they are ecological phenomena whose complexity was not anticipated because we know now what happened—someone has discovered the principles that govern such events. Many other examples could be cited, e.g., long-range effects of introducing new species of organisms into a given habitat, wide-spread crop diseases resulting from attempts to increase yield by reducing genetic diversity.

More Direct Examples: Micro-Ecology

There are analogies and examples that are closer to our primary level of analysis. In one case, an ornithologist with a European zoo wished to add a bird called the bearded tit to the zoo's collection.[1] Armed with all the relevant information he could find about the tit, the ornithologist went to great pains to build the right setting. Introducing a male and female to the setting, he noted that, by all behavioral criteria, the birds functioned very well. Unfortunately, soon after the birds hatched babies, they shoved the babies out of the nest, onto the ground, where they died. This cycle, beginning with mating and ending with the babies dead on the ground, repeated itself many times.

The ornithologist tried many modifications of the setting, but none forestalled the infanticide. After many hours of direct observation of tits in the wild, the ornithologist noted three patterns of behavior that had missed everyone's attention. First, throughout most of the daylight hours in the wild, the parent tits were very active at finding and bringing food

---

[1] I am indebted to Robert B. Lockard for this story. If the story has lost or gained anything in the present use, the fault is mine. Lockard's recent paper (1971) on the "fall of comparative psychology" also offers strong corroboration of the present suggestions.

for the infants. Second, the infants, with whose food demands the parents could hardly keep pace, spent the same hours with their mouths open, apparently crying for food. The third pattern was that any inanimate object, whether eggshell, leaf, or beetle shell, was quickly shoved out of the nest by the parents. With these observations in mind, the ornithologist went back to observe his captive tits, and he found that during the short time a new brood of infants lived, the parents spent only brief periods feeding them by racing between the nest and the food supply, which the ornithologist had provided in abundance. After a short period of such feeding, the infants, apparently satiated, fell asleep. The first time the infants slept for any length of time during the daylight hours, the parents shoved them (two inanimate objects, after all) out of the nest. When he made the food supply less abundant and less accessible, and thereby made the parents work much longer and harder to find food, the ornithologist found that the infants spent more daylight time awake, demanding food, and that the tits then produced many families and cared for them to maturity.

There are several important implications of this story. The first is the subtlety and elusiveness of the interdependencies among: (1) some aspects of a total environment, (2) the ongoing, short-range behavior of the birds, and (3) some long-range outcome. The second is that neither the designer's good will nor the technologist's respect or concern for his subjects will themselves ensure his creating the right environment. The third implication is more complex and has to do with the criteria that are used in making evaluative inferences about intervention efforts. All the indicators in the behavior of the parent tits suggested that their captive environment was congenial and hospitable and that it fulfilled their needs. Yet, the long-range criterion of survival of the captive representatives of the species (a surprise, a shock to the ornithologist) pointed to a very different conclusion about the environment. It is easy to look in the wrong place for indicators of success in intervention. We must pick and choose our criteria with the greatest care, perhaps flying in the face of what common sense, accepted social wisdom, and even past success with our technologies tell us is humane, important, and worthwhile. The last implication points to methodology. Since it involves behavior and behavior-environment relations, the case of the bearded tit and its human analogs would be of direct interest to the psychologist. And yet, our traditional methods of research on humans hardly put us in a position to elucidate the real-life interdependencies of behaviors and environments. We say that systems concepts, complex dependencies, reciprocity, and extended time-related cycles must be entertained as descriptive and explanatory terms, but they almost never show up in the actual reports of our research. By and large, we continue to study behavior as though its important phenomena were simple, single-file, and relatively short-term.

The behavior of the predators of lemmings in Alaska is also instructive (Sears, 1969). Living and breeding under the snow, lemmings have a cyclical population record, in which high and low density alternate in fairly regular fashion. When the snow melts, they are preyed upon by a variety of animals, including the jaeger, a kind of sea hawk resembling a gull. When the lemming population is low or average, the jaegers space their nests and consume their prey in orderly fashion. But, when the lemming population is at its peak, so that food is no problem, there is a great deal of fighting over nesting space and food among the jaegers. Few of them raise normal broods and their numbers decline, but not from lack of food. Plenty is not the road to biological success among the jaegers, and their behavioral development is somehow involved in this paradox. Again, the governing principles, the interdependencies, are little understood.

Several years ago, Proshansky, Ittelson, and Rivlin attempted to increase the therapeutic effectiveness of psychiatric facilities through environmental design (Chapters 3 and 43 in Proshansky, Ittelson, and Rivlin, 1970). They focused their efforts on one ward of a state mental hospital. The ward was laid out on one long corridor, with a nurses' station at one end, near the entrance, and a solarium at the other end, with bedrooms, a bathroom, and a dayroom in between. The solarium, which was meant to be a place of relaxation and recreation, was overheated, poorly furnished, and generally unappealing, with intense sunlight pouring in through a bank of uncovered windows. It was used very little, even though there was a TV set there. Just about the only thing patients did consistently in the solarium was to stand alone for long periods of time in a state of preoccupation, detachment, and withdrawal—that singular behavior pattern in which severely disturbed persons engage so much. This isolated standing was one of the behavior patterns that the hospital staff wished to change. The psychologists changed the solarium by adding furniture, drapes, and other small accessories. Immediately, larger numbers of patients began spending longer periods of time there and the solarium took on the air of a pleasant recreational and social area. More importantly, the rate of isolated standing behavior went down so that very little of it now occurred in the solarium. The psychologists had achieved their purpose—for the solarium. However, all they had succeeded in doing was to change the *location* of the isolated standing behavior—a great deal of it now took place at the other end of the corridor, by the nurses' station. Luckily, these intervention agents did not restrict their focus to the solarium, but studied a whole environment-behavior *system,* of which the solarium was only one component. Creating the environmental conditions for reducing the level of troubling behavior in one part of the system had only shifted the behavior to another part.

Some years ago, New York City police, in work with gangs, engaged in a program of intervention whose purpose was to break up the gangs and their fighting behavior. Several troublesome and unanticipated phenomena accompanied their systematic intervention: outbreaks of vandalism, isolated drug-taking, feelings of alienation, and serious crimes of assault (Philip G. Zimbardo, personal communication). These phenomena beg for further research, but if the accompanying phenomena can be attributed to the intervention, then they point again to the system-like complexity of behavioral phenomena.

At CCNY in 1965, a student snack bar was closed for several months in mid-year to permit remodeling. On the basis of independent observation and tallies of seating patterns and occupancy before and after the remodeling, it was possible to ascertain that the proportions of occupancy by blacks and whites and the cross-racial seating patterns that had reached a very stable level before the closing never reinstated themselves afterwards (Zimbardo, unpublished).

Some General Implications

Other examples and the key aspects of the ecological perspective on behavior are presented elsewhere (Barker, 1965; 1968; 1969; Willems, 1965; 1973; in press). However, if we think of the implications of such phenomena and what they suggest (emphasis on suggest) about human behavior in general, and if we think about the growing pressure to apply known behavioral technologies, the following observation emerges: we have become fairly conservative and sophisticated about introducing new biotic elements and new chemicals into our ecological systems, but we display almost childish irresponsibility in our attitudes toward behavioral and behavioral-environmental systems. I am thinking here about many of our favorite sacred cows: (1) intensive psychotherapy upon single, perhaps arbitrarily selected, members of social and behavioral networks, (2) poverty programs, (3) social change programs in which simplistic measures of attitudes or values provide the criteria of change, (4) managerial and industrial consultations in which we intrude arbitrarily into organizational-behavioral systems about which we know little, (5) educational programs, and (6) yes, even that most solidly empirical of sacred cows— contingency management in the modification of behavior. Applied behavior modification is an astonishingly simple and successful technology of behavior change. However, its precision and objectivity depend, in large part, upon its application to single dimensions of behavior, one at a time. The questions of larger and unintended effects within interpersonal and environmental contexts and over long periods of time beg for evaluation and research because lessons learned in other areas suggest that we should always be sensitive to "other" effects of single-dimensional intrusions.

It is becoming clear in the ecological literature that "we can never do merely one thing" (Hardin, 1969), that every intervention has its price, no matter how well intentioned the agent of intervention may be. The counter-argument often is: "Don't try to immobilize us with all that alarmist talk. We'll deal with side effects when they come up. After all, we're not stupid!" However, when we think in terms of environment-behavior *systems*, we can see that there is a fundamental misconception embedded in that popular term, "side effects" (Hardin, 1969). This phrase means, roughly, "effects which I hadn't intended, hadn't foreseen, or don't want to think about." What we so glibly call "side effects" no more deserve the adjective "side" than does the "principal" effect—they are all aspects of the interdependencies that we need so badly to understand. But it is hard to think in terms of systems, and we eagerly warp our language to protect ourselves and our favorite approaches from the necessity of thinking in terms of interdependent systems. It is quite foreign to us to think of the physical and behavioral environment as inextricable parts of the behavioral processes of organisms and as relating to them in ways that are extremely complex.

For the student of behavior, there is much to be learned from this emerging ecological orientation, but if the lessons are learned, then there is an immediate and pervasive need for an expansion of perspective. Until a few years ago, technologists believed that most, if not all, of their develop-ments would be useful in a rather direct and simple sense. We know now that this is not necessarily true—feasibility and even intrinsic success are not sufficient grounds for immediate application. This widening aware-ness—the ecological perspective—suggests that many things that *can* be done either should not be done or should be done most judiciously, and that more technology will not provide solutions to many technologically induced problems (Dubos, 1965, 1970–1971; Eisenberg, 1972). Before we can be truly effective at alleviating human suffering, we must know much more about the principles that characterize and govern the systems into which such alleviating efforts must, of necessity, intrude. Seeking that knowledge raises a host of theoretical, metatheoretical, and methodologi-cal problems.

One implication of this line of argument may well be a conservatism with regard to intervention in behavior-environment systems and the clear hint that the most adaptive form of action may sometimes be *in*action.

The problem is that we know little as yet about the circumstances under which the price for action outweighs the price of inaction and vice versa. So, if we give the above examples and arguments a slight interpretive twist, we arrive at a second implication that is even more important. This is the clear suggestion that we need a great deal more basic research and theoretical understanding that take account of the ecological, system-like principles that permeate the phenomena of behavior and environment. There is immediate need for a systematic basis to plan behavioral interventions and technologies in such a way that they will not produce unanticipated negative costs in behavior-environment systems.

THE PROBLEM OF EFFECTIVE BEHAVIORAL TECHNOLOGY

A frequent and inevitable accompaniment of progress in basic scientific understanding is the transformation of that understanding into technology. When technology is developed, there follows the understandable predilection to apply it and explore its range of application. This is just as true of behavioral technology as it is of medical procedures, pharmaceutics, cleaning agents, insecticides, electronics, food preparation, and agriculture. This tendency is even more reasonable in the case of behavior modification, because the paradigms of research and application are so closely intertwined. As the procedures of intervention become more powerful, more sophisticated, and more precise, their *intended* effects become easier to specify. However, most technological interventions also have *unintended* effects. One would think that increased power, sophistication, and precision would ensure greater ability to specify and anticipate unintended effects. But they do not. From the ecological standpoint, this is a fundamental issue, and it may call for mounting investigative efforts that have not been designed as yet.

The ingenuity involved in the widespread use of various forms of applied behavior modification need not be documented here. Together with some techniques of psychopharmacology, the contingency-management paradigm probably represents the most powerful technology of behavior change available today. This admirable power and precision, which has been demonstrated hundreds of times over and which is the great strength of the approach, is also the reason for greatest concern. First, there is the problem of the metaphor of the world as a vast, programmed, learning situation and the problem of failures and partial successes. When operant technology is applied with a particular behavioral outcome in mind and the result is outright failure, marginal success, or some vexing behavioral drift over time, it is easy to assert that no larger, system-wide problem or no *theoretical* problem has arisen; that there is only the need for more technological ingenuity and for more rigorous programming and control of contingencies. I submit that there is a theoretical issue here that has to do with assumptions and predictions not borne out and with the overall adequacy of the operant view of behavior to deal with behavior-environment phenomena. As an ecologist, I would prefer that behavior analysts became involved in clarifying the profoundly complicated and theoretical nature of the simplified interfaces they arrange between organisms and environments. The behavior modifier is justified in his pride over the power of contingencies of reinforcement and in arguing eloquently for his simple solutions to many pressing social and behavioral problems. I just wish that he and others could *join* in reflecting upon and probing into the principles and laws that govern what must surely be very complicated systems in which organisms, behavior, environmental events, *and* the technologist's programmed intervention are all implicated. I say this partly because such a strategy has been very fruitful in other areas of science, and partly because we also know that, depending upon the time, the place, the organism, the state of the organism, and many other as yet unknown properties of natural settings, the behavior analyst has degrees of success that range from extremely high down to zero.

Clearly, the theoretical issue and the implications of partial success boil down to a matter of preference. The devotee of behavior modification can certainly disregard those questions and go about his work productively. However, the second reason why this behavioral technology gives me pause is less a matter of personal preference and more a matter of unavoidable professional and practical importance. This is the problem of the possible implications of success. What we admire so much about the behavior modification approach is the rigor of the paradigm and the explicitness with which a successful outcome can be specified and evaluated. What worries me is the distinct possibility of unanticipated accompaniments of success. In part, I am arguing by analogy from such phenomena as the insecticide problem, but there are examples from behavioral research that are also suggestive.

Recently, I heard a description of some attempts to modify the behavior of parents of troubled children. One subject-mother was observed to nag (emit commands) at rates of up to 100 or more per hour, and the child complied at a very low rate. The rate of mother's commands was reduced to an average of 15 per hour, and, correspondingly, the proportion of compliance on the part of the child went up. This was the outcome that had been designated as successful. However, the investigator went on to report difficulty in dealing with this case. As the study progressed and as the shaping of nagging succeeded, the mother's rate of eating went up, she gained weight, and she reported frequent anxiety and tension. Finally, she abandoned the child and left town. These events were seen by the investigator as only an unfortunate and vexing interruption of the treatment program.

In the Probation Department of Los Angeles, some explicit use has been made of token systems and other behavior modification techniques in dealing with deviant behavior among adolescent boys.[2] The probation officers were successful in reducing the rates of petty vandalism, such as stealing hubcaps and items from stores. However, as the petty vandalism went down, the rates of more serious offenses, such as stealing cars and destroying property, went up. It goes without saying that such phenomena beg for further research before any definitive statements can be made about their causal linkages. However, that is precisely my point: the phenomena beg for research, but they beg for research that: 1) *admits the possibility* of unanticipated complexities, 2) uses models that lead us to look for them and define them as real phenomena, and 3) adds procedures that allow their detection and measurement when they occur.

Arguing against a simplistic interpretation of operant behavior control, Wahler (unpublished) raises the possibility of *indirect* stimulus control, i.e., that one set of behaviors can be maintained or affected by reinforcers applied directly to other behaviors. He argues that these phenomena can occur because of unaccounted and unmeasured covariations among naturally occurring behaviors. One commonly accepted form of complex covariation is chaining, wherein a sequence of behaviors is maintained by a single reinforcer following the last response. More interesting for present purposes are other covariations that do not readily fit the chaining model because they do not always occur in the same temporal order (e.g., Buell et al., 1968). Wahler et al. (1970) showed that parents' successful efforts to reduce nonspeech deviant behaviors by their children also led to reductions in stuttering and that this "side effect" was not due to differential reinforcement of stuttering and fluent speech. Wahler uses the term *response class* to denote naturally occurring, covarying, functional units of behavior that arise by means of processes that are unknown at present, and he argues:

> Not only are developmental and maintenance features of the response class unknown, but predictions about which behaviors will become so

---

[2] Personal communication from Mr. Caldwell M. Prejean, who was a probation officer in Los Angeles for three years.

organized are equally vague. When a clinical investigator restricts his operations to one child behavior, he has no way of knowing what other behaviors emitted by the child will be affected by that operation. Unless his baseline observations encompass multiple behaviors, including a correlational analysis of these observations, the complete outcome of his intervention procedures cannot be predicted in most cases. . . . Simply stated, these guidelines first require the investigator to monitor more than a single troublesome behavior presented by the child. However, rules concerning what other behaviors to record are necessarily vague at this point.

It is from such phenomena that unanticipated effects of interventions are made. At present, we know almost nothing about the properties of situations, places, persons, and interactions that affect and maintain such complex covariations in nonlaboratory behavior.

Another clear example comes from the work of Sajwaj, Twardosz, and Burke (1972), who found various "side effects" of manipulating single behaviors in a preschool boy. For example, using ignoring by the teacher to reduce the child's initiated speech to the teacher in one setting of the preschool led to systematic changes in other behaviors by the child in the same setting and in another setting as well. Some of the "side effects" were desirable (increasing speech initiated to children, cooperative play), while some were undesirable (decreasing task-appropriate behavior, increasing disruptive behavior), and some were neutral (use of girls' toys). The investigators were able to show that the covarying effects were not due to differential contingent attention by the teacher applied directly to those behaviors, but were somehow (as yet, mysteriously) a function of modifying another single dimension of behavior. Sajwaj et al. consider it distinctly possible that modifying one behavior modifies the properties of the larger setting, thus changing the system of contingencies and the opportunity for reinforcers to contact behaviors. We know almost nothing as yet about governing principles in such systems or about the ways in which behaviors and behaviors and environments form clusters or covarying units in the everyday world. Such system-like ecological phenomena must be elucidated if we are ever to substitute rational anticipation and planning in the use of operant approaches, where we now fight only brush fires on unintended results.

COMMONALITIES AND SOME IMPLICATIONS

The ecological and behavior modification points of view seem to operate from quite different values and assumptions. Differences, strongly stated, may stimulate research and thus progress, but the explicit phrasing of commonalities is a step toward another form of scientific progress–the common formulation of principles and procedural styles (see Krantz, 1971).

Shared Values

Contrary to some widely held views, the ecological perspective is not a single, unified body of theory, nor is it defined by any particular method (Willems, 1973). Rather, it is an orientation, a set, a perspective, that leads the investigator to do his research, ask his questions, and view his phenomena in certain distinctive ways. Behavioral ecology as an enterprise has some distinctive features, even though it is not *a* model or *a* theory (Menzel, 1969; Willems, 1965, 1973). Here are several values that behavioral ecology and the behavior modification movement hold in common.[3]

1. Empiricism and Objectivity In general, the ecologist and the applied behavior analyst are socialized to place a great deal of emphasis upon empirical data, especially if they must choose between complex, speculative theories and an empirical base. For both, the ratio of empirical data to theory is higher than it is for many other subdisciplines, and both prefer to base their generalizations on extensive data sets. However, if we add the criteria of explicitness and rigor, then, at least in psychology, it is quite clear to me that the behavior analyst has it over the behavioral ecologist. The behavioral ecologist admires and aspires to the behavior analyst's objectivity, but does not often achieve it. Both are known to say, "Let's look at the facts," but there may be some intriguing differences in the facts they seek.

2. Environment as Selective Both emphasize a transactional view of behavior, i.e., that the organism's functioning is mediated by behavior-environment interaction. This transactional credo, which is foreign to many scientists, is so dear to both that Skinner might as well be speaking for both when he says: "The environment is obviously important, but its role has remained obscure. It does not push or pull, it *selects*, and this function is difficult to discover and analyze . . . the selective role of the environment in shaping and maintaining the behavior of the individual is only beginning to be recognized and studied" (1971, p. 25). The implications of this view are widespread (see Platt, 1972), but two that are accepted by the behavioral ecologist and behavior analyst are: 1) that behavior is largely controlled by the environmental setting in which it occurs, and 2) that changing environmental variables results in the modification of behavior.

---

[3] It should not be implied from this listing of shared values that other professionals would not share some or all of them.

3. Importance of Site Specificity   One offshoot of the transactional character of behavior and its responsiveness to environmental selection is the phenomenon of site specificity of behavior. Both the behavioral ecologist and the behavior analyst assume site specificity, know it from their own work, and urge other professionals to recognize the strong linkages between place and behavior (see Barker, 1968; King, 1970; and Sells, 1969 for the ecologist's argument). "The correlation between site and activity is often so high that an experienced ecological psychologist (or behavior analyst)[4] can direct a person to a particular site in order to observe an animal exhibiting a given pattern of behavior" (King, 1970, p. 4). Furthermore, the behavior analyst offers the behavioral ecologist a very promising model for understanding site specificity. Whether the governing principles must always be labeled *contingency control* or *stimulus control* is a separate issue.

4. Baseline Data on Behavior   Both the behavioral ecologist and behavior analyst tend to focus upon what organism *do,* defined quite physicalistically, in relation to the environment and tend to deemphasize what organisms feel, think, and say about their behavior and environment. A common value follows from this behavioral emphasis, i.e., both attach fundamental importance to gathering extensive, reliable, relatively atheoretical data as a starting point for their work. Both tend to begin by obtaining unusually extensive observations of their phenomena of interest because they insist upon documenting the frequency and distribution of behavior and upon understanding the descriptive character of the behavior with which they are working. Their activities diverge sharply after such baseline observation, but this commonality is worth noting (see also Bijou, Peterson, and Ault, 1968).

5. Environmental Measurement   Closely related to the baseline observation of behavior is the emphasis of both groups upon explicit documentation, measurement, and recording of the environment of behavior. The fact that they conceptualize the environment quite differently is less interesting than the fact that both actually *carry out* environmental measurement as part of their work, i.e., that both usually engage in observation of the objective environment of behavior.

6. Commonplaceness   Perusal of the writings of the behavioral ecologist and behavior analyst indicates that, to an unusual degree, both accept common, ordinary, everyday behaviors as primary phenomena to be described, counted, understood, explained (ecologist), and manipulated (modifier). Both proceed on the basis that "science advances by relentless

---

[4] My addition.

examination of the commonplace; that some of its greatest discoveries have been made through fascination with what other men have regarded as not worthy of note" (Henry, 1971, p. xix). Thus, the naturalistic observation of the ecologist and the baseline observation of the applied behavior analyst bulge with reference to such ordinary phenomena as location of persons, eating, talking, resting, fighting, reading, holding and handling objects, participating in activities, making mistakes, etc. The fact that each tends to do different things with commonplace events should not becloud the fact that both attach fundamental scientific importance to the common, mundane behavior repertoires of persons, rather than to highly abstract, rarified concepts.

7. *Common Sense and Principles of Behavior*   Beyond the emphasis on commonplace events is another shared value. Everyone has some intuition regarding his behavior and the behavior of others. Conventional social wisdom and commonsense principles of how things work and what is right, good, and humane permeate what people say about behavior and behavior change. Beyond the value placed on common behaviors as primary data, I detect that both the behavioral ecologist and behavior analyst display an unusual openness to accepting, pursuing, and discovering explanations and governing principles that are counter-intuitive and violate common sense. Furthermore, once the principles have been found to hold, it is probably true that both show an unusual degree of willingness to promote pragmatic programs that violate conventional social wisdom or commonly held views of what is humane. The phenomena of punishment (Baer, 1971; Birnbrauer, Burchard, and Burchard, 1970), contingent love (Baer, 1969), and amount of effort (bearded tit example above) illustrate what I mean.

8. *Intervention and its Effects*   Finally, the behavioral ecologist and behavior analyst share a common value—maybe even a converging fate—at the level of studying the effects of intervention. Even the most narrowly focused behavior modifier is (or should be) interested, case by case, in creating the conditions for shaping and maintaining a particular level of functioning in a behavior-environment system. We know little as yet about the extent to which he does that successfully in the long run. We do know what he does extremely well—achieving categorical outcomes in behavior by means of dimensional management of contingencies. He says, "Show me the specific troublesome behavior," and then applies a highly specific remedy to it. This approach satisfies a fundamental principle of applied ecology: control measures that are as specific as possible to the particular troubling events are always preferable (see Odum, 1963, pp. 106–107). However, another fundamental principle of applied ecology and an objec-

tive of ecological research is: we must improve our ability to predict the results of intrusions in ecological systems, and thereby more intelligently prescribe or avoid the removal of vital behaviors or the inadvertent addition of dysfunctional ones (Odum, 1963, p. 27). Thus, far more than other strategies of behavior change, the work of the behavior modifier fulfills one ecological principle. The work of the behavioral ecologist emphasizes the second. This should be seen as a logical and productive opportunity, rather than a diversion of basic values. Logic would dictate that the behavioral ecologist and the behavior modifier link efforts to fulfill both principles.

Interdependent Effort

The behavior modifier and behavioral ecologist are both deeply concerned with interfaces between behavior and environment. Now, both must formulate and promote a new kind of interface—the interface between their separate and mutual concerns, skills, and efforts. The time has come to demand of the behavior modifier that he provide information and insight regarding the ways in which the effects of his interventions ramify across other phenomena that may extend widely into physical, social, and behavioral space and across time. He need not do this alone, of course, but he must open up his domain to disconcerting questions and outside interests. Analogously, the time has come to demand of the behavioral ecologist that he open up his domain, that he articulate his questions and principles in such a way that they can be evaluated in the arena of real behavior problems and real attempts to apply behavioral technology, and that he accept the results of replicated experiments and intervention attempts as valuable and crucial data (Willems, 1973).

Not only is it scientifically critical that the behavior analyst and ecologist engage in new forms of cooperative effort, joint-event research, or piggybacking (Eisenberg, 1972; Kranzberg, 1972), but the practical products will be worth the investment of effort and ingenuity.

The ecologist and the behavior modifier work differently, they work with different objectives, they tend to use their data very differently, *but* they have much to offer each other. The strength of the one is that he restricts himself to an intervention and what he considers to be its direct, immediate characteristics. The strength of the other is that he focuses on the *context* of intervention, on the characteristics of context and person, and what he suspects might be the indirect and unintended effects of intervention, i.e., ecological indicators of the functioning of an interdependent system. Just as the lion tamer and the ethologist both contribute much to the understanding of behavior control, so should the behavior modifier and the ecologist jointly be able to contribute much to the understanding of behavior control in such a way that costs and benefits can be balanced.

SOME PROBLEM AREAS

Exhortations and propaganda are of little use unless their implications for concrete work can be spelled out. The general arguments about behavioral ecology and behavioral technology suggest some points of sharp disagreement and some concrete areas for action. I shall attempt to spell out several such areas in terms of a brief list of issues whose pursuit should benefit both movements. The intent is that each issue be made into an empirical problem that can be developed with mutually acceptable data.

1. Long Time Periods

In keeping with some of the characteristics of behavior-environment systems and the kinds of behavioral dimensions with which he often works, the behavioral ecologist, like his counterparts in other areas of ecological science, pays attention to unusually long time periods. Time is not a functioning variable for him, but many of the phenomena to which he is attuned evolve over long periods. This concern is quite different from the more traditional developmentalist's concern with early and remote antecedents, because the ecologist always aspires to fill in the functional account of the sequence. We know by now from other areas, e.g., crop diseases, insecticides, that empirical monitoring of very long sequences can be both scientifically illuminating and pragmatically critical. Somehow, the behavior modifier must become willing to participate in such long-range concerns. The fact that the behavioral sciences cannot match the sophistication of ecological biochemistry is no excuse to wait.

The most ready and reasonable response by the behavior modifier, a function of his view of behavior and his view of the world, will probably be: "Whatever happens before or after my technological intervention, whether good, bad, or indifferent, is a function of chaotic or unfortunate programs of contingency or, at the least, programs of contingency that are out of my explicit control. *Ergo,* those occurrences are none of my business, by definition." He should make them his business, because we do not know when that response is an evasion of direct responsibility. Some behavioral interventions might unwittingly disrupt desirable things or set undesirable things in motion that become clear only over long periods of time.

2. "Other" Data

Closely related is a dilemma that surrounds effective technologies of all kinds and, therefore, applied behavior analysis, whose great strength comes from its concreteness, specificity, and narrowness of focus. The dilemma derives from the fact that the more narrow and specific the technological application becomes, the greater the array of phenomena its practitioners tend to disregard. So, while the behavior analyst would tend to assert that we should not bother him with arguments about unintended effects and "other" data—that he should take them all with so many grains of salt—the ecologist would argue that "other" data are worth gathering or may even be the most important.

The behavior modifier seems to be operating from strength when he says that the other-data argument comes from *absence* of data, from behavioral rates as yet unknown. My rejoinder is threefold. First, scientific progress sometimes follows from simply raising new questions—"I wonder what would happen if . . ." Second, behavior analysts themselves sometimes acknowledge the problem of unintended effects. Third, behavior modifiers themselves also argue from the absence of data, e.g., "We observed no ill effects. Therefore, our intervention procedure must be clean." Reporting that there were no unintended effects measured within a circumscribed, preset category system is just as unconvincing as the high proportion of studies that do not allude to unintended effects at all. Furthermore, the prescription to engage in multi-dimensional observation in behavior modification studies is not enough. We need to formulate and carry out new forms of research, because, as Wahler (unpublished) points out, there is, at present, no a priori basis for choosing behaviors to monitor. It is embarrassing to be unable to spell out what kinds of behavior to monitor. We do not know enough yet about behavior-environment systems, but finding out will be just as important to the technologist as to the ecologist.

Altogether new, system-wide domains of data seem indicated because: 1) successful modifications may produce unintended effects in the repertoire of the target person, 2) failures or marginal successes may be governed by variables that have not even been contemplated as yet, 3) with varying degrees of success on the target person, there may be unintended effects in the larger social or environmental network, 4) success may be temporary for reasons that are little understood, and 5) success may be situation-specific for reasons that lie beyond simple contingency principles.

For purposes of illustration, here is a classification of some of the kinds of unintended effects that may occur in behaviors that are not manipulated directly by the behavior modifier: 1) desirable, neutral, or undesirable behaviors may be affected, 2) the behaviors may increase or decrease, 3) the target subjects, other persons, or both may be affected, 4) effects may occur in the setting where the manipulation occurred, other settings, or both, and 5) effects may occur immediately, somewhat later, or much later. Cross-classifying these outcomes (3×2×3×3×3) results in 162 possible kinds of "side effects" from this classification alone, e.g., decrease in a desirable behavior by target subject, occurring somewhat later in the same setting. This analysis illustrates the magnitude and complexity of the other-data problem. The classification should be expanded by taking account of kinds of behaviors. Then, extensive research should be conducted to ascertain which *kinds* of unintended effects occur most frequently and *why* they occur so that practitioners can begin to predict such effects and plan their interventions with these effects in mind.

3. When to Rearrange

There has been an expansion in behavior modification circles from traditional forms of reinforcement and punishment, such as candy and slaps, toward more subtle behavioral forms, such as smiles, frowns, attention, timeouts, and eye contacts. Not only are these commodities readily available, but they can be very powerful when delivered in strictly contingent fashion. However, what happens to the personal and interpersonal system in the long run with so many effective principles of behavior change available for application?

> . . . adult practitioners must train themselves to inhibit spontaneous expressions of emotion in favor of expressions arranged to produce some desired behavior in the child. And assuming that the child 'learns' to produce that which may never even be openly demanded of him, he may also eventually learn that smiles and frowns are not genuine signs of reflexive emotions, but rather are signals indicating how well he is conforming to authority . . . the legitimate emotional meaning of facial expressions may become corrupted for both adults and children (Rappoport, 1972, Preface).

The work of the Brelands (Breland and Breland, 1966) pointed out long ago that what organisms can be *made* to do in the short run may be very arbitrary and dysfunctional in the *long* run (see Lockard, 1971, for a similar argument). Ethological and cross-cultural evidence suggests that various forms of individual and interpersonal behavior occur in relatively invariant, reciprocal units that have adaptive value or, perhaps, even survival value. Also, the behavior-modification work of investigators such as Sajwaj et al. (1972) and Wahler (unpublished) suggests that we have little understanding of the covariations among behaviors between and within persons, between events, and over time. If that is so, then we should work hard to discover their full array and their functional value and not only rush to disregard them by rearranging them.

4. Diagnostic Observation

We marvel at the observational skill, astuteness, and hunch-generating skill displayed by many students of behavior. What is chaos to others yields functional and critical dimensions of behavior to them. Within this context, I marvel at the least publicized and least explicit part of most behavior modification studies—the observational process by which the investigator views complicated behavior systems, selects certain dimensions for study, and bets successfully that they will be amenable to contingency control. In fact, since the systematic application of contingency programs is explicitly designed to be simple and straightforward, demanding mostly self-control and tenacity by the manager, I would even hypothesize that it is the accuracy of the initial observing-selecting-betting process that distinguishes between successful and unsuccessful behavior modification studies in many cases. Knowing that many studies fail, I marvel, for example, at the unpublicized ingenuity of a behavioral technologist who observes the behavioral scene in the ward of a residential treatment center for retardates, picks four or five behavioral dimensions from the chaos, babble, and rubble, subjects the dimensions to a multiple contingency program, and ends up being successful. His skill and ingenuity in picking crucial behaviors and deciding upon category systems needs to be made more public and explicit, and it needs to be subjected to study. It is, after all, diagnosis *par excellence,* and both the behavior modifier and ecologist could benefit greatly from more explicit rules for analyzing the critical aspects of behavior-environment systems and diagnosing the specific ways in which they function suboptimally.

5. Setting-behavior Linkages

Just as behavior and its behavioral consequences can be shown to form selective, interdependent systems, so do behavior and its physical context link up in almost inextricable ways. Furthermore, all of these elements concatenate in ways that we understand poorly at present, and which need to be investigated. For example, we might expand our investigations to consider the ways in which particular behavioral and educational outcomes in a classroom evolve as a combined function of: 1) shape, distribution, and crowding of furniture, 2) mutual delivery of interpersonal reinforcers and punishers, 3) proxemics, and 4) classroom activity format. The designing of functional environments awaits such information, which should be of interest to both the behavioral technologist and ecologist.

6. Outcomes versus Antecedent Conditions

Applied behavior modification involves more than a technology. It participates in a theoretical (yes, theoretical) movement whose view of behavior rests on assumptions of environmentalism, instrumentality, and contingency control. One of the pitfalls here is that information gleaned from interventions into troubling behavior may lead to misleading inferences back to the general model of behavior. The potential error lies in building and confirming a model of behavior on the basis of what works in treatment, or inferring causes from effectiveness of treatment. Does the fact that aspirin alleviates headaches mean that the deficiency of aspirin causes headaches (Bernard Rimland, personal communication)? Likewise, does the fact that reinforcement contingencies alleviate troubling behavior mean that the troubling behaviors are caused by fouled-up contingencies of reinforcement? It is illogical to infer too much about etiology from the nature of effective treatment (Davison, 1969). It is entirely possible that there are fundamental differences between the conditions under which an organism comes to behave in a certain way and the conditions under which he can be *made* to behave in that way or another way. The issue here is that we need to understand both sets of conditions far better than we do now (see Lockard, 1971). Troubling behavior certainly suggests that something is wrong, but it does not necessarily suggest that the problem resides in the sequential microstructure of behavior and its consequences. We need more wisdom about such matters and they are matters of concern for both the technologist and the ecologist. More complete *contextual* understanding of troubling behavior can only lead to increased predictability and success in intervention.

CONCLUDING COMMENTS

Partly by analogy and partly from some general ecological concerns, I have argued that the behavioral technologist in general and the behavior modifier in particular are implicated in problems that extend far beyond their elegantly simple though successful working models and procedures, but also that the technologist and ecologist have much to offer each other by way of orienting questions, modes of analysis, and cooperative effort.

Sometimes in jest, sometimes with irony, the physician is told, "You can *bury* your mistakes." However, this semi-humorous comment presupposes that either the physician or someone else, or both, recognize when the physician has made a mistake, i.e., that they have enough complete technical information to judge when a medical technique has been mis-applied. If the arguments of this paper are tenable, then the practitioners and consumers of applied behavior analysis do not have enough perspective as yet even to *judge* whether a mistake has been made, much less to bury it. Within the larger context of behavioral ecology, self-defined successes may actually be failures, wherein unintended harm follows from short-term or narrowly circumscribed good. Perhaps, the ecologist and behavior modifier together can acquire the kind of complete contextual ability to judge between good and harm that follows from a mutual, scientifically defensible acceptance of the complexities of everyday human behavior and thereby, develop the capability to anticipate the effects of intervention.

Skinner (1971) argued that, "The task of a scientific analysis is to explain how the behavior of a person as a physical system is related to the conditions under which the human species evolved and the conditions under which the individual lives (p. 14). . . . A scientific analysis naturally moves in the direction of clarifying all kinds of controlling conditions (p. 21)." Living up to this credo will require all the investigative ingenuity and cooperation we can muster.

ACKNOWLEDGMENT

I wish to thank Gerald Grateh, Larry Brandt, William LeCompte, and Sander Martin, who read early drafts of the paper and made helpful suggestions.

LITERATURE CITED

Baer, D. M. 1969. An operant view of child behavior problems. *In* J. H. Masserman (ed.), Science and psychoanalysis, Vol. 14. Childhood and Adolescence, pp. 137—146. Grune and Stratton, New York.
Baer, D. M. 1971. Let's take another look at punishment. Psych. Today 5:32—37, 111.
Barker, R. G. 1965. Explorations in ecological psychology. Amer. Psychologist 20:1—14.
Barker, R. G. 1968. Ecological Psychology. Stanford University Press, Stanford, Cal.
Barker, R. G. 1969. Wanted: An eco-behavioral science. *In* E. P. Willems and H. L. Raush (eds.), Naturalistic Viewpoints in Psychological Research, pp. 31—43. Holt, Rinehart, and Winston, New York.

30   Willems

Bijou, S. W., Peterson, R. F., and Ault, M. H. 1968. A method to integrate descriptive and experimental field studies at the level of data and empirical concepts. J. Appl. Behav. Anal. 1:175–191.

Birnbrauer, J. S., Burchard, J. D., and Burchard, S. N. 1970. Wanted: Behavior analysts. In R. Bradfield (ed.), Behavior Modification: The Human Effort, pp. 19–76. Dimenions, San Rafael.

Breland, K., and Breland, M. 1966. Animal Behavior. Macmillan, New York.

Buell, J., Stoddard, P., Harris, F. R., and Baer, D. M. 1968. Collateral social development accompanying reinforcement of outdoor play in a preschool child. J. Appl. Behav. Anal. 1:167–173.

Davison, G. C. 1969. Appraisal of behavior modification techniques with adults in institutional settings. In C. M. Franks (ed.), Behavior Therapy: Appraisal and Status, pp. 220–278. McGraw-Hill, New York.

Dubos, R. 1965. Man Adapting. Yale University Press, New Haven, Conn.

Dubos, R. 1970–1971. The despairing optimist. Amer. Scholar 40:16–20.

Eisenberg, L. 1972. The *human* nature of human nature. Science 176:123–128.

Hardin, G. 1969. The cybernetics of competition: A biologist's view of society. In P. Shepard and D. McKinley (eds.), The Subversive Science: Essays Toward an Ecology of Man, pp. 275–296. Houghton Mifflin, Boston.

Henry, J. 1971. Pathways to Madness. Random House, New York.

King, J. A. 1970. Ecological psychology: An approach to motivation. In W. J. Arnold and M. M. Page (eds.), Nebraska Symposium on Motivation, pp. 1–33. University of Nebraska Press, Lincoln, Neb.

Krantz, D. L. 1971. The separate worlds of operant and non-operant psychology. J. Appl. Behav. Anal. 4:61–70.

Kranzberg, M. 1972. Scientists: The loyal opposition. Amer. Scientist 60:20–23.

Lockard, R. B. 1971. Reflections on the fall of comparative psychology: Is there a message for us all? Amer. Psychologist 26:168–179.

Menzel, E. W., Jr. 1969. Naturalistic and experimental approaches to primate behavior. In E. P. Willems and H. L. Raush (eds.), Naturalistic Viewpoints in Psychological Research, pp. 78–121. Holt, Rinehart, and Winston, New York.

Murdoch, W., and Connell, J. 1970. All about ecology. The Center Magazine 3:56–63.

Odum, E. P. 1963. Ecology. Holt, Rinehart, and Winston, New York.

Platt, J. 1972. Beyond freedom and dignity: "A revolutionary manifesto." The Center Magazine 5:34–52.

Proshansky, H. M., Ittelson, W. H., and Rivlin, L. G. (eds.) 1970. Environmental Psychology. Holt, Rinehart, and Winston, New York.

Rappoport, L. 1972. Personality Development. Scott, Foresman, Glenview, Ill.

Sajwaj, T., Twardosz, S., and Burke, M. 1972. Side effects of extinction procedures in a remedial preschool. J. Appl. Behav. Anal. 5:163–175.

Sears, P. B. 1969. The inexorable problem of space. *In* P. Shepard and D. McKinley (eds.), The Subversive Science: Essays toward an Ecology of Man, pp. 77–93. Houghton Mifflin, Boston.

Sells, S. B. 1969. Ecology and the science of psychology. *In* E. P. Willems and H. L. Raush (eds.), Naturalistic Viewpoints in Psychological Research, pp. 15–30. Holt, Rinehart, and Winston, New York.

Skinner, B. F. 1971. Beyond Freedom and Dignity. Alfred A. Knopf, New York.

Wahler, R. G. 1972. The indirect maintenance and modification of deviant child behavior. Unpublished paper presented to a symposium ("The Child in His Environment") of the Houston Behavior Therapy Association, May, 1972.

Wahler, R. G., Sperling, K. A., Thomas, M. R., Teeter, N. C., and Luper, H. L. 1970. The modification of childhood stuttering: Some response-response relationships. J. Exp. Child Psych. 9:411–428.

Willems, E. P. 1965. An ecological orientation in psychology. Merrill-Palmer Q. 11:317–343.

Willems, E. P. 1973. Behavioral ecology and experimental analysis: Courtship is not enough. *In* J. R. Nesselroade and H. W. Reese (eds.), Life-span Developmental Psychology: Methodological Issues, pp. 195–217. Academic Press, New York.

Willems, E. P. Behavioral Ecology et al. In press.

Zimbardo, P. G. 1966. Physical integration and social segregation of northern Negro college students (1953, 1963, and 1965). Unpublished paper presented to the Eastern Psychological Association.

COMMENT

A Note on the Absence of a Santa Claus in any Known Ecosystem: A Rejoinder to Willems

Donald M. Baer

In general, the preceding discussion is a usefully irritating argument, cogently and gracefully presented, and it should be published. However, in this reviewer's opinion, four major complaints can be specified. The paper merits publication even if it does not answer these complaints. However, it would have more effect on its audience of behavior analysts if it avoided imputations they will not accept as characteristic of them, or recommendations they cannot follow. Because this argument should be as effective as it possibly can be in modifying its audience's behavior, I wish that Willems had written the paper differently. This is not for the author's sake, but for his readers', and their clients in the society. The author will recognize this as an ecological view.

1. For too many pages, Willems advises the reader to do something about the apparent shortsightedness of the typical behavior analysis approach to social problem-solving. Some of his readers—eminently behaviorists, after all—will be impatiently wondering just what they are supposed to *do* (other than close down the entire discipline and practice of behavior modification). For in those pages, the author does not specify a *behavioral* remedy. Instead, he recommends "expansion of perspective," an "understanding that takes account of the ecological, system-

Reprinted by permission from Journal of Applied Behavior Analysis, 1974, 7:167–170.

like principles (relevant)," a "systematic scientific basis to plan behavioral interventions . . . ," "mounting investigative efforts that have not been designed as yet," "reflecting upon and probing into the principles and laws . . . ," and using "models that lead us to look for (unanticipated outcomes of behavior modification applications);" and he recommends that ecologists and behavior analysts "link efforts (to simultaneously solve problems and predict the 'side effects' of the solution)." None of these are behaviors; they are metaphors, and the Journal of Applied Behavior Analysis (JABA) audience is exactly the wrong one to offer metaphor instead of procedure. It is reasonable to call for solution of a problem even when the means to that solution cannot be anticipated. Nevertheless, the ecological consequences of pairing an indictment of behavior analysis with only metaphors describing the necessary reform may well be dysfunctional for the argument: ignoring, discounting, forgetting, or not finishing are the likely reactions of many readers.

Predictably, Willems does better than metaphor. Under the heading "Some Problem Areas," he presents six reasonably behavioral prescriptions for behavior analysts to consider as revisions or additions to their research practices. The existence of *this* class of argument is the major importance of the paper. Thus, the author might well have done two things before its appearance: he could have eliminated the metaphors of the early pages, and he could have told his readers clearly at the outset that there would be six behavioral recommendations to consider later on.

In this reviewer's opinion, there are not truly *six* behavioral recommendations; there are only four. (But four are still more than enough for a valuable argument.) The third recommendation, labeled *"When to rearrange,"* is not a behavioral specification, but simply a restatement of Willems's often stated caution and of the first two recommendations (collect long-term data, and collect diverse measures of outcome over that long term). For this reviewer, the only valid way to evaluate when to, and when not to, rearrange behavior-environment interactions is to proceed experimentally with the rearrangement *and* with recommendations 1 and 2. The sixth recommendation, labeled *"Outcomes versus antecedent conditions,"* is a recommendation that is not required by most behavior analysts, who in fact regularly make the same recommendation to their (beginning) students, and regularly explain it to psychoanalytically oriented critics. Of course the etiology of a behavior may be different than its current maintaining contingencies; of course the means that successfully modifies a problem may have no relevance to the means that created the problem. (We frequently modify behavior by means other than those that we intend to support the behavior change after our program stops, and if *we* can do that in solving a problem, then surely it could have been done in creating the problem.) There is little point in this recommendation because there is no issue in it.

2. This paper recurrently points out that there may well be unanticipated costs to any behavior change (indeed, it appears to insist that there always will be), and that behavior analysts should become better students of those costs than at present. That recommendation cannot be denied, in this reviewer's opinion. However, there is another cost, equally important and equally ecological in its nature. It is the cost of *not* modifying behavior, when the behavior is a problem. Assessment of the cost of modification plus unintended side effects should always be conducted concurrently with assessment of the cost of nonmodification. Willems values analogies; so does the reviewer. Consider this one: in the production of drugs, there will be events such as penicillin and thalidomide. Great care in assessing all the side effects of a new drug before putting it into practice will make the thalidomide cases very infrequent— but it will also make the penicillin cases infrequent, in the sense of late. The disasters that we avoid by keeping thalidomides out of use are to be considered alongside the disasters that we allow by delaying the use of penicillins. For example, this reviewer has a daughter who very probably would be dead except for the existence and use of penicillins. That does not mean that we should free the drug developers to put every one of their hopefuls to use as soon as they manufacture it. It merely reminds the reviewer—and everyone else who finds the analogy sound—that caution in the assessment of ecological consequences of any new technology is in itself disaster-prone. Some societies, waiting for a complete understanding of the modification programs they might be applying to their behaviorally dispossessed citizens, may find themselves burned down by those citizens, in the name of caution. Surely it is a basic tenet of ecology that there is no Santa Claus *anywhere* in an ecosystem.

3. Willems has not been very explicit on where the research that he calls for is to take place. Perhaps there is an implication that it will be "safe" laboratory research that investigates unanticipated side effects, rather than applied research in the social arena. In this reviewer's opinion, that is not likely to be a fruitful course. The excellence of Willems' argument is that it has implications for the conduct of applied behavior analyses in the real-life settings where trouble is found. If that research were conducted according to his (four) recommendations, the field of applied behavior analysis might profit in immensely valuable ways. But past experience suggests to applied behavior analysts that laboratory analogs too often are not possible, and too often are not analogs. If this

research is to be done at all, and have meaning for real life, then very likely it will have to be done in real life. Indeed, eventually it must be situated in real-life settings, no matter where it originates—and the reviewer bets that it might as well start in real-life settings, at this point in the development of the field. It can.

4. The reviewer agreed (3, above) that pursuing ecologically oriented behavior analysis might yield immense profit. Now is the time to underline *might*. As Willems suggests, a little research looking for response classes and response chains has turned up some puzzling ones that would have been hard to predict. We know something about response classes and chains—not enough to predict them, perhaps, but enough to state the procedures for making new response classes and new response chains. Unfortunately, our understanding of chains shows that we can make as arbitrary, diverse, and bizarre chains as anyone cares to specify. Thus, to the extent that environment can be capricious, the resultant response chains can be equally capricious. Then it will be difficult to predict the response chains of the client from such an environment. Similarly with response classes, perhaps. On the other hand, the environment may operate very similarly on most of our clients, such that they tend to share quite similar chains (or classes). In that case, an actuarial study of *typical* chains (classes) may be fruitful, and the predictions that Willems calls for may in fact be possible and practical. It all depends, obviously, on some unknown facts about the environment. The author and the reviewer can agree that it is very worthwhile to try collecting those facts—but perhaps we had better prepare ourselves for the possibility that there will not be a useful ecological outlook for applied behavior analysts. They may have to cope from now until who-knows-when with unpredictable brushfires, simply because the nature of the environment does not offer a choice. However, even if this should be true, no one could confidently assert today that it is. Consequently, Willems' argument is the proper one for today.

PART II
UNPLANNED CHANGE:
IS THERE
CAUSE FOR ALARM?

3

Steps Toward an Ecobehavioral Technology

Edwin P. Willems

Several significant developments have been compressed into the last few years. First, both in sporadic bursts and at a steady and geometric pace, the circle of influence of applied behavior analysis has been widening. At an astonishing rate, areas of human performance and human difficulty that once were intractable and shrouded in mystery and pseudoscientific mumbo-jumbo have yielded their functional secrets to the relatively simple management techniques of applied behavior analysis. Second, accompanying this growth and to an extent that may not be clear to its practitioners, the productive skepticism of behavior analysts has permeated large portions of behavioral science. "I won't go along with it until I see some proof" has become the working rule for many in the newer generation of scientists and practitioners. Third, as a result of forces from inside and outside the behavior analysis movement, its conceptions, guiding principles, and technical procedures have been scrutinized, and some provisional steps have been taken to place them within the context of impingements and constraints that are extrinsic to the technologies themselves (see Mahoney, Kazdin, and Lesswing, 1974; Reppucci and Saunders, 1974; Willems, 1973a, 1974). Fourth, in ways that are troubling and demand serious attention, new questions are being raised from many parts of society about containing and controlling the practice of applied behavior analysis. It is still unclear which of these issues are legal ones, which are moral and ethical ones, which are a function of professional jealousy, and which are the result of irritation over careless or thoughtless

Work on this paper was supported in part by Research and Training Center No. 4 (RT-4), Baylor College of Medicine and by Texas Institute for Rehabilitation and Research, funded by Rehabilitation Services Administration, USDHEW.

practices by behavior analysts. Fifth, Robert Wahler (1975a) has summarized the decline and fall of the operant conditioning therapies, and Leonard Krasner (1976) has offered the eulogy at the funeral of behavior modification. Sixth, just when I was getting my feet planted firmly on the solid pilings of objective behavior, Montrose Wolf (1976) had the temerity to invite subjective data into behavior analysis.

Finally, a number of things have happened since the publication of my earlier papers on applied behavior analysis (Willems, 1973a, 1974; see Chapter 2 of this volume). As a result of the torrent of feedback that followed (oral comments, written notes, shared papers), I can testify that behavior modification works. I have been labeled as an enemy of behavioral analysis (untrue), as working to shut it down (untrue), and as dealing in unclear metaphors and analogical arguments (true and untrue, but no apologies). I have been hailed as a prophet by the right persons (fortunately) but also by the wrong persons for the wrong reasons (unfortunately), and I have been invited to bed down with some strange fellows (invitations declined). More productively, I have been told that I am on the right path, but that my description of the path and the steps we might take along it are too vague and not concrete enough (see Baer, 1974, and Chapter 2 of this volume). The results of this shaping process are: 1) a stronger commitment to some major elements of the perspective of behavior ecology, 2) a stronger sense of alliance and common fate with applied behavior analysis, 3) a stronger inclination to modify applied behavior analysis in some distinctive ways, and 4) the recognition that we will mature together in direct proportion to the clarity, explicitness, and concreteness with which we can prescribe new forms of action.

Against that background, the purpose of this chapter is to sharpen what was in dim focus in 1974. I have not reviewed here the earlier published papers, but I have tried to build on them and on my intervening experience to extend the arguments and make them as concrete as possible. Thus, I have tried to spell out some steps toward an *ecobehavioral technology*. [1] The first section to follow presents a sharpened reminder of the ecological perspective that has guided my thinking. The second section describes some things we can actually do, but of a conceptual and strategic sort. The third section spells out some concrete procedural and empirical steps that follow from the general arguments. Some of the steps are difficult to classify into the conceptual and procedural categories, but further discussion should help to clarify where they belong.

---

[1] The only rationale for the ordering of the words in this label is grammatical ease. For example, *behavioral-technological ecology* or *behavior-analytic ecology* sound awkward.

THE QUESTIONS FROM BEHAVIORAL ECOLOGY

On September 14, 1976, a commentator on an NBC news program spoke of some recent findings regarding aerosols and then said: "So often these days, we hear of severe and sometimes permanent damage being done by the very things we have been invited to use and consume. Where are the scientists ahead-of-time?" That question and what we can do to answer it in terms of techniques for behavior change are the overall agenda for this chapter. Often, science is sold in terms of the technological innovations it can produce, and technological innovations are sold in terms of their basis in scientific research. People are beginning to see that many of these innovations have indirect and secondary effects that are far greater than anticipated. Being closely linked, science and technology have both come under a cloud of suspicion. The credibility of science should worry us, but that is not my primary concern. Rather, we should ask ourselves for substantive, theoretical, and professional reasons, "Where are we ahead-of-time, with some anticipatory understanding of the effects of our behavioral technologies?" Gaining such anticipatory understanding is a central issue in behavioral ecology.

Ecological principles often can be dramatized best by demonstrating that a given intervention or change leads to complicated and unintended ramifications. The same is true for the systems with which behavior analysts work. One of the significant features of many social, physical, and biological systems is that they function as integrated wholes; manipulation of any part of such a system will affect each of the other parts and change the whole. Even the most positively motivated intrusions into interdependent systems can lead to all sorts of unanticipated effects, many of which are unpleasant and pernicious. To label these unintended effects as "side effects" only compounds the problem. Anticipated and unanticipated effects are all functions of the system's process. Side effects do not occur in the real world. They exist in our images of events for which we *expect* some things and not others.

In the face of growing awareness of ecological phenomena, we are reluctant to introduce new biotic elements and chemicals into our ecological systems, but we do not yet display the same judiciousness about intervening in behavioral and behavior-environmental systems. Almost every day we hear of projects or technologies being changed, slowed down, stopped, or disapproved on ecological grounds, because of the known complexity or delicacy of ecosystems. The location of a proposed factory is switched, a bridge is not built, a planned freeway is rerouted, a smokestack is modified, someone is restrained from introducing a new animal into an area, or a pesticide is taken off the market. Those who think that no changes are required in the behavioral sciences, or that arguments for a new effort in behavioral ecology are just so much window dressing should ask just one question: How often have I heard of a program or project, whose target is human behavior, being changed, slowed down, stopped, or disapproved on *behavioral*-ecological grounds, because of the known complexity and delicacy of ecobehavioral systems? The answer should sober us quickly.

I will not argue that we should rush to shut down all of our programs of behavioral intervention. However, I will argue that we know too little at present about the functional characteristics of ecobehavioral systems and too little about unanticipated and indirect effects of intervention. Thus, we must generally stand silent on the issue of weighing costs and benefits and on the issue of when and when not to intervene. Rather than recite illustrative examples from applied behavior analysis (see Willems, 1974, 1975, 1976a), I will simply stick by my assertion of 1974:

> One would think that increased power, sophistication, and precision would ensure greater ability to specify and anticipate unintended effects. But they do not. From the ecological standpoint, this is a fundamental issue, and it may call for mounting investigative efforts that have not been designed as yet (p. 156).

Spelling out some of those investigative efforts is one of my objectives in this chapter. Before that, let me try to summarize what I mean by "the ecological standpoint," or behavioral ecology, which runs through all of the arguments to follow. Fuller explication of behavioral ecology and its major assumptions are offered elsewhere (Alexander, Dreher, and Willems, 1976; Willems, 1973b, 1976b, 1976c). Among the central themes of behavioral ecology are:

1. Human behavior must be conceptualized and studied at levels of complexity that are quite atypical in behavioral science.
2. The complexity lies in systems of relationships that link person, behavior, social environment, and physical environment.
3. Such systems cannot be understood piece meal.
4. Such behavior-environment systems have important properties that change, unfold, and become clear only over long periods of time.
5. Tampering with any part of such a system will probably affect the other parts and alter the whole.
6. We must develop an ecological grasp of the many ways in which
   a) simple intrusions can produce unintended effects,
   b) indirect harm may follow from narrowly defined good, and
   c) long-term harm may follow from short-term good.

7. The focal challenge is to achieve enough understanding of such systems so that the effects of interventions and planned changes can be anticipated in comprehensive fashion.

To the extent that these themes have merit, the behavior analyst is implicated just as strongly as the behavioral ecologist. It is in this very specific sense that I would argue that we must develop an ecobehavioral technology and get on with the business of outlining some of the steps in that development. I turn now to my current view of these steps, first at a conceptual level and later at a more procedural level.

WHAT WE CAN DO: CONCEPTUAL-ORGANIZATIONAL STEPS

After some of the reactions to my paper of 1974, I feel like I am putting my hand on the griddle by presenting conceptual or speculative steps for consideration. For example, Baer (1974; also, Part I comment of this volume) says that the audience of behavior analysts "is exactly the wrong one to offer metaphor instead of procedure" and "ignoring, discounting, forgetting, or not finishing are the likely reactions of many readers" (p. 167). However, I am obstinate and will offer some conceptual-thematic steps for two reasons: 1) they merit the kind of debate that will test their translatability into more concrete behaviors, and 2) I intend to follow the conceptual steps with some procedural-behavioral ones that will help to answer and defuse the question, "Where are the scientists ahead-of-time?"

Balanced Technology Assessment

In typical ecobehavioral fashion, the most frequent response to my paper of 1974 was one that I neither predicted nor intended to elicit. I argued generally that we must be cautious about intervening in human behavior, and specifically, that we must learn enough about indirect, secondary, or unanticipated effects of interventions so that those effects can be taken into account in deciding when, where, and how to intervene. In responding, many persons seemed to assume, at best, that I wanted behavioral technologists to wait, immobilized, until all of that new learning had taken place, or, at worst, that I wanted behavioral technologists to stop their work entirely. Neither is true. This experience has impressed upon me the importance of balanced, judicious, and careful assessment and evaluation of technology.

Often, the arguments of ecologists crop up in the form of criticisms and disconcerting questions after the fact, only after technologists, de-

signers, engineers, and other practitioners have been hard at work.[2] Therefore, the responses of ecologists sound like carping, second-guessing, and
Monday-morning quarterbacking. The ecologist frequently pounces on the
work of others and says, "Hold on just a minute! I've got you with your
unintended effects showing!" Also he may tend to overgeneralize from his
newly found hindsight about someone else's work. Productive technology
assessment is a challenge for all of us. Spelling it out and doing it is a step
we can take. To do it well, the behavioral technologist must take a broader
view of his work than is necessary for the solution of a specific problem,
and the behavioral ecologist must take a narrower view of his task by
focusing more on actual problems and less on problems that are hypo-
thetically possible.

Computers and automatic switchboards enable astounding human
performances, penicillin saves lives and reduces human misery, seat belts
save lives more efficiently than educational programs, birth control pills
reduce family size, insecticides suppress malaria, fertilizer and irrigation
carve productive garden spots out of deserts, and behavioral technologies
reduce or eliminate maladaptive human performance. And yet, the emergence of resistant bacteria and insect strains is speeded up through overuse
and injudicious use of antibiotics and insecticides; garden spots disappear
and deserts grow larger because of human artifice; and so on. The underlying dilemma for us lies in the following statements, both of which are
true (Dubos, 1973):

1. From our vantage point as human animals, undisturbed nature often
    produces clumsy and painful solutions.
2. Troublesome ecological consequences of past and present human
    intervention indicate the need for greater knowledge and respect of
    natural laws.

It is just as bad to argue that behavioral technology is a neutral means as to
argue for some romantic version of the tautology that nature knows best.

Somewhere among us we must find the principles for the productive
and balanced assessment of behavioral technology. American society is
shifting slowly with regard to technology assessment (Dubos, 1976). After
a period of shrill cries, breast beating, finger pointing, and witch hunting,
some productive campaigns and studies are in the works to anticipate,
minimize, and correct the negative effects of technology. Although they

---

[2] This is true of ecologists generally and not only behavioral ecologists. In fact,
this parasitic activity probably has been responsible for making ecology a faddish and
controversial enterprise.

may be difficult to organize and produce, statements of environmental impact represent a model of action that will be followed more and more. Together, in gradual approximations, we must do the work that will enable us to provide *ecobehavioral impact statements*. From the present vantage point within applied behavior analysis, this sounds clumsy and onerous, but shifting to that mode should foster studies that will provide criteria for weighing our practices, classifying them in terms of benefit and cost, and modifying or withholding those that are technically possible but ecologically and socially objectionable.

Widening Conceptualizations

In her recent comments about living with applied behavior analysts, Horowitz (1975) said:

> Applied behavior analysis has solved some of the simpler problems of an applied technology. . . . A fully developed system of technology requires the combination of a basic understanding of the principles of the phenomenon with the principles of technology and with the development of delivery systems. Applied behavior analysis incorporates some of the principles of technology and is entering more and more into the field of good delivery systems. But its application of technology will continue to be primarily to remedial problems or to relatively gross behaviors, unless it develops systems for keeping abreast of the basic research (p. 11).

Horowitz is speaking of insularity, and she goes on to present some specific ways in which the conceptions of the applied behavior analyst should be opened up to influences from outside.

Largely because of the precision of its focus and its procedural rules, applied behavior analysis is ideally suited to working within a phenomenon. As scientists and practitioners, we often seem to accept the doctrine of the organization of the world in terms of levels. For example, having picked the level of analysis that clusters tightly around the person and his behavior, applied behavior analysts tend to work *within* that level and not *with* it. They do little to investigate that level of behavior as it relates to the whole environment and as it extends farther away from the person and over time.

> When we elect, wittingly, or unwittingly, to work *within* a level . . . we tend to discern or construct . . . only those kinds of systems whose elements are confined to that level. From this standpoint, the doctrine of levels may not only fail to be heuristic, it may actually become anti-heuristic, if it blinds us to fruitful results obtainable by recognizing *systems that cut across levels* (Duncan, 1961, p. 141).

Applied behavior analysts have been very effective at defining the principal dimensions of their work and at stating their consensual criteria of success and failure (Baer, Wolf, and Risley, 1968; Stolz, Wienckowski, and Brown, 1975). However, in starkest terms, applied behavior analysis is far too important and too widespread in its implications to be left to the current conceptions of behavior analysts. In its present versions, it is not well suited to working *with* its conceptions. I think applied behavior analysts can become much more eclectic, more like libertines who poach freely from the conceptions of others. The basic strength need not suffer in the process, and the ratio of reinforcers to punishers probably will be much higher than anticipated. Behavior analysis not only can, but *should* push out beyond its internal concepts and internal criteria for effectiveness.

Franks and Wilson (1975) argue that "New conceptual frameworks need to be boldly erected, frameworks which are more adequately representative of the person as a complex bio-psycho-social series of systems in continuing dialogue with each other within a diversity of environments" (p. 310). Two examples will illustrate what I mean by pushing beyond current concepts.

Professional Image   To a great extent, the caricature of applied behavior analysis that comes across to the outsider is analogous to workers in a light bulb factory that has some quality control built in: the major concern is with producing operational light bulbs at rate x and with demonstrating successful production at rate x. That is, the preoccupation seems to be: *does* it work? Many other behavioral scientists are interested in whether or not things work, but they often are more preoccupied with *how* and *why* things work. Like those outsiders, behavior analysts could display more openness about and concern with understanding the processes, mechanisms, and ingredients that enter into successful and unsuccessful production. Not only would that give the rest of the world something to which to link in terms that it understands, but it might give something of a workable nature. For example, in my research on the longitudinal aspects of patient performance in a rehabilitation hospital, I want to find out why patient behavior displays such powerful place specificity, or dependence on settings (Willems, 1976b). I am hard pressed to identify clear discriminative stimuli or contingency control. However, unless I present behavior under stimulus control, my acquaintances in behavior analysis are reluctant to talk to me about it.

Synergism   Mixed and confusing findings can be just as important as demonstrations and explanations of success and failure. We can probably agree on several statements: 1) behavioral technologies work (demonstrated); 2) behavioral technology and its results can be very complicated (demonstrated, e.g., Herbert et al., 1973; Sajwaj, Twardosz, and Burke, 1972); 3) often, we do not know why the complex and confusing results occur (demonstrated). "The phenomena occur because . . ." is almost anyone's guess and we need much more work.

I think applied behavior analysis can benefit from the use and the implications of the concept of *synergism*, the combined action of discrete agents such that the resultant effect is greater than or different from the sum of the effects of the agents taken singly or independently. In environmental pharmacology, this concept has become so much a part of the conceptualization that it is seldom mentioned any more. Several hundred drugs, insecticides, herbicides, hormones, carcinogens, and other environmental chemicals are now known to enhance, inhibit, and become involved in complex interactive effects with ingested drugs in both man and animals (Conney and Burns, 1972; Lichtenstein, Liang, and Anderegg, 1973). Assuming synergism, environmental pharmacologists have pressed for explanations. At present, one common denominator appears to be the variable nature of liver enzymes that process and deal with chemicals having diverse structures and diverse biological effects. Many synergistic effects of chemicals are now predictable. In behavioral technology, we have made only a few bare attempts to ask questions about synergism, and there are even fewer answers. Adopting the assumption of a synergistic world is a step we can take.

New Partnerships

In addition to conceptual cross-seeding, we also can benefit from symbiotic work and new partnerships. Behavior, the principal means by which organisms carry on commerce with the environment, is embedded in and related to phenomena at many levels, which themselves form hierarchies of embedded systems: molecules, cells, tissues, organs, organ systems, organisms, settings, facilities, institutions, political systems, and economic systems. Behavior is a mid-range phenomenon here; what organisms *do* is the principal means by which they relate to the various levels of context. Thus, the full contextual understanding of behavior requires models and approaches developed by persons who study the various levels of embeddedness. "The division of labor in the economy of science is, after all, a historical product and not the reflection of logical necessity. As science progresses, old partnerships . . . are dissolved, and new ones . . . come into being" (Kaplan, 1964, p. 31).

One step we can take is to develop new forms of intensive, problem-oriented collaboration and cooperation in our work. I realize that, in one sense, applied behavior analysts already work with persons from outside their discipline more frequently than most professionals. They have worked with teachers, parents, administrators, neighborhood organizers, medical personnel, and so on. In most cases, however, those other persons have been involved in identifying and defining a problem to be solved, or they have been consumers of the technology. Kagel and Winkler's (1972) proposals regarding behavioral economics come closer to what I am talking about—mutual, behavioral interdependence and overlap between behavior analysts and behavioral ecologists in working on a problem of intervention or research.

A Priori Prediction of Effects

We need not start from scratch in puzzling out the complexities for every problem of applied behavior analysis. Among us, we have more relevant collective wisdom, past experience, working models, existing data, and explicit theories than we give ourselves credit for. In other words, in some areas, we need not work in complete mystery; we can use our accumulated experience and hypotheses to predict various effects that might occur with an intervention. At the very least, we can predict *some* and then monitor their occurrence. One step we can take toward an ecobehavioral technology is to make that collective wisdom more explicit, case by case, and use it to anticipate effects. One example will illustrate what I mean.

Zelazo, Zelazo, and Kolb (1972) studied the infantile walking response and found that, if held under the arms with his feet touching a flat surface, a newborn infant will perform coordinated walking movements. Generally, the response disappears by about the eighth week after birth. Stimulation (practice) of the response during the period from the second through the eighth week after birth resulted in significant reductions in the ages at which the infants began to walk alone. The investigators described a number of possible benefits that could result from the development of early mobility, particularly the promoting of competence and independence.

Based partly on prior developmental data and theory and partly on his own judgment, Gotts (1972) indicated that to accelerate the onset of walking might prove undesirable. Detrimental effects might result. For example, "at the naturally occurring mean age for solo walking ... the average infant's posterior fontanel is closed and his anterior fontanel is closed or nearly closed. ... To accelerate the onset of walking would thus unnecessarily expose younger children, who have less complete fontanel closure, to possible central nervous system injury" (p. 1057). Gotts mentioned several other predictions of possible effects. Whether or not we agree with Gotts is less interesting to me than the illustration of before-the-fact predictions of indirect and secondary effects. There must be many possibilities of this sort that would allow us to anticipate and measure a higher proportion of what are, at present, unanticipated effects.

WHAT WE CAN DO: PROCEDURAL AND EMPIRICAL STEPS

The behavior analyst says, "Specify the behaviors. Describe for me what I can *do* differently to increase the likelihood of solving the problems you keep harping about." In this section, I propose some procedural and empirical steps. Where they are still too ambiguous or programmatic, further discussion should render them operational. Not only are these proposals more procedural than many of my previous arguments, but I, for one, will deliver reinforcers when I see the behaviors emitted.

Analysis of Contexts

Horowitz (1975) notes that "Behavior analysts are notorious for ignoring the nature of the organism with which they are working" (p. 14). This complaint implies that behavior analysts work primarily with organisms. I would argue that behavior analysts do not work primarily with organisms. They work with behaviors and with the environments of those behaviors. No behavior analyst has ever asked me to point out the kind of person about whom he should be concerned. He identifies a target *behavior* and sets up ways to manipulate the *environment* of that behavior in order to control it and change it. Thus, I would shift Horowitz's friendly complaint to make a different friendly complaint: "Behavior analysts are notorious for ignoring the nature of the environmental settings with which they work." It has been demonstrably fruitful for them to conceive of environments in terms of discriminative stimuli, stimulus control, and management of the consequences of behavior. However, I do not agree that such dimensions and their derivatives characterize all of the behavior-relevant environment.

In order to clarify what I am arguing, we need to make a distinction between intrabehavioral complexities and ecobehavioral complexities. Intrabehavioral complexities are the complicated effects and behavioral outcroppings that arise as a function of behavior-behavior relationships, such as response chains and response classes. Such complexities should be (and have been) of great concern because they operate in producing unintended effects of interventions. However, they are largely intrinsic to repertoires of behavior. Ecobehavioral complexities are the complicated effects and discontinuities in behavior that arise as a function of behavior-environment relationships and the properties of settings. Thus, ecobehavioral complexities are at least partially extrinsic to repertoires of behavior. Since the complexities are at least a partial function of the properties of settings, they are very poorly understood because so little effort has been devoted to the analysis of contexts. One specific problem—place specificity or setting dependency—will illustrate what I mean.

Where organisms are located is never unimportant because behavior and place concatenate into lawful, functioning systems (Barker, 1963; Moos, 1973; Wicker, 1972; Willems, 1976b, 1976c). In the conduct of everyday affairs, not only do we depend upon location specificity in behavior for predictability and social order, but we often use departures from such correlations to label persons as being sick, crazy, or deviant, and in need of help or control. Barker (1963) points out that place-behavior systems have such strong principles of organization and constraint that their standing patterns of behavior remain essentially the same although individuals come and go. Wicker (1972) calls this "behavior-environment congruence." Barker (1968) calls it "behavior-milieu synomorphy" and argues that the appropriate units of analysis for studying such relationships are behavior settings, whose defining attributes and properties he has spelled out in detail (1963, 1968).

A clear example of the importance of place dependencies is found in the work of Raush and his colleagues in their studies of normal children and children diagnosed as hyperaggressive or disturbed (Raush, 1969; Raush, Dittmann, and Taylor, 1959a, 1959b; Raush, Farbman, and Llewellyn, 1960). By observing the children for extended periods of time in various settings and then examining the frequencies of various kinds of behavior by the children toward peers and adults, the investigators were able to demonstrate several aspects of place dependency. First, the inter-personal behavior of all the children varied from one setting to another. Second, and perhaps most revealing, the place dependency of behavior was much stronger for normal children than for disturbed children. That is, the influence of the setting was greater for normal children. Finally, as the disturbed children progressed in treatment, the place dependency of their behavior came to approximate the normal children more and more.

Wahler (1975b) observed two troubled boys periodically for three years in home and school settings. He found: 1) that behaviors clustered differently in home and school settings, 2) that the clusters within each setting were very stable over time, and 3) that different patterns of deviant behaviors occurred in stable fashion in the two settings. Lichstein and Wahler (1976) observed 16 behaviors of an autistic child and six behaviors of adults and peers for approximately six months. Observations were made in three different settings, and covariation of behaviors across time and settings was analyzed by means of cluster analysis. Again, the investigators found that the child's behavior was relatively stable across time within a given setting and that none of the child's behavior clusters appeared in more than one setting.

From the evolutionary standpoint, it makes sense to argue that behavioral responsiveness to settings is selected for, because location-appropriateness of behaviors is crucial to adaptation in many settings (Sells, 1969; Skinner, 1971). The implications of such phenomena are widespread. First, behavior is largely controlled by the environmental setting in which it occurs. Second, changing the environmental setting will change behavior. The third implication is related to methodology. This is the investigative problem of describing and classifying the types and patterns of congruence between behavior and environment and formulating principles that account for the congruence. Such an effort is important because it promises to contribute much to programs of environmental design. To accomplish this goal, investigators must become more persistent in adding descriptions and codes for locations and contexts to their measures and descriptions of behavior.

These principles are illustrated and elaborated by my program of research on persons with spinal cord injuries (Willems, 1976b). First, when we look at distributions of patient behavior within different settings, we find that these profiles of behavior vary dramatically from one setting to another (LeCompte and Willems, 1970; Willems, 1972a, 1972b). Some behaviors that occur in one setting never occur in others, and the relative frequencies and percentage weights of behavior show strong variation between settings. What patients do varies systematically from one setting to another.

Second, in addition to these topographical dependencies on settings, we find setting dependencies in the more dynamic aspects of patient behavior. From the observations, we extract behavioral measures of *independence*, i.e., the proportion of performances that patients initiate and execute alone. Because an increase from very low rates in this measure reflects a relative normalizing of the patients' behavior repertoires, it relates closely to important goals of the hospital's treatment system. Many traditional, person-based theories of human behavior assume that independence is largely a matter of individual motivation and thus should reflect a high degree of personal constancy across situations. We find instead that behavioral independence varies dramatically when patients move from one hospital setting to antoher.

Third, we find in many cases that differences between settings account for more variance in patient performance than do differences between patients. Fourth, and most interestingly, there are powerful variations among settings in the rate of behavioral growth and development displayed by individual patients over time. That is, patients show much more change of behavior in some hospital settings than in others. Thus, not only do we find that persons perform differently in different settings when we make simple comparisons between settings, but we find that persons change in different ways and at different rates in different settings.

These are important phenomena toward which we all should take some procedural and empirical steps because there is too much mystery surrounding them. As a behavioral ecologist, I am intrigued by place dependency as a fundamental issue in ecobehavioral relationships. More specifically, I am concerned about place dependencies in the rehabilitation hospital, for several reasons. For one thing, we have discovered that the place of dependency in patient behavior affects staff judgments and assessments of patients, and, therefore, probably influences their treatment of patients. More importantly, we hope to determine the properties of the settings and the processes in the settings that produce the specificities so that they can enter into the design of treatment.

Understanding these phenomena is also very important to the applied behavior analyst. One example is the problem of generalization. I applaud the behavior analyst's emphasis on generalization and maintenance and on the variables that promote generalization. However, most demonstrations of generalization probably still fall into the train-and-hope variety (Stokes and Baer, in press): train, wait, hope, celebrate when successful, groan when unsuccessful. We still do not know much about how and why generalization occurs or does not occur. Generalization probably is intimately related to the setting specificity of behavior, which means that you need to understand setting specificity as well.

We need data to reduce the mystery. We should develop some classifications of settings, situations, or contexts so that different investigators will be focusing on similar environmental units. We should share our various measures of the structure and organization of settings, from which we might identify variables that influence behavior. We should be more persistent at including notations for intersetting shifts when they occur in the behaviors we monitor. Then, we should begin choosing among various processes or combinations of processes to account for setting specificity, e.g., specific stimulus relationships, pattern learning, feedback at molar levels of behavior, specific contingencies, vicarious learning, learning of rules.

New Kinds of Data

By definition, indirect effects are different from targeted effects, and unintended effects are effects that the investigator or practitioner does not predict. Because complex effects are part and parcel of the phenomena with which we work, they must be measured and understood. From this, it would follow that one concrete procedural step we should take is to expand our measurement systems. It is impossible to offer a priori specification of the degree of expansion for each and every study. However, I think we can agree on a general procedural guideline: Always gather as many data as are feasible rather than obtaining only the minimum number necessary to demonstrate the targeted effectiveness of a treatment.

Although some consensus on this general principle is perhaps the most important step here, I can offer some suggestions regarding the kinds of data to obtain. With some exceptions, the focus of the behavior analyst seems to be on a few kinds of behavior, on their rates, and on the ways in which environmental manipulations affect those rates. I would recommend that, wherever possible, we expand the data systems in the following ways:

1. Increase the number of behavior categories. Measuring complex effects suggests monitoring of more than a few behaviors. These can be identified from preliminary observations, interviews with subjects and companions, theoretical considerations, or even common sense.
2. Increase the number of persons observed. Complex effects may occur in the behaviors of persons other than the target.
3. Observe other dimensions of behavior in addition to its type. Complex effects can show up in those other aspects, e.g., was the behavior done alone or with the aid of someone, who instigated it, how long did it occur, etc.
4. Lengthen the time period of observation. Complex effects sometimes show up only after some lapse of time.
5. Increase the number of settings in which the observations are made. Complex effects may show up across different settings.

A study by Spyker, Sparber, and Goldberg (1972) illustrates the importance of expanding data systems to study complex effects. Noting that neurological dysfunction is the official criterion for recognizing a case of methylmercury poisoning and for setting allowable standards, the investigators gave pregnant mice small injections of methylmercury and later (at 60 days after birth) conducted extensive neurological tests on the offspring. There were no differences between these animals and animals whose mothers had received injections of saline solution. However, the investigators expanded their data system to include open-field and swimming tests. The slightly poisoned group displayed significant negative differences on these behavioral criteria.

In my research program, we have used data from our direct observations of spinal cord patients to assess the effects of changes in hospital treatments (Willems, 1973c, 1976d). In one case, there was no effect on the *kinds* of patient behavior, but there were powerful effects on other aspects of the behaviors, such as the number of settings they entered and the rate at which they behaved without the direct, hands-on involvement of someone else.

One important principle that we have established in my research program is that extensive, relatively open, and heuristic data systems can be maintained for long periods of time. We have developed a streamlined version of the specimen record approach (Barker and Wright, 1955; Wright, 1967). For our narrative system (sequential, on-the-spot recording by an observer, separate coding), we have solved the problem of measuring interobserver agreement (Crowley, 1976; Dreher, 1975; Willems, 1976b), and our agreement rates hover around 90–92%. Our turnaround time is now down to two hours between an observation and the production of usable data. We observe each patient for 15 hours per week throughout his hospital stay (average 95 days). From this data system, we derive 30 behavioral and behavioral-environmental measures on a regular basis.

Data-Based Predictions of Effects

Earlier, I suggested that we might use theories and collective wisdom to predict some intervention-produced effects. At a more procedural and empirical level, we can take the step of data-based predictions of "other" effects that will accompany our interventions. The clearest paradigm for this step comes from the work of Robert Wahler's group and, to a lesser extent, from my research program.

Studies by Wahler (1975b), Lichstein and Wahler (1976), and Kara and Wahler (in press) suggest that, if baseline data are extensive enough in time and number of measures, they can be used to predict complex changes in behaviors that are not manipulated directly in the subsequent treatment. For example, Kara and Wahler (in press) monitored 14 categories of a child's behavior during baseline. By means of factor and cluster analysis, the investigators identified the clusters that occurred during baseline. One constituent behavior was selected from one of the clusters to be put on an extinction schedule during the intervention phase, while the other constituent behaviors were maintained on their baseline schedules. The important point for present purposes is that, as the focal behavior followed the extinction-reinstatement manipulation in the multiple reversal design, the other behaviors in the cluster increased *and* decreased in ways that were predicted from the directions of their interrelationships in the baseline cluster analysis. Behaviors that were positively related to the target behavior in the cluster decreased when the target behavior went on extinction, whereas behaviors that were negatively related to the target behavior *increased* when the target behavior went on extinction. In other words, by using some extensive baseline data and some unusual statistical operations on the data, Kara and Wahler were able to predict some intervention-produced effects that otherwise would have remained hidden (without the extensive measurement) and unanticipated (without the unusual statistical analysis). In our longitudinal research with spinal cord patients, we have been conducting similar cluster analyses as a basis for identifying key constituents of patient performance, for anticipating the specific ways in which performance will be affected by events such as illnesses, and for selecting the best predictors of post-hospital adjustment (Alexander, 1977; Willems, 1976e).

With these developments, several things are becoming clearer. First, complex effects do occur that cannot be accounted for in terms of direct stimulus changes. Second, and more important, vague and analogical arguments about unintended effects and "other" data (e.g., Willems, 1973a, 1974) are now slowly giving way to data and procedures. There is sufficient promise here for us to take some major procedural steps. Two words of caution: First, the demonstrations to date have focused on behavior-behavior relationships. In the long run, we should expand this work to include intersetting shifts and complex effects caused by dependencies of behavior on settings. Second, it is important to remember that this procedure for translating unanticipated effects into anticipated effects is bounded completely by the categories of behavior that enter into the baseline observations. We should note that our present category systems may not include measures of other effects. All I can recommend at present is some extensive trial-and-error with relatively extended, open data systems.

Selective Expansion

Having presented some new approaches to measurement, prediction, and specification of complex effects, I can now make much more precise some recommendations that have been too vague. I have no complaint with, and make no recommendation about, the actual tactics of treatment and intervention used by most applied behavior analysts. In fact, I applaud the ingenuity and elegance that most of the treatments display. In other words, what the behavior analyst actually does to change behavior is none of my business. However, I do have some recommendations to make about what else he does surrounding his treatments and what he says about the treatments.

On the basis of analogical arguments and on the basis of recent data, it is becoming clear that, in and around treatments, many behavioral phenomena occur that can neither be accounted for conceptually nor dealt with empirically in terms of a simple model of stimulus control. The fact that this awareness has grown from measurements and data tells us something important, i.e., the data are shaping our views. For the moment, consider three domains: 1) models that give us a running conceptual account of how behavior works, 2) procedures for intervention and treatment, and 3) measurements and data that tell us how the treatments are going and what is happening in subjects' behaviors. My specific recommendation is that expansion of our work be carried out selectively and that we begin by designing and using far less simplistic systems of measurement and less simplistic techniques for analyzing the data. Recent work tells me that we can do this almost immediately. Perhaps in repeated cycles over time, the second step is to let the results of the new data systems shape our models of how behavior works. It is important to note that, first, I am recommending that we change one accompaniment of treatment immediately and gradually change another, both into less simplistic versions. Then, perhaps in the longer run and in ways that cannot be anticipated now, the expansion of these accompaniments of treatment will actually lead to changes in systems of treatment and delivery.

In summary, I have tried to specify what, as a behavioral ecologist, I want most from applied behavior analysts. Convinced that you intervene in complex systems, I want most for you to be less simplistic in measuring what happens when you intervene and less simplistic in what you say about the complex systems. Not only will that be informative to me, but I think it will be very important to you. For the present, I am much less concerned about changing the specific manner in which you intervene. In the long run, that will be taken care of.

CONCLUDING COMMENTS

In this chapter, I have tried to sharpen and up-date some themes that I outlined in my earlier papers on the relation between behavioral technology and behavioral ecology (Willems, 1973a, 1974; also see Chapter 2 of this volume). I have tried to clarify: 1) some conceptual-strategic steps that can be taken, and 2) some tactical, procedural, and empirical steps that should be taken soon. My argument boils down to the following: applied behavior analysts should continue to carry out their treatments. (I am sure they will do that anyway, with or without my blessing.) However, they must expand the kind of information they gather surrounding their treatments and expand what they say about their treatments.

Two things still disturb me. First, I wish that I were incisive and astute enough to translate the important and sometimes confusing principles of behavioral ecology into more precise implications for applied behavior analysis and vice versa. I believe strongly that these two orientations have a great deal in common because they come to the same complexities from somewhat different origins and because they share some important values. This chapter outlines what I currently can specify with enough clarity and conviction to share. Second, position papers and comparative analyses like this chapter often tend to communicate a particular spirit: what's mine is mine and what's yours is negotiable. Let me announce clearly that what's mine is negotiable, too. The maturation of my ecological perspective depends just as much on how you influence it as the maturation of applied behavior analysis depends on how I influence it in turn.

A number of significant steps have been taken toward an ecobehavioral technology during the last four years, and I have tried to spell out some steps that will help to answer the question "Where are the scientists ahead-of-time?" John Ciardi once said, "There is no answer: seek it lovingly." One might well ask of the interface between behavioral technology and behavioral ecology, "But *precisely* what must we do?" The current state of our art is such that I cannot answer with great precision, but I am more convinced than I was four years ago that we must pursue it lovingly and tenaciously. Whatever it is we must do, it cannot yet be prearranged in an exact way. Persons cannot be lined up in tidy rows and given directions from printed sheets. We will not get it done by instructing each researcher or practitioner to make this or that piece of the puzzle, or by means of committees fitting the pieces that are made.

What it needs is for the atmosphere to be made right, or if you will, for the general investigative environment and the reinforcers to be made right. If you want a bee to make honey, it won't help to issue proclamations on solar navigation or on the chemistry of carbohydrates. You just put the bee to work with other bees, and you do what you can to arrange the general environment around the hive. If the general environmental conditions are right, then the ecobehavioral technology will come.

LITERATURE CITED

Alexander, J. L. 1977. The wheelchair odometer as a continuous, unobtrusive measure of human behavior. Unpublished masters thesis, University of Houston, Houston.

Alexander, J. L., Dreher, G. F., and Willems, E. P. 1976. Behavioral ecology and humanistic and behavioristic approaches to change. *In* A. Wandersman, P. Poppen, and D. Ricks (eds.), Humanism and Behaviorism: Dialogue and Growth, pp. 307–359. Pergamon, Elmsford, New York.

Baer, D. M. 1974. A note on the absence of a Santa Claus in any known ecosystem: A rejoinder to Willems. J. Appl. Behav. Anal. 7:167–170. Reprinted as Part I Comment in this volume.

Baer, D. M., Wolf, M. M., and Risley, T. R. 1968. Some current dimensions of applied behavior analysis. J. Appl. Behav. Anal. 1:91–97.

Barker, R. G. 1963. On the nature of the environment. J. of Soc. Iss. 19(No. 4):17–38.

Barker, R. G. 1968. Ecological Psychology. Stanford University Press, Stanford, Cal.

Barker, R. G., and Wright, H. F. 1955. Midwest and Its Children. Harper and Row, New York.

Conney, A. H., and Burns, J. J. 1972. Metabolic interactions among environmental chemicals and drugs. Science 178:576–586.

Crowley, L. R. 1976. Development and assessment of an alternative to the narrative observation. Unpublished masters thesis, University of Houston, Houston.

Dreher, G. F. 1975. Reliability assessment in narrative observations of human behavior. Unpublished masters thesis, University of Houston, Houston.

Dubos, R. J. 1973. Humanizing the earth. Science 179:769–772.

Dubos, R. J. 1976. The despairing optimist. Amer. Scholar 45:168–172.

Duncan, O. D. 1961. From social system to ecosystem. Sociolog. Inquiry 31:140–149.

Franks, C. M., and Wilson, G. T. 1975. Commentary, *In* C. M. Franks and G. T. Wilson (eds.), Annual Review of Behavior Therapy Theory and Practice, pp. 310–316. Brunner/Mazel, New York.

Gotts, E. E. 1972. Newborn walking. (Letter). Science 177:1057–1058.

Herbert, E. W., Pinkston, E. M., Hayden, M. L., Sajwaj, T. E., Pinkston, S., Cordua, G., and Jackson, C. 1973. Adverse effects of differential parental attention. J. Appl. Behav. Anal. 6:15–30.

Horowitz, F. D. 1975. Living among the ABAS—Retrospect and prospect. *In* E. Ramp and G. Semb (eds.), Behavior Analysis: Areas of Research and Application, pp. 3–15. Prentice-Hall, Englewood Cliffs, N.J.

Kagel, J. H., and Winkler, R. C. 1972. Behavioral economics: Areas of cooperative research between economics and applied behavioral analysis. J. Appl. Behav. Anal. 5:335–342.

Kaplan, A. 1964. The Conduct of Inquiry. Chandler, San Francisco.

Kara, A., and Wahler, R. G. Organizational features of a young child's behaviors. J. Exp. Child Psych. In press.

Krasner, L. 1976. On the death of behavior modification. Amer. Psychologist 31:387–388.

LeCompte, W. F., and Willems, E. P. 1970. Ecological analysis of a hospital: Location dependencies in the behavior of staff and patients. In J. Archea and C. Eastman (eds.), EDRA-2: Proceedings of the 2nd annual environmental design research association conference, pp. 236–245. Carnegie-Mellon University, Pittsburgh.

Lichstein, K. L., and Wahler, R. G. 1976. The ecological assessment of an autistic child. J. of Abnorm. Child Psych. 4:31–54.

Lichtenstein, E. P., Liang, T. T., and Anderegg, B. N. 1973. Synergism of insecticides by herbicides. Science 181:847–849.

Mahoney, M. J., Kazdin, A. E., and Lesswing, N. J. 1974. Behavior modification: Delusion or deliverance? In C. M. Franks and G. T. Wilson (eds.), Annual Review of Behavior Therapy Theory and Practice, pp. 11–40. Brunner/Mazel, New York.

Moos, R. H. 1973. Conceptualizations of human environments. Amer. Psychologist 28:652–665.

Raush, H. L. 1969. Naturalistic method and the clinical approach. In E. P. Willems and H. L. Raush (eds.), Naturalistic Viewpoints in Psychological Research, pp. 122–146. Holt, Rinehart, and Winston, New York.

Raush, H. L., Dittmann, A. T., and Taylor, T. J. 1959a. The interpersonal behavior of children in residential treatment. J. Abnormal and Soc. Psych. 58:9–26.

Raush, H. L., Dittmann, A. T., and Taylor, T. J. 1959b. Person, setting and change in social interaction. Human Relations 12:361–379.

Raush, H. L., Farbman, I., and Llewellyn, L. G. 1960. Person, setting and change in social interaction: II. A normal-control study. Human Relations 13:305–333.

Reppucci, N. D., and Saunders, J. T. 1974. Social psychology of behavior modification: Problems of implementation in natural settings. Amer. Psychologist 29:649–660.

Sajwaj, T., Twardosz, S., and Burke, M. 1972. Side effects of extinction procedures in a remedial preschool. J. Appl. Behav. Anal. 5: 163–175.

Sells, S. B. 1969. Ecology and the science of psychology. In E. P. Willems and H. L. Raush (eds.), Naturalistic Viewpoints in Psychological Research, pp. 15–30. Holt, Rinehart, and Winston, New York.

Skinner, B. F. 1971. Beyond Freedom and Dignity. Knopf, New York.

Spyker, J. M., Sparber, S. B., and Goldberg, A. M. 1972. Subtle consequences of methylmercury exposure: Behavioral deviations in offspring of treated mothers. Science 177:621–623.

Stokes, T. F., and Baer, D. M. An implicit technology of generalization. J. Appl. Behav. Anal. In press.

Stolz, S. B., Wiencowski, L. A., and Brown, B. S. 1975. Behavior modification: A perspective on critical issues. Amer. Psychologist, 30: 1027–1048.

Wahler, R. G. 1975a. The decline and fall of the "operant conditioning" therapies. Paper presented to the Southeastern Association for the Advancement of Behavior Therapy, Atlanta, Ga.

Wahler, R. G. 1975b. Some structural aspects of deviant child behavior. J. Appl. Behav. Anal. 8:27–42.

Wicker, A. W. 1972. Processes which mediate behavior-environment congruence. Behav. Sci. 17:265–277.

Willems, E. P. 1972a. The interface of the hospital environment and patient behavior. Arch. Phys. Med. and Rehab. 53:115–122.

Willems, E. P. 1972b. Place and motivation: Complexity and independence in patient behavior. In W. J. Mitchell (ed.), Environmental Design: Research and Practice, pp. 4-3-1 to 4-3-8. University of California at Los Angeles, Los Angeles.

Willems, E. P. 1973a. Go ye into all the world and modify behavior: An ecologist's view. Rep. Res. in Soc. Psych. 4:93–105.

Willems, E. P. 1973b. Behavioral ecology and experimental analysis: Courtship is not enough. In J. R. Nesselroade and H. W. Reese (eds.), Life-span Developmental Psychology: Methodological Issues, pp. 195–217. Academic Press, New York.

Willems, E. P. 1973c. Changes in the micro-ecology of patient behavior over three years: Direct observations of patient behavior. Paper presented to American Psychological Association, Montreal, Quebec.

Willems, E. P. 1974. Behavioral technology and behavioral ecology. J. Appl. Behav. Anal. 7:151–165.

Willems, E. P. 1975. Lonely genius is not enough: Thoughts on the content and organization of social ecology. Paper presented to a colloquium, Program in Social Ecology, University of California, Irvine, Cal.

Willems, E. P. 1976a. Behavioral ecology: One hope for psychology. Paper presented to the Guest Lecture Series, Southwest Texas State University, San Marcos, Tex.

Willems, E. P. 1976b. Behavioral ecology, health status, and health care: Applications to the rehabilitation setting. In I. Altman and J. F. Wohlwill (eds.), Human Behavior and Environment: Advances in Theory and Research, pp. 211–263. Plenum, New York.

Willems, E. P. 1976c. Behavioral ecology. In D. Stokols (ed.), Psychological Perspectives on Environment and Behavior, pp. 39–68. Plenum, New York.

Willems, E. P. 1976d. Patient performance as a criterion of change in hospital programs. Paper presented to American Psychological Association, Washington, D.C.

Willems, E. P. 1976e. Longitudinal analysis of patient behavior. In W. A. Spencer (ed.), Annual report of Research and Training Center No. 4, pp. A6–A53. Texas Institute for Rehabilitation and Research, Houston, Texas.

Wolf, M. M. 1976. Social validity: The case for subjective measurement or how applied behavior analysis is finding its heart. Paper presented to the American Psychological Association, Washington, D.C.

Wright, H. F. 1967. Recording and Analyzing Child Behavior. Harper and Row, New York.

Zelazo, P. R., Zelazo, N. A., and Kolb, S. 1972. "Walking" in the newborn. Science 176:314–315.

4

The Moral Risk
and High Cost of
Ecological Concern in
Applied Behavior Analysis

Jacqueline Holman

The early growth of behavior modification was accompanied by polemical and political outcry (London, 1972), and scientific and public acceptance has come slowly. At first, criticisms came largely from dynamically oriented therapists, who charged that behavior modification was too simplistic and that dealing with surface symptoms did not solve clients' problems because other symptoms undoubtedly would emerge (Bookbinder, 1962), or who charged that behavior therapists were not qualified to deal with complex human processes (Raush, 1954). These varied charges produced both theoretical defences (Eysenck, 1954; Yates, 1958) and attempts to respond on empirical bases: by testing whether or not behavior modification effects were merely placebo outcomes (Davison, 1968); by documenting the absence of symptom substitution (Baker, 1969); by comparing behavior modification to traditional forms of therapy (Paul, 1966); and by demonstrating that bizarre, seemingly psychotic behavior patterns could be developed and maintained by contingent reinforcement (Ayllon, Haughton, and Hughes, 1965). As late as 1966, Astin, in a bitterly satirical paper, deplored the tenacity of opposition to learning-theory based solutions to social problems, and concluded that "the principle of functional autonomy will permit psychotherapy to survive long after it has outlived its usefulness . . ." (p. 77).

63

Such controversial issues have never been entirely resolved and some of the original reactionaries are still presenting their positions (Eysenck, 1970). Nevertheless, the number of publications devoted to the evaluation of behavior modification has increased from approximately 12 per year in 1967 to 42 per year by 1972 (Mahoney, Kazdin, and Lesswing, 1974). During this last decade, however, there has been a shift in emphasis: the success of treatment techniques is now rarely disputed, and the efficiency of the varied programs is infrequently challenged. Behavior modification has become an established reality with a wide literature attesting to its benefits (e.g., Bandura, 1969; O'Leary and O'Leary, 1972; Sherman and Baer, 1969). Furthermore, the frontiers are being extended from single responses with single organisms to groups, communities, and the natural environment (Franks and Wilson, 1975).

This success, efficiency, and extended territoriality are responsible for the shift in critical emphasis. As noted by Baer (1971), early criticisms of behavior modification could be handled on an empirical basis, and continual demonstrations of success led to an acceptance of the fact that behavior *can* be modified. More difficult to contest are criticisms based on the moralistic premise "you shouldn't," because such premises cannot be debated on scientific grounds. These moralistic contentions continue to be argued today, both in the popular media (Hilts, 1974) and coupled with legal considerations (Wexler, 1973). Such criticisms are not merely an inconvenience to behavior analysts: if the public and legal profession conspire against the field (however well meaning), they may eventually discourage a valuable technology.

It seems that behavior modification is not yet destined to a peaceful (and presumably fruitful) existence because with these early issues still unsettled, the 1970s are recording an attack from yet another quarter—the ecologists. Ecological criticisms of applied behavior analysis are as subtle and problematic to handle as the moralistic ones, and in some ways more dangerous because they also profess to be scientifically based. It seems that "ecology now" is the fad of the 1970s; Jordan (1972) noted that more books treating man and the environment from a wholistic or ecological viewpoint have appeared since 1968 than during the three decades prior to that year. These concerns cover many crucial issues such as pollution, the depletion of natural resources, and environmental insults (technological changes that may produce short-term benefits and long-term disasters, e.g., the use of DDT or thalidomide). It is this last issue that becomes the focus when examining behavior modification because it is feared that the very efficiency of behavioral solutions to human problems may indicate a need for caution and the possibility of long-term failures.

THE HISTORICAL EMERGENCE
OF ECOLOGY AND ITS PERSPECTIVE

To understand the genesis of the ecologist's concern with the procedures and outcomes of behavior modification, it may be helpful to trace the emergence of the ecological perspective.

Human ecology has developed from three main sources: 1) plant and animal ecology, 2) geography, and 3) studies of the spatial distribution of social phenomena (Theodorson, 1961). This latter category probably accounted for the earliest studies (e.g., patterns of crime in England between 1830 and 1860, Levin and Lindsmith, 1937), but it was not until 1921 that the term "human ecology" was introduced (Theodorson, 1961) to help develop a systematic theory of human communities. Throughout the 1920s and 1930s, human ecology remained largely the domain of sociologists. Despite many attempts to clarify both theoretical and methodological aspects of this emergent science, major issues of the field remained unclear. For example, Quinn (1939) asserted that the diversity of literature published under the label of "ecological" had led to confusion and that "the nature of human ecology does not seem so clear today as it did a decade and a half ago" (p. 135). By 1944, Hawley, a sociologist, charged that human ecology, despite 20 years of existence, "remains a crude and ambiguous conception," and that furthermore, it had become "isolated from the mainstream of ecological thought" (pp. 144–145).

The link between human ecology (as represented by these sociologists) and ecological psychology (on its subsequent emergence) appears to lie in a mutual emphasis on the distribution of phenomena in nature. In fact, it seems that this concern with naturalistic occurrences is what prompted Barker's (1963, 1968) conception of ecological psychology, and what underlies an early ecological paper by Edwin Willems (1965) in which the field of general psychology is urged to adopt ecological principles.

This chapter is concerned primarily with the arguments and criticisms of behavior modification, as presented by Willems (1974). Before examining these closely, however, it may be instructive to look at where Willems' viewpoint fits into the broader context of his own chosen field, as well as to consider his viewpoint from a behavioral orientation. After all, if one is recommending that a particular branch of science broaden its framework to include concepts of a different nature, then it is surely functional to examine the stability and integration of those concepts. Thus, if behavior analysts are to adopt ecological principles, it may be important to estimate the cohesiveness of such principles. This goal may be partially achieved by reviewing some theoretical and empirical reports in the current literature. Such a review suggests (to this author) that while most (self-proclaimed) ecologists share some overlapping tenets, there is in fact little homogeneity among writers.

Is There a Cohesive Ecological Psychology?

Any examination of the field of ecological psychology must acknowledge the contributions of Roger Barker and his colleagues, whose findings have been recognized as not only important but unique (Moos, 1973). In perhaps his most comprehensive work, Barker (1968) pointed out that "psychologists know little more than laymen about the distribution and degree of occurrence of their basic phenomena: of punishment, of hostility, of friendliness, of social pressure, of reward, of fear, of frustration" (p. 2). Barker conceptualized behavioral ecology as being concerned "with molar behavior and the ecological context in which it occurs" (1968, p. 12). The essence of Barker's notion would seem to be that behavior is coerced by the setting in which it happens.

An important conception is that of "behavior settings." As developed by Barker (1968) and extended by Gump (1971), this concept implies an approach to the study of environment that is independent of, while concerned with, both the physical milieu and the attributes of individual subjects and their behavior. An ecological approach, as proposed by these researchers, urges an examination of settings. This permits a description of molar ecological units and patterns, as they are constrained by ongoing activity patterns or by standing patterns of behavior. Research conducted from this basis implies a transducer approach to question-asking and data-gathering. This strategy demands that subject-specific variables be set aside, and that other, more general concepts of psychological theory, such as personality traits of authoritarianism, aggression, etc., be replaced by units that are descriptively and empirically based, in the notion of the "setting."

Setting-based research has been undertaken on both large and small scales. For example, Barker and Schoggen (1973) compared two whole towns as their settings, Barker and Gump (1964) compared large and small schools, and Wicker (1969) replicated the Barker and Gump study in a different milieu in his study of large and small churches. Other setting-based research has been concerned with smaller units such as the intrasetting analysis of specific classrooms (Gump, 1969). These various studies are collectively valuable in that they all illustrate the importance of extra-individual factors, i.e., they show that the behavior of individuals varies predictably from setting to setting and that different individuals in the same setting display similar behavior. The implications of this statement are that the primary determinants of at least some kinds of behavior are not related to individual differences but to the environment itself.

Thus, the focus of setting-based research is on the complexity of behavior and the interdependence of the organism and the environment. The conclusion that individuals are constrained by settings and behave differently across them would not be disputed by operant conditioners. After all, it is well known that principles of learning favor the occurrence of discrimination rather than generalization (Baer and Sherman, 1970). Furthermore, some researchers have suggested that by paying greater attention to ecological factors militating against therapeutic gains, behavior modifiers might promote desired goals more efficiently (Wahler, 1972). Hence, the methodology of Barker and his colleagues is not incompatible with the goals of applied behavior analysis and may even be facilitative. Nevertheless, it may be difficult and extremely costly to implement ecological behavioral programming, if the aim of such programming is not only to produce more effective therapeutic gains but also to satisfy the apparent requirements of ecologists such as Willems.

These potential communalities are considered later in this chapter. Here, the concern is still to define an ecological viewpoint. The Barker school has undoubtedly been an influential one, yet it usually has presented its findings objectively, without incorporating a missionary zeal to convert other, less enlightened psychologists. Collaboration with, or even direct opposition to, behavior modification has not been a primary goal. Among other ecological authors, the goals have been different.

In 1969, Auerswald, a psychiatrist, argued that intervention efforts involved in alleviating social problems could only be truly effective if they were guided by ecological principles. Auerswald attempted to present the usefulness of an ecological, as opposed to an interdisciplinary, approach. For Auerswald, the merit of the ecological position was that its wholistic, nonexclusive nature minimized the dangers of excessive selectivity in the collection of data and allowed for greater explanatory clarity. As an example of such value, Auerswald presented a case history of a juvenile runaway. Auerswald argued that the delinquent's ultimate fate (being committed to a state hospital, diagnosed as a childhood schizophrenic) could have been avoided if an ecological assessment, rather than an interdisciplinary one, had been made. Auerswald's description of an ecological approach, especially its wholistic perspective, has elements in common with the Barker school; yet, in practice, his focus is on the "systems" operating within the environment. Hence, for Auerswald, being ecological is equated with a concern for the transactions taking place between identifiable systems.

Basing his ecological approach significantly on Auerswald's theorizing, Dockens (1975) argued that the integration of such theory and behavior analysis was a "necessary extension for the application of operant principles to the design of cultures" (1975), p. 426). Thus, Dockens' philosophy reflects a pragmatic basis—the need to implement social change. Interested in the application of operant principles to the solution of social problems, Dockens recognized, however, that the implementation of such principles was not simple. The primary goal, therefore, in adopting an ecological outlook, was to program generalization of therapeutic gains. Dockens (unpublished) noted that "this concept of the experimenter as programmer places a heavy stress on the analyst's ability to describe precisely the behavior that he observes, and the conditions under which he observes it" (p. 45). For Dockens, the value of an ecological approach is that it can generate efficient delivery systems; by helping in the specification of stimulus control factors (and not only operating contingencies), therapeutic benefits may be maintained. As an example of the importance of understanding the total, ecological context of behavior, Dockens (1975) described the successful development of an operant treatment program for amphetamine addicts. Ironically, an attempt to implement the same program with methadone patients resulted in failure because "the stimulus properties of methadone were of such a nature as to set up strikingly different behavioral patterns" (1975, p. 438).

Thus, Dockens' notion of an ecological perspective is clearly different from Barker's, although both are interested in whole environments. Furthermore, the notion of programming (unlike Auerswald's concentration on social networks) relies on direct and extensive manipulation of both subject variables and stimulus settings. Another example of an ecological orientation is provided in recent sociological literature. Michaels (1974) drew attention to the fact that human ecology and behavioral social psychology have employed "similar orienting strategies and have produced strikingly parallel general concepts and propositions" (1974, p. 313). Specifically, he discussed the "feasibility and desirability of a symbiotic relationship between human ecologists and behavioral social psychologists and other sociologists who have begun applying the concepts and principles of operant conditioning to the analysis of social process and social organization" (1974, p. 313). Michaels concluded that the major barrier to such a relationship was the discrepancy in the size of the social systems each studied but he offered few suggestions for overcoming this barrier (although he apparently felt this would be beneficial).

This very selective review has illustrated a number of points:

1. The term "human ecology" initially emerged as a sociological concept.
2. The label of "ecological psychology" came independently to reflect a very specialized school of thought (Barker et al.) that emphasized nonmanipulative examination of organism—environment interdependencies.
3. Ecological (implying a need to examine "networks" of relationships), as opposed to interdisciplinary, diagnosis has been promoted by some psychiatrists.
4. Applied operant research has attempted to maximize generalization by pursuing a behavioral ecology.
5. The possibility of uniting sociological and behavioral notions of ecology has been discussed in current sociological literature.

Thus, a variety of differing disciplines has produced a variety of different definitions of what it means to be "ecological" or to adopt an "ecological perspective." True, there are many overlapping components, but the essential fact remains that an ecological orientation can be conceived of from many different perspectives. The overlapping core is a set of principles that, by itself, leads to no action but, in conjunction with *your* own set of principles, leads to clear conclusions that are different, depending on *your* principles. It is conceivable then, that armed with the same basic tenets, researchers working for totally different goals might all achieve success (according to their own criteria), yet be regarded by each other as somewhat misguided. Hence, one might easily imagine a psychologist, trained in the Barker mode and examining behavior modification programs, arguing for caution and restraint in implementing such procedures. Conversely, a skillful operant researcher, realizing the value of such principles, would undoubtedly capitalize on such knowledge and thereby facilitate behavioral gains. Thus, being ecological is a somewhat ambiguous entity because knowing and understanding the elements of an ecological perspective do not define the actions that may result from such knowledge.[1]

Within this overall context, Willems, in a series of papers, has recommended that general psychology (1965), and, more explicitly, behavior

---

[1] This thesis is not an extravagant one and should be well understood by operant conditioners. After all, the applied technology of operant conditioning (behavior modification) itself has many formulations, although there is always one essential point of agreement: behavior can be changed by altering the controlling environmental contingencies. According to Skinner, "Such a technology is ethically neutral.

modifiers (1973a, 1973b, 1974), adopt an ecological viewpoint. Such recommendations have been presented as though there was one, homogeneous, ecological thesis (complete with a set of commandments, or at least a standard text) ready to be adopted. Even a superficial review of the literature reveals, however, that such assumptions are too simplistic. Indeed, perusal of the literature shows, all too clearly, that most proponents of an ecological perspective are concerned only with *their own* definition of ecological. Rarely do such proponents recognize each other's existence (as indicated most obviously by their lack of cross-references to one another).

Undoubtedly, there are problems in providing a simple definition of an ecological perspective. Yet, perhaps the problem is not such a great one; perhaps this author's attempts to understand the genesis of such a position have been misguided. To examine Willems' recommendations in this larger context may be pointless; it may be more fruitful to examine and evaluate them quite independently.

Willems' Ecological Perspective

Despite the current independence of Willems' assertions, their basic development owes much to the Barker ecological school. This is partially reflected in the development and change of focus of Willems' philosophy and orientation over a 10-year period. It may be instructive to examine this change. In 1965, in a paper presented primarily to the field of general psychology, Willems argued that experimental psychology was essentially a laboratory science. He went on to assert that in many instances, laboratory findings may not generalize to the everyday lives of organisms: the difference between artificially contrived (although highly controlled) situations and the complexities of the natural environment are sometimes too great. Willems supported his claims by citing a variety of studies in which experimental findings did not generalize to the natural environment. The reasons for lack of generalization varied. In some cases, both experimental and ecological measurements would show identical outcomes but for different reasons. For example, Willems reported a study by Washburn (1963) showing that, when two or more baboons were grouped together, a leader emerged. However, in the experimental zoo setting, the leader emerged by intimidation or brute force; whereas in the natural setting,

---

It can be used by villain or saint." (1971, p. 150). Thus, a knowledge of such principles potentially can lead to different outcomes, but usually will lead to changes deemed good or bad. The ecological example is more complicated because it is less easy to place a value judgment on the outcomes. Rather, such principles may result in varying actions: their value will depend on the judge.

leaders usually based their power on superior cunning, sexual prowess, and "attractiveness."

Another example illustrative of the inadequacy of experimental data arises when variables are artificially tied in ways that would never occur naturally. Willems cited an example provided by Gump and Kounin (1960), who tested the effects of various kinds of control techniques used by teachers in college classes. It was found that punitive (rather than supportive) teacher techniques (in dealing with stooge students who were deliberately tardy) resulted in lowered student evaluations of the instructor's competence, likeability, and fairness. Later questionnaires, however, showed that students were surprised by the instructor's behavior, and, thus, their responses were evaluations based on their perception of "atypical" behavior rather than evaluations of supportive and punitive techniques. Willems provided many other examples to illustrate the inadequacy of a purely experimental approach and to illustrate the value, as he sees it, of an ecological approach. Certainly, his criticisms of many experiments in the general psychological field are valid and are supported by other investigators urging naturalistic research (Menzel, 1969; Sells, 1969), as well as by studies from a different perspective, e.g., the literature on demand characteristics (Orne, 1962, 1969) and experimenter bias (Rosenthal, 1969).

Willems further asserted that he was not attempting to denounce experimental research as such, but merely attempting to point out that many answers cannot be found if experimental methods are the only ones used. Willems then attempted to define the ecological orientation. In summary, it seems that this perspective implies that a researcher: acts as a transducer of information; uses sensitive, noninterfering techniques; measures units of behavior as they present themselves; utilizes richer, higher-order, more multi-dimensional concepts; and thus yields statements about what exists in the behavioral world unaltered by the investigator or the investigation. The essence, then, is description rather than manipulation.

Willems' arguments are persuasive: obviously, psychology, if it is interested in establishing truth (the presumed god of science), must attend to more than artificial demonstrations of possibilities. It must expand its horizons beyond the realm of introductory psychology students participating "voluntarily" in experiments (usually as a course requirement). Granted the validity of this persuasion, the problem of how to do so still remains. Since the ecological orientation proposes to "incorporate phenomena of different levels into one conceptual scheme" (Willems, 1965, p. 333) the problem of measurement is immense. Willems discussed Barker's (1963) specimen-record technique as one possible solution. Essentially, a specimen record is an observer's verbal transcript of the behavior and interactions of a focal subject (minute by minute). To be meaningful, it also itemizes the objects, places, people, and events involved in the ongoing behavior. The wealth of information that may be provided by a specimen record is not in dispute at this point. However, it should be noted (because of crucial relevance to later issues) that Willems himself raised the question, "What can be done with it?" (1965, p. 335). Willems has cited some possibilities. For example, Fawl (1963) analyzed behavior disruptions and frustrations measured in 16 day-long, specimen records, that preserved over 200 hours of sequential behavior. Fawl summarized the frequency, duration, and intensity of disturbance that were evoked in the ongoing behavior of children by objects, events, and people in their environment. It was concluded that frustration (defined as goal-blockage) was not severe, i.e., that only an average of 16.5 blocked goals occurred daily. Further, such blockages rarely produced disturbed states on the child's part.

This author is not disputing the validity of Fawl's chosen methodology or the interest of the findings. However, the goal of behavior analysis is to eliminate problem behaviors as efficiently as possible. Therefore, a retrospective analysis cannot be used because it is no longer a measure of the current situation. Furthermore, though measurement for 16 days would not be an unusual baseline for behavior modifiers to assess, the cost of focusing on one behavior sequence (goal-blockage and possible subsequent frustration) for 200 hours of analysis, would make many studies incredibly expensive. It is difficult to see how this kind of measurement system could be implemented in the context of an applied analysis of behavior

Between 1965 and 1973, Willems' target audience shifted somewhat. Leaving the realm of general psychology, Willems began appealing to a more specialized area of psychology (and perhaps from his viewpoint, a more crucial one)—behavior modification. Two papers published by Willems in 1973 are dealt with briefly here. Their titles give a feel for the content: 1) Behavioral ecology and experimental analysis: Courtship is not enough, and 2) Go ye into all the world and modify behavior: An ecologist's view. A fourth paper, published in 1974, is considered in greater detail.

THE ECOLOGICAL CHALLENGE TO BEHAVIOR MODIFICATION

Behavior modification is generally referred to as a technology rather than a therapy (Zifferblatt and Hendricks, 1974). This is not surprising: it is easy to conceptualize the procedures and methods from a technological view-point and to describe much of the research in terms of social engineering. The term therapy is usually restricted to the somehow more human values of such states as rapport, transference, and growth. Another reason for subsuming behavior modification under the technological label is the effectiveness of the implementations. It is probably this latter point that encourages concerned persons to fear the potential outcomes of too much success and of procedures implemented too widely. After all, therapies that are useful only with very small populations, and that may take a very long period before a cure is pronounced, need not be feared because their impact is minimal. It seems ironic that success thereby prompts cautionary critiques—critiques that frequently are argued on the analogous basis of long-term disasters documented as occurring within the natural sciences.

This seems to be the flavor of Willems' 1973a paper. His stated purpose is to advocate the adoption of an ecological perspective and to urge an interdependent methodological and procedural pluralism in the active pursuit of important problems of behavior and development. Willems admitted in this paper that the ecological perspective is a difficult one to define, and he noted two stereotypes: 1) the ecological perspective involves direct observation of children, and 2) it involves nonexperimental techniques for gathering data. These, Willems claimed, are inadequate characterizations. He stressed that a precise definition of the ecological perspective was impossible, partly because it is neither a method nor a theory but rather a viewpoint. This somewhat perplexing position is partially elucidated by Willems' use of examples from the biological sciences. This author offers the following extract, from a different source, with a similar intention:

> In Malaya, an attempt to eliminate malaria nearly caused an outbreak of plague and certainly made a lot of roofs fall in. In spraying the malaria-carrying mosquitoes, they also reduced the number of roaches, which in turn reduced the number of geckos, and this in turn reduced the number of cats. With fewer cats, the rats increased and with them the plague-bearing lice. At this stage, the obvious—but fatal—thing to do was to put down rat poison. This would have caused the lice to look for new homes and they would have moved to human beings. Fortunately, World Health Organization officers were on the spot: they did the right thing. They parachuted in more cats and the plague was averted.
>
> And the roofs? A side effect of all this was that a leaf-eating caterpillar which lived on the thatched roofs increased exceedingly, probably because the wasp which preys on it was also decimated by DDT—though the geckos may have helped to keep it down too. Freed from their predators, the caterpillars munched away until they brought the roofs down . . . (Taylor, 1970, p. 78).

Willems reported similar examples of disastrous, unanticipated effects occurring because of technological intrusions. For example, the building of the Aswan Dam on the Nile River resulted in a reduction of the annual sardine catch in the Mediterranean from 18,000 tons to around 500 tons per year and also led to an increase in the incidence and virulence of schistosomiasis. Other small-scale problems are noted in his paper, such as the impossibility of the bearded tit (a rare European bird) rearing chicks in captivity because its environment was *too* comfortable (allowing the parents to satiate the chicks, which would never have occurred in nature, and precipitating an infanticide cycle when the parents threw their sleeping offspring from the nest). Perhaps such stories have value in partially clarifying the importance of mutual interdependencies and the delicacy of the balance points in nature.

Willems (1973b) presented another, similar thesis, but his challenge to behavior modification was more specific. Again citing examples from both macro- and micro-ecology, Willems urged that if such examples exist in biology, it is likely that similar principles operate in human behavior. Furthermore, he pointed out that neither love nor humanitarian interests guaranteed the appropriateness of any technological intervention. In fact, Willems rather scathingly referred to the "almost childish irresponsibility displayed by psychologists dealing with behavior and behavioral-environment systems" (1973b, pp. 96–97). It is time, he asserted, to display greater care when interfering with behavior, even when the interferer is "that most solidly empirical of sacred cows—behavior modification" (1973b, p. 97).

Perhaps the greatest significance of Willems' 1974 paper (see Chapter 2 of this volume) is its publication outlet—the *Journal of Applied Behavior Analysis.* Through this source, possibly the most prestigous and widely distributed among applied operant researchers, Willems challenged behavior modifiers in one of the most direct ways possible. The paper was primarily a reiteration of the 1973 thesis; he again utilized examples from social and engineering sciences to point to the potential for unanticipated outcomes of large-scale interventions and additionally noted some cases of side effects or unpredicted outcomes in behavior modification programs. For example, he cited a case in which a subject-mother was trained to reduce her rate of nagging (verbal commands) from 100 or more per hour to 15 per hour. The result was an increase child compliance (the target goal). However, as the case continued, the mother's rate of eating, anxiety, and tension also increased, and the final outcome was that the mother deserted the child. Willems mentioned some other troublesome studies in behavior modification and restated a number of warnings:

1. There is no possibility of "simple" intervention, because the interfaces between organisms and environments are complex and often subtle.
2. Neither technological ingenuity and capacity, nor humanitarian motives provide a license for action.
3. Within the context of behavioral ecology, short-term successes may underlie irreparable long-term harm.
4. There is an urgent need to develop creative, meaningful criteria to evaluate intervention efforts—perhaps "flying in the face of what common sense, accepted social wisdom and even past successes with our technologies tell us is humane, important and worthwhile" (Willems, 1974, p. 153).

In conclusion, it seems that Willems has come very close to asserting that behavior modifiers should abandon intervention programs until a more complete contextual understanding of behavior is acquired.[2] Very close, but not quite! Rather than condemn all behavior modifiers to the valley of extinction—perhaps because such instant commitment would itself comprise an intervention and disturb the delicate ecology of many existing behavioral programs, or more likely because attempted extinction usually results in an increased, albeit brief, burst of output—Willems holds out the opportunity for collaboration between behavioral ecologists and analysts. Such collaboration, Willems suggests, *may* avert catastrophic outcomes, but only if behavior analysts are willing to work within a system of long-term dependencies. The important phenomena of behavior (from Willems' perspective) are not merely single responses or even response classes. Ironically perhaps, it is when behavior modifiers deal with single-unit (molecular) behavior that they least offend ecologists because the potential ramifications of such "simplistic" interventions are presumed to be less disastrous. However, when behavior modifiers (being aware of ecological factors and not merely contingencies) design a treatment package focused on molar behavior in the total environment, they are most vulnerable to ecological attack because they are maximizing their chances of producing far-reaching changes and, thus, of disturbing the existing ecological schema.

In addition to suggesting collaboration, Willems (1974) does offer behavior analysts some possible guidelines:

1. Information gleaned from behavioral interventions into troublesome

---

[2] Willems has argued, recently, (see Chapter 3 of this volume) that his earlier papers have been misunderstood). Nevertheless, it seems reasonable to note that his later writings represent substantially modified versions of his earlier opinions.

behavior may be misleading if used to infer causality on a general behavioral basis.

2. There is a need to collect long-term data and diverse behavioral measures.

3. Unanticipated costs of intervention are almost inevitable; therefore, caution and foresight are essential.

4. Unanticipated effects of behavioral interventions, documented so far, beg for research, and it may very well be that such a need is greater than the literature to date suggests.

If applied behavior analysts reject these recommendations or attend only superficially to them, Willems implies that much harm may eventuate and that finally behavior analysis, like comparative psychology, may die (Lockard, 1971).

The ecological challenge is a disturbing one, partly because examples from the natural sciences are frightening, and partly because there is already a hint of such potential effects in the existing behavior modification literature. These warnings and hints cannot be ignored: Baer (1971) noted that when behavior modification became the target of moral, as contrasted with empirical, criticism, the field could not afford to put its audience on extinction; the issue of morality had to be (indeed, continues to be) debated. So it is with the ecological challenge: the challenge must be accepted; ecology's basic tenets must be treated with respect; the possibility of long-term disastors should be noted with awe; and the field should be prepared to learn from its ecological colleagues. After all, ecological considerations may be useful in maximizing treatment gains as well as in anticipating and predicting problems. However, despite the fact that this author has much sympathy for Willems' viewpoint, the time has not yet come for total despair. This reviewer finds doomsday prophecies to be somewhat dysfunctional and therefore takes issue with Willems on a number of points. These include:

1. A rejection of the implication that behavior analysts do not distinguish between etiology and the maintenance of behavior by current controlling contingencies.

2. The possibility that the negative outcomes so far reported may reflect a lack of sophistication in the techniques implemented, rather than a basic flaw in the behavior analysis model.

3. The likelihood that the cost of implementing an ecological viewpoint (potentially acceptable to critics such as Willems) may be prohibitive and, thus, paralyze remediation efforts for little (at least inestimable) social benefit.

These issues all deserve serious consideration and will be debated in the following pages.

A RESPONSE TO THE ECOLOGICAL CHALLENGE

The primary concern of this section is to examine carefully the points presented by Willems. As noted earlier, there are some objections to be raised. It is hoped that these objections will convince an impartial audience that applied behavior analysis is neither totally naive of scientific principles nor hopelessly blind to potentialities beyond an immediate modification.

Outcomes versus Antecedent Conditions

In raising the issue of outcomes versus antecedent conditions, Willems noted that applied behavior modification rests on certain assumptions of environmentalism, instrumentality, and contingency control. He asserted that a pitfall of this theory was "that information gleaned from troubling behavior may lead to misleading inferences back to the general model of behavior" (1974, p. 163). Willems is disturbed that behavior modifiers might confirm a model of behavior on the basis of treatment. To illustrate his point, Willems cited an example provided by Rimland: "Does the fact that aspirin alleviates headaches mean that the deficiency of aspirin causes headaches?"

Baer's (1974) rejoinder to this assertion is both succinct and competent. (Reprinted as Part I Comment of this volume.) In essence, he claimed that there was no issue. Perhaps, however, the point should be considered further, not because this reviewer believes that such an issue exists, but because it is distressing to suppose that behavior analysts are considered to be so naive that they are not granted the basic respect due to any scientist, i.e., that judgments and conclusions are based on rational deductions and empirically validated data. (If behavior analysts were presumed to have an ego, it would surely be deflated by now!)

In this author's opinion, to confuse the distinction between etiology and behavior maintained by the current controlling contingencies would reflect not only scientific naivite but a deficiency in logical deductive powers. As Willems sought to clarify his assertion by using Rimland's example of headaches, it seems just to attempt a rebuttal using another Rimland-associated example, that of autism.

There are two primary theories of autism: 1) that of organic etiology proposed by Rimland (1964) who traced the problem to a single critical disability "cognitive dysfunction," and 2) an alternative explanation presented by Ferster (1961, 1965), who has argued that an autistic repertoire *could* be accounted for in terms of past reinforcement history. To date, the question of the etiology of autism remains unanswered. However, there are many examples in the literature of behavior modification effecting relief, improvement, hope, and understanding when other orientations have offered only an apparent understanding (see Koegel and Schreibman, 1974; Lovaas et al., 1966; Risley, 1968; Schreibman, 1975). As yet, medical science has not provided an explanation of the cause of autism. While recognizing that organic etiology is a possibility, and may even be accompanied by a cure (as with the problem of phenylketonuria), it has not yet happened. If such a situation did eventuate, then behavior modifiers could afford to bypass attempts to examine reinforcement histories potentially responsible for the development of autism: they would still be left with the existing autistic population. Unless, or until, medical science provides both an explanation and a cure for this condition, behavior analysts should continue to develop and refine their technology to produce effective behavioral change, *and they manifestly can do so in the ignorance of etiology.*

In this example, behavior analysts have provided a "possible" explanation of etiology; they have by no means asserted that this is the only explanation. There are surely many other examples that could be considered in a similar fashion. It is discouraging to think that fellow psychologists do not grant one the status of belonging to a scientific community based on logical principles. Perhaps, after all, Baer's comment was the only appropriate response: "There is no issue" (1974, p. 168).

Do Behavior Modification Procedures
Lead to Unpredictable or Unanticipated Outcomes?

Whether this question is analyzed from the viewpoint of a behavior analyst or from the viewpoint of an ecologist, its implications are critical. For the ecologist, the focus is not simply on the directly measured outcomes of a particular intervention, but also on outcomes that may emerge indirectly (perhaps at a later time) and that probably have not been included within the existing measurement system. The ecologist is concerned with whether or not the "system" has been inappropriately disrupted. These concerns are valid, and in many instances (though for different reasons) they are shared by behavior modifiers. The behavior analyst usually has two major therapeutic concerns: 1) does the procedure work to change the target behavior? and 2) will such change maintain across diverse settings and over time?

These questions are of inestimable importance to the field of behavior modification: unless answers are sought (and eventually found) behavior modification will probably cease to exist by default because it will not have provided permanent solutions to social problems. This is the issue of generalization, i.e., how to maximize the gains of any therapeutic endeavor so as to gain the most positive behavioral effects. Thus, generalization might simplistically be conceived of as achieving the initial goal and positively extending the treatment effects. However, there is another possibility. The treatment goal may be achieved but be accompanied by negative outcomes (usually, perhaps euphemistically, referred to as side effects).

The issue of generalization is no longer a luxury because applied behavior analysis has long since demonstrated dramatic skillfulness in effecting behavioral change. For the most part, however, these changes have been limited to discrete responses and stimulus situations, and, while these results provide a strong and necessary foundation for a still develop-ing technology, it is unlikely to adequately sustain that technology. It is therefore essential to develop a technology which will specify more pre-cisely the conditions that favor the occurrence of appropriate generaliza-tion. The need to develop a generalization technology is supported by those studies that, while achieving success in the training situation, show zero or minimal evidence of transfer to the untrained setting. Examples of failure have been reported for both individual and group treatment pro-grams: Birnbrauer (1968) and Lovaas and Simmons (1969) independently showed that punishment can successfully reduce self-destructive and ag-gressive responses in retarded and psychotic subjects. Regretably, the punishment effects were highly specific across both situations and people. Wahler (1969) reduced deviant behavior and increased cooperative behav-ior of two oppositional children at home, but this did not affect classroom deviance.

On the other hand, some studies have recorded generalization effects that were not specifically programmed. Such fortuitous benefits have been categorized in a recent review of generalization by Stokes and Baer (1977) as "train-and-hope" procedures. In such instances, the target behavior is modified (trained), and it is hoped (though not necessarily expected) that such training will result in generalized change. An example of this category is provided by Kirby and Shields (1972), who modified an academic response by combining immediate praise and immediate correctness feed-back on arithmetic response rate. Concurrently, measures of attending behavior were taken. It was hoped that attending would increase along with an improvement in the academic response. Indeed, both the immediate goal and the desired collatoral changes were achieved.

The Stokes and Baer (1977) review has examined and classified almost 300 studies of generalization and has provided at least seven techniques for promoting behavioral gains. The review provides considerable evidence that a technology of generalization exists, because, although half the cited studies fall into the "train-and-hope" category, these studies tend to be the earlier, less sophisticated, investigations. Recently, studies of generalization have been more extensive and complex and have displayed substantial evidence of therapeutically desirable outcomes. Why such effects were obtained is not of immediate concern here. What should be noted, is that within the narrow confines of a behavior modification system, unpredicted (although desirable) changes were shown to occur along with the directly targeted response. For Stokes and Baer (indeed, for all behavior modifiers), such outcomes seem promising because they herald the more elaborate development of a generalization technology. However, for an ecologically oriented researcher, the documenting of such unanticipated results (no matter how positive) suggests a need for caution because it is obvious that simple modifications are not necessarily leading to simple results. Consider the case in which behavior modification procedures lead not only to successful modification of the targeted response, but also to unanticipated negative effects, i.e., effects that may be either directly or indirectly harmful to a subject. In considering this situation, it seems instructive to examine the literature to determine whether or not such negative outcomes exist.

If one accepts that ecological concepts are important, then documenting the number of reported unfavorable studies is not of immediate concern because even a very low number of negative outcomes establishes a baseline for needed evaluation. Thus, the following studies are not meant to represent an exhaustive literature review. Rather, they are a sample, illustrative of a fairly simple fact: behavior modification techniques can, and sometimes do, lead to undesirable or troublesome outcomes. Furthermore, these are outcomes that are detectable "within" the measurement technology of the applied behavior analysis model. Rarely do these studies detect disruptions of a subtle, interdependent nature. Such subtle disturbances (if they exist) may require a more sophisticated, or at least a different, procedural analysis.

A cursory perusal of current literature does suggest that behavior modification is not always successful. Specifically, there appear to be four main types of failure:

1. Procedures that work some of the time do not work consistently for all subjects.
2. A procedure may work initially, for a limited period, but be unsuccessful over time.
3. A procedure established under restricted laboratory conditions may work in such a limited setting but fail to generalize to a more natural community.
4. A procedure may work to achieve a targeted goal but be accompanied by unanticipated, undesirable side effects.

All of these types of failure need to be experimentally analyzed and understood by behavior analysts because only then can therapeutic benefits be maximized. The last category, however, most nearly approximates an ecological concern. All four types are considered here.

Some Failures of Behavior Modification

Inconsistent Effects of Procedures Sometimes procedures that are efficient and effective across varied subjects and situations will prove ineffective with similar subjects. For example, implementing a token economy program has been shown to result in: improved self-help skills of chronic schizophrenics (Lloyd and Garlington, 1968); reduced apathy for psychotic males (Henderson and Scoles, 1970); increased classroom attending behavior (Walker and Buckley, 1968); more appropriate social and academic behaviors by delinquents (Phillips, 1968); and decreased incidence of stuttering (Ingham and Andrews, 1973). Despite such general success, however, a large number of studies also report that certain patients were unresponsive to such procedures. Ayllon and Azrin (1965) reported that 18 percent of their patients were relatively unaffected by the procedures, while Lloyd and Garlington (1968) reported a failure figure of only 8 percent. Kazdin (1973) reviewed the problem of failure to respond and (while noting a failure rate ranging from 7.7 percent to 75 percent) suggested that the percentage was relatively consistent. Just why such failures occurred is not at issue here; rather, the point to be made is that even well established procedures may not lead to predictable outcomes.

In the case of token economies, the unpredictable effect noted was simply "no" effect. However, there are other documented examples of procedures that, while generally successful, are sometimes accompanied by quite serious consequences. For example, differential social attention from adults is frequently used in modifying child behavior. A variety of behaviors has been successfully modified in this way, e.g., study behavior (Hall,

Lund, and Jackson, 1968) and inappropriate behaviors (Wahler, 1969). By contrast, using just this procedure, Herbert et al. (1973), in two independent parent training projects, trained mothers to use differential attention procedures to increase appropriate and decrease inappropriate child behaviors. For five out of six children, the procedure failed to produce desirable effects; additionally, substantial increases in deviant behavior emerged in four of the subjects. Furthermore, this distressing result reflected a change not only in rate but in quality of deviance, i.e., there was a topographical shift in the behaviors exhibited, such that the children displayed behaviors that were never before noted by the parents, that were aggressive, self-destructive, and dangerous. The authors were unable to account for these disturbing findings but offered their conclusions as a warning against adopting too simplistic an attitude toward behavior modification procedures. They urged workers in the field to engage in careful evaluation of all implementations.

An interesting example of superficial training and application of behavior modification principles is provided by Goldstein (1974). Dormitory counselors in a Bureau of Indian Affairs Navajo boarding school requested, and were given, a workshop in behavior problems. Following the workshop, a child with whom a counselor had been working began to be truant (a behavior nonexistent prior to the workshop). The counselor was neither able to place the "running away" behavior under control, nor obtain control of "attending" in class, the original target goal. Based on the workshop principles, the counselor had chosen "eye contact" as an initial behavior in the chain toward shaping attending behavior. Apparently, this initial choice was a basic error: traditional Navajos feel a profound sense of intrusion when eye contact is sustained in a manner which the predominant white society regards as appropriate. Navajo children are told the myth of a terrible monster called He-Who-Kills-With-His-Eyes when quite young, and they are taught to avert their eyes to avoid bringing harm to people. Thus, the counselor had inadvertently chosen a behavior which was entirely inappropriate within the existing cultural context. This lack of sensitivity to cultural norms (although used with a well intended intervention program) actually magnified an existing problem rather than providing a remedy. This example suggests two important considerations:

1. Perhaps behavior modification techniques should not be taught so casually. While the procedures are frequently declared to be simple (as opposed to the intensely deeper meaning claimed by traditional psy-

chotherapies), they usually require fairly sophisticated programming to be successful.

2. Behavior modifiers dealing with minority groups need to be especially sensitive to the requirements of a cultural milieu.[3]

Temporary Successes A therapeutic intervention, to be regarded as genuinely successful, should be able to demonstrate durability over time (Baer, Wolf, and Risley, 1968; Keeley, Shemberg, and Carbonell, 1976; Lovitt, 1975). Unless this requirement holds, then a procedure—no matter how brilliant, creative, or efficient—will generally be deemed of little value. This criterion of success, however, cannot be said to be a strong point of behavior modification programs. This does not necessarily imply that immediate successes are long-term failures, but it does definitely suggest that long-term successes have been documented infrequently. A reasonably skeptical audience might begin to wonder if behavior analysts merely change the initial presenting problem and do little to change the final outcome. There is at least preliminary evidence to suggest that this might be true. For example, Quirk (1974) reported a study in which the initial, successful treatment (by behavioral means) of a case of exhibitionism resulted in inadequate maintenance. Initially, the patient was cited as a successful case and maintained this status through a three-month follow-up period. Shortly after this time limit, however, the frequency and intensity of the patient's acting out behaviors again increased. This resulted in the patient entering an aversive conditioning program, that apparently was also unsuccessful. Approximately nine months later, a biofeedback desensitization procedure appeared helpful. The patient was treated over a three-year period and subsequently was followed for an additional two years. At that time the presenting problem appeared to be under control, but, in the clinician's words, "it does not seem proper to comment on this case since, in such work, who knows what tomorrow might bring" (1974, p. 431).

This case is an interesting example because the client involved was essentially tracked over a 14-year period. The point to be made is not

---

[3] An alternative route would be to teach Navajo children that awesome consequences are not necessarily associated with making eye contact. To do so, however, would obviously be more difficult, because such training would not be supported in the natural community. Furthermore, there is a growing awareness that minority groups should be encouraged to maintain their cultural heritage, rather than simply conform to majority norms. Hence, pragmatic, as well as social, value judgments dictate that some response other than eye contact be selected. Eye contact is merely an arbitrary element, and not a necessary component, of the original target (attending).

merely that behavior modification procedures sometimes fail (as other therapeutic endeavors do also), but that the final outcomes of behavioral interventions should be assessed as carefully as their initial baselines and, additionally, that long-term changes need to be documented for the benefit of the behavior modification field. Of course, even this recommendation cannot stand unqualified. Long-term maintenance should generally be regarded as crucial for behavioral problems that require extinction. Thus, in the example given, exhibitionism is not regarded as appropriate within the cultural milieu: successful therapy therefore means extinction or suppression of the response. A similar case could be made for a variety of other behaviors, such as self-destructive patterns. But success is not always defined by maintenance of a therapeutically induced change. For example, a preschool child may be classified as a social isolate and taught to play cooperatively by soliciting peer interactions. Success, in this case, would be defined as an increase in cooperative play, and one would hope to observe maintenance (at least occasionally). However, the outcome of a 10-year follow-up could not be deemed desirable if it was shown that the subject (now 15 years old) was displaying cooperative patterns appropriate to a preschooler. In this situation, a clinically valuable result would be to observe that the subject "could" engage in social interactions, i.e., that this skill was available in the subject's repertoire for use when so desired. (It might be very difficult, however, to argue that this success was the direct outcome of the early therapy.)

Competing Variables in the Natural Community   The importance of the natural community in maintaining therapeutic change has been discussed in the behavioral literature (Baer and Wolf, 1970; Seymour and Stokes, 1976). The negative natural-community pressures are less often noted, although recently there have been attempts to specify these factors. Thus, Reppucci and Saunders (1974) have argued that behavior modifiers in natural settings face a series of problems that are either nonexistent, or relatively inconspicuous, in the laboratory. They suggested that such problems may often account for program failures (when intervention efforts are attempted directly in a community, as opposed to a research, setting) and offered a list of potentially damaging setting variables to guard against (e.g., institutional constraints and external pressure).

A variety of studies support the need to attend to these issues. For example, Burtle, Whitlock, and Franks (1974), using behavioral techniques with hospitalized women alcoholics, succeeded in modifying the women's low self-esteem. Following return to the community, however, most of these gains were lost by the 16-week follow-up. Miran, Lehrer, and Koehler (1974) reported dramatic short-term improvement in the school adjustment of deviant adolescents. Despite the obvious success of the program, social pressures within the community resulted in withdrawal of financial support and the effectual collapse of the program. Both studies point to a need to attend to extra-therapeutic variables. Thus, Burtle et al. suggested establishing halfway houses within the community to support treatment gains, and Miran et al. urged workers to examine ways of improving institutional motivation. As behavior modifiers become increasingly involved in large-scale community programs (see Tharp and Wetzel, 1969) they will need to deal effectively with the bureaucratic structure of long-established institutions. Otherwise, wide-scale successes may not often be achieved.

Unpredictability of Techniques This category most closely approximates an ecological concern because it documents the existence of unpredictable, possibly negative changes accompanying the intended behavioral change. Several kinds of difficulties have been reported, e.g., the sequential development of problem behaviors. Balson (1973) reported that two weeks after eliminating encopretic behavior in an eight-year-old boy, violent temper tantrums emerged. This subsequent emergence is reminiscent of the notion of symptom substitution. However, such problems are not necessarily serious, provided they can be successively modified. It would be expected that eventually such substitutions would cease (with individual subjects varying in their creative efforts to display new responses).

Other difficulties are more complicated. For example, Pendergrass (1972) used timeout to suppress self-stimulatory behaviors in two very withdrawn, retarded children. However, this reduction was accompanied by a collatoral lowering of social responsiveness. This outcome can hardly be considered positive for children whose social repertoire is already extremely restricted.

Additionally, several studies have reported effects that are difficult to explain in terms of known learning principles. Wahler, Sperling, Thomas, and Teeter (1970) modified stuttering behavior in two children by dealing with secondary behavior problems (oppositional behavior in one child and hyperactivity in the other). By training the parents to respond differentially to these secondary problems, control of stuttering was also obtained, i.e., verbal disfluencies decreased when the secondary problems were reduced. These changes were not explainable on the basis of the verbal and nonverbal behaviors sharing any observed common stimulus-control properties.

Sajwaj, Twardosz, and Burke (1972) specifically recorded diverse and multiple behaviors (while modifying only one of them) to examine the possibility of widespread, unanticipated outcomes. When a teacher ignored the excessive conversation of a young, retarded boy during free play, teacher-directed conversation decreased. Along with achieving this goal, however, cooperative peer interactions increased (a positive effect) and use of girls' toys decreased (possibly a neutral effect). Additionally, and undesirably, appropriate classroom behaviors decreased, and disruptions increased during group academic time. These results are partially understandable, i.e., it could be that peer interactions increased simply because the child was now spending less time with adults. However, it is perplexing to understand why play with girls' toys, or inappropriate responding during an academic period, would covary with the manipulation.

It might be possible to present tenable hypotheses explaining the above effects. Nevertheless, these studies collectively suggest that perhaps the modification of behavior is not such a simple matter. It is true that many of the procedures are simple to implement; it is also true that success (meaning modification of the target response) is often recorded. However, it is not yet clear if the failures of operant technology (as classified above) are sufficiently serious to warrant either behavioral or ecological concern. The next section considers this issue.

The Need for Concern about Behavioral Interventions

Undeniably, the evidence indicates that behavior modification techniques do not always work. Having established this and having tentatively categorized some types of failures, a different question arises: "What do we do now?" Behavior modifiers are dedicated to developing further a technology to correct social problems, but can the failures be defended or ignored? Or are these issues so serious that our technology should be disbanded until perfect implementations are possible and no unknown outcomes will ever emerge? Stated more simply, are behavior modifiers acting irresponsibly?

It is this author's contention that many of the reported failures may reflect a lack of sophistication in the techniques implemented, rather than a flaw in the behavior analysis model as such. Consider the types of failure noted, e.g., that the therapy does not always work, or that it works initially but fails in the long term. This is true of any therapeutic endeavor (including some widely prescribed medical treatments as well as a variety of psychotherapies). This surely does not establish that all potential successes should be sacrificed. Rather, it implies a need for more creative analyses of resistant cases and an urgent need to refine maintenance techniques. Similarly, if programs fail when introduced into social institutions (as opposed to the more controlled research settings), therapists must learn to deal with and to work within the established institutional structure, rather than attempt to impose an arbitrary, unnatural structure that unquestionably will be resisted.

However, all the issues noted above reflect the concern of a therapist, i.e., reflect the perspective of maximizing treatment gains. They are not the essential concern of the ecologist. The ecologist is as likely to be concerned by therapeutic success as failure (because of its potential long-term disruptive system effects). Furthermore, the ecologist will be concerned by failures of treatment which display obvious harmful effects as well as unpredicted outcomes (the so-called side effects). As we have seen, behavioral research has documented such effects. They are complex, difficult to understand, and seemingly do not obey the usual, or at least well understood, laws of learning. This issue cannot yet be resolved on a data base. Indeed, the potential ramifications are complex, and any decision almost inevitably must rest on a value judgment. Perhaps, then, it is the value judgments that must be examined and that may define a set of alternative actions.

ALTERNATIVE COURSES

The ecological challenge to the field of behavior modification is at least a call to sober reflection and cautious evaluation. Both reflection and evaluation have been attempted in this chapter. If the issues cannot be resolved simply on an empirical basis, it is time to consider options. Therefore, three main alternatives are considered below:

1. Behavior modifiers cease all action.
2. Behavior modifiers satisfy *all* ecological concerns and continue therapeutic interventions.
3. Or, behavior modifiers adopt a well tempered ecological perspective.

Action versus Inaction

Willems (1973) suggested that perhaps the most adaptive form of action may be inaction. Adopting this course implies that behavior modifiers cease all technological programming until it can be unequivocably demonstrated that all potential effects, intended and unintended, can be predicted in advance of interventions. Such a stand would guarantee that the disruption of existing systems would never occur as a planned procedure. Unfortunately, such a stand also implies maintenance of the status quo, at least temporarily, and possibly permanently.

If there were considerable agreement that after some temporary period of investigation and clarification of learning principles, operant technology would be *totally* predictable, then it might be reasonable to wait. However, it is very doubtful we will ever have a technology that can predict *all* the complexities of even known schedules and response classes. Analogies of mistakes made in the natural sciences offer little hope. Thus, the repercussions of introducing DDT "might" have been avoided if this insecticide had first been used on a small scale and observed over a very long period. However, it is possible that the undesirable outcomes would never have been noticed *until* the usage was large-scale. Hence, with a behavioral technology, there may be unpredictable and undesirable outcomes that accompany intended changes, but these effects may not be predictable in advance. Perhaps unanticipated (if undesirable) changes will have to be dealt with only after they arise.

Willems claimed for ecologists an "unmistakeable undercurrent of direct moral concern and involvement in prescriptive and proscriptive guidelines for human action" (1973a, p. 208). It seems that the proscriptive guidelines are abundant and the prescriptive ones are scarce. Furthermore, the claim of "direct moral concern," while a laudatory one, is of little use to a therapist whose (surely equally valuable) moral concern depends on action. Indeed, if moral concern is to be made the basis of selecting an active or inactive course, one might debate the morality of a laissez-faire policy: after all, how morally responsible is it to maintain the status quo? It might be simpler to ask the question about a specific, atypical population such as mental retardates. How responsible is it to withhold from this group a technology that can remediate some of their deficits? Should they be left to vegetate (presumably in an institution where their existence is noticed only by the few), or should some useful responses, e.g., self-help skills, be developed? A similar question might be raised about destructive responding such as head-banging (a not infrequent behavior of autistic children). Is it better to allow such responding rather than implement a change that substitutes more normal behavior? In counting the cost of withholding such assistance, one should calculate not only the current state of the population being considered but also the network of society involved: parents, professionals, and paraprofessionals. The costs are not measureable only in terms of money; they are far more complex. Indeed, the costs suggest the possibility of horrendous future problems, as well as the continued existence of a totally undesirable state. For this author, inaction is ethically unacceptable. (It might be added here that even those ecologists who point out that waste is natural, admit that some forms of waste are more acceptable than others (see Hardin, 1963).)

Behavior Modifiers Become Ecologists

This alternative proposes that whenever a therapeutic endeavor is planned the measurement system should be sufficiently sophisticated to detect ecological outcomes *as* they occur. Thus, operant therapists need not be prevented from action, as long as they act like wise ecologists. Very few researchers have attempted to do this, and the few available data hold minimal hope for this becoming a viable option.

Wahler (1975) provided one of the few examples of ecological research that might derive from Willems' conception. This study was designed to explore regularly occurring interrelationships between deviant behavior and other events in a child's social environment. Wahler presented two cases of within-family behavior modification. A coded observation system permitted scoring 19 child-behaviors and six social-environment categories. Baseline measurement demonstrated that each child showed a group of behaviors that covaried and that the groupings were specific to the home and school settings. When contingency management procedures were introduced into one setting, across-setting effects were recorded and experimentally replicated. Molar analyses of the results suggested that the problem behaviors could be appropriately modified. Additionally, however, the planned changes in one setting were accompanied by unplanned changes in the second setting. For one subject, increments in classroom schoolwork were grossly associated with increments in home self-stimulation and reduced social interactions; for a second subject, modification of oppositional behavior at home was accompanied by increases in peer interaction and reduced opposition at school. No viable explanation of these across-setting changes, in terms of environmental determinants, were found.

This study is important in providing yet another example of unanticipated outcomes accompanying behavior modification procedures. It is additionally important because of the complexity of the measurement system used which coded 25 events across settings (home and school) and over a long time period (three years). Unfortunately, this study does not really provide support for behavior modifiers adopting such measurement systems. Consider the findings. An incredibly expensive analysis of behavior was conducted, and the conclusions were only that: 1) in one case, contingency management procedures were accompanied by positive effects, and 2) in a second case, they were accompanied by mildly disturbing effects. Each of these unanticipated outcomes was noticed by relevant persons in the environment: by the teacher, who expressed delight at improved school progress, and by the family, who expressed some reservations about increases in solitary behavior during treatment. The point to be made here is that this complex and costly analysis of behavior produced results detectable by other concerned individuals in the subject's environment. While it is true that these people were unable to explain why the behavioral covariations occurred, it is also true that the measurement system could not do so either.

Thus, it does not seem likely that this is a valuable route for behavior modifiers to take.[4] If such a complex system could have explained why elaborate covariations occurred, it might have been worth pursuing. As it did not, this author doubts the worth of pursuing such a course because it seems that the cost of implementing an ecological perspective (potentially acceptable to critics such as Willems) increases at a rate greater than its ability to satisfy that perspective. Thus, to adopt such a plan would potentially paralyze all behavioral remediation efforts, for little apparent social benefit.

An additional theoretical point may be argued here: essentially, it is impossible to satisfy the ecological perspective. If behavior analysts, attempting to do so, engage in a prohibitive research (as well as a therapeutic) endeavor, they can only definitively confirm the existence of a negative instance. Thus, having demonstrated some successfully targeted change, an experimental analysis might also reveal (as has been noted) that unanticipated (sometimes undesirable) effects accompanied such change. If no undesirable, or unintended effects are noted (and even if positive ones are) the behavior modifier remains open to the charge that the measurement system utilized was too primitive to detect these potentially subtle and dangerous outcomes.[5] Furthermore, since Willems has suggested that the outcomes of any particular intervention must be sought creatively—"perhaps flying in the face of what common sense, accepted social wisdom, and even past success with our technologies tell us is humane, important and worthwhile" (1974, p. 153)—this writer seriously

---

[4] Research by Wahler and his colleagues represents a skillful and dedicated attempt to experimentally specify the kinds of environments that support certain clusters of behaviors. The criticisms raised within this chapter in no way negate the value of such data. Rather, the criticisms are meant to illustrate that this kind of research is still in a formative period and that the paradigm cannot, as yet, be accepted by all applied behavior analysts.

[5] This problem is reminiscent of Sidman's (1960) discussion of systematic replication by "affirming the consequent." Since such a procedure is logically fallacious, although potentially very persuasive, one can never convince a confirmed doubter of the adequacy of the evidence.

doubts the ability of the most ingenious behavior analyst to modify Willems' opinion.

Tempering the Ecological Perspective

As noted earlier in this chapter, the ecological challenge to behavior modification is a disturbing one, and cannot be lightly discarded (see Baer, 1974). Nevertheless, while retaining considerable sympathy for the viewpoint expressed by Willems (1974), the thesis presented in this chapter is essentially a negative one: to cease behavioral programming (and thus maintain the status quo) would be unethical, and for behavior modifiers to satisfy the ecological perspective would be a pragmatic (and theoretical) impossibility. It might be noted here that some ecologically oriented scientists are themselves aware of the difficulties inherent in oversimplifying the ecological viewpoint. Thus, Ward and Dubos (1972), while criticizing the widespread dispersion of DDT, argued that simply banning its use would not necessarily solve the problem because pests do eat crops—in fact, in Asia a quarter of the harvest may go to feed predators rather than humans. Ward and Dubos suggest that it is important to "avoid being tunnel minded in our retreats from technology" (p. 63) and that answers will not be found in broad generalizations.

Perhaps a compromise is possible, and perhaps that is all Willems intended. After all, it is clear that any behavioral intervention may be a highly complex affair and one that should not be pursued cavalierly. Any behavioral intervention should be accompanied by careful assessment of change, not only in the sense of measuring the specified target goal, but by being generally attuned to the whole experimental situation and to all relevant people. Thus, despite the essentially negative thesis of this chapter, it may be possible that a relatively new approach in behavior modification—the assessment of "consumer satisfaction" with the procedures and results of any behavioral program—may prove useful in at least the detection and loose specification of undesirable ecological outcomes. The technique may not be a strong one, but, in the absence of more specific guidelines from ecology, it may yet be of value.

The technique has not been widely discussed in the operant literature, but it has been in use with well established programs for some time. For example, organizers of Achievement Place, a community-based program for juvenile offenders, regularly evaluate the effect of their program in the wider community context. Phillips et al. (1972) pointed out that routine, formal evaluation of a program was a means of obtaining feedback from the delinquents involved, from their parents, and from members of various agencies that served the youths (teachers, probation officers, and welfare workers) regarding their opinions of the program's quality, effectiveness, and usefulness in accomplishing its objectives. Indeed, they claimed that neglect to carry out at least an annual evaluation may be an attempt to hide failure and/or malpractice.

It is perhaps unfortunate that the use of program evaluation is not widely reported in the literature, particularly when it is carried out in practice (see Wolf, 1976). One recent, though limited, example is provided by Fawcett and Miller (1975) whose training package effectively increased the public-speaking skills of low-income paraprofessionals. Additionally, these researchers measured audience ratings of public-speaking performance and the self-confidence of the participants before and after training. These measures were shown to improve, along with the targeted goal of public speaking. (An additional example, related to the training of conversation skills, is provided by Minkin et al. 1976.)

A primary value of current satisfaction-assessment instruments is their simplicity and cheapness of design and administration (as opposed to the extremely complex and costly method of behaviorally measuring unanticipated effects). Additionally, and perhaps the most valuable aspect of questionnaire assessment of outcomes is its potential "openness" to detecting any unpredicted side effects. Undoubtedly the route which should be taken by behavior analysts interested in assessing behavioral interventions and their possible ramifications is to maximize this potential for openness. There are many ways of pursuing this goal: Wallis and Roberts (1956) suggest that one useful technique is to ask a main question, e.g., "What did you think of this program?" and then, depending on the response, to probe for some index of an opposite opinion. Thus, if a respondant's answer was positive, a probe might take the form, "What features of the program did you find troublesome or unpleasant?" A negative response might be followed up by asking, "What aspects did you find valuable or useful?" This brief description is not meant to contain all the important considerations necessary in satisfaction-questionnaire design; rather, the key point to note is that this technique has some value for program assessment *if* the pursuit of openness is maximized.

Questionnaire design should not be conducted superficially because an approach that is too simplistic will be of little value. It is probably always possible to phrase a question in a way that invites only a positive response. For these reasons, it is not easy to specify just what questions should be asked, and of whom, or to supply some kind of general questionnaire that will suit every research project. Such decisions will have to be made by an individual investigator in the context of the ongoing study. The available psychological and sociological literature on attitudinal assessment should prove helpful to researchers attempting to acquire skills in this area (see Schuman and Duncan, 1974). Adopting these procedures will impose an additional response cost on behavior analysts, yet surely such demands are not too onerous. A behavior modifier interested in effecting widespread social change should be willing to engage in some independent assessment of the technology being implemented and to be sensitive to unanticipated ecological fallout. Unwillingness to accept the spirit of public account-ability may force some programs out of existence, if, as the ecologists fear, unanticipated, undesirable outcomes eventually emerge. Conversely, adopting these procedures now, and thereby detecting possibly undesirable effects as they emerge (if not in advance) may very well protect behavior modifiers at least against the charge of irresponsible manipulation.

CONCLUSION

This chapter has examined a challenge to the behavior modification field, one that argued that behavioral interventions may result in unanticipated, ecological effects. A review of some current behavior modification studies revealed that intervention outcomes are not always predictable and that unanticipated (possibly undesirable) effects sometimes occur. Neverthe-less, this writer has argued that behavioral programming should continue, because to cease such action implies acceptance of the status quo—an ethically intolerable state. Furthermore, it seems economically impractical for behavior modifiers to become thoroughgoing ecologists and theoreti-cally impossible for this field—or any field— to satisfy the ecological perspective. A compromise (essentially suggesting a more sensitive and diverse evaluation of all behavioral programs) has been proposed, and behavior modifiers are urged to adopt this procedure and thereby reduce (if not avoid) ecological and behavioral irresponsibility.

LITERATURE CITED

Astin, A. W. 1966. The functional autonomy of psychotherapy. Amer. Psychologist, 16:75−78.

Auerswald, E. H. 1969. Interdisciplinary versus ecological approach. *In* W. Gray, F. J. Duhl, and N. D. Rizzo (eds.), General Systems Theory and Psychiatry, p. 373−386. Little, Brown, and Co., Boston.

Ayllon, T., and Azrin, N. H. 1958. The measurement and reinforcement of behavior of psychotics. J. Exp. Anal. Behav. 8:357−383.

Ayllon, T., Haughton, E., and Hughes, H. B. 1965. Interpretation of symptoms: Fact or fiction. Behav. Res. and Ther., 3:1−7.

Baer, D. M. 1971. Behavior modification: You shouldn't. *In* E. A. Ramp and B. L. Hopkins (eds.), A New Direction for Education: Behavior Analysis, p. 358–367. The University of Kansas Support and Development Center for Follow Through, Department of Human Development. University of Kansas Press, Lawrence, Kan.

Baer, D. M. 1974. A note on the absence of a Santa Claus in any known ecosystem: A rejoinder to Willems. J. Appl. Behav. Anal. 7:167–170.

Baer, D. M., and Sherman, J. A. 1970. Behavior modification: Clinical and educational implications. In H. W. Reese and L. P. Lipsitt (eds.), Experimental Child Psychology, p. 643–672. Academic Press, New York.

Baer, D. M., and Wolf, M. M. 1970. The entry into natural communities of reinforcement. *In* R. Ulrich, T. Stachnik, and J. Mabry (eds.), Control of Human Behavior, Vol. II, p. 319–324. Scott, Foresman, and Co., Glenview, Ill.

Baer, D. M., Wolf, M. M., and Risley, T. R. 1968. Some current dimensions of applied behavior analysis. J. Appl. Behav. Anal. 1:91–97.

Baker, B. L. 1969. Symptom treatment and symptom substitution in enuresis. J. Abnorm. Psych. 74:42–49.

Balson, P. M. 1973. Encopresis: A case with symptom substitution. Behav. Ther. 4:134–136.

Bandura, A. 1969. Principles of Behavior Modification. Holt, Rinehart, and Winston, New York.

Barker, R. G. 1963. The stream of behavior as an empirical problem. *In* R. G. Barker (ed.), The Stream of Behavior, p. 1–22. Meredith Publishing Co., New York.

Barker, R. G. 1968. Ecological psychology. Stanford University Press, Stanford.

Barker, R. G., and Gump, P. V. 1964. Big School, Small School. Stanford University Press, Stanford.

Barker, R. G., and Schoggen, P. 1973. Qualities of Community Life. Jossey-Bass, San Francisco.

Birnbrauer, J. S. 1968. Generalization of punishment effects—a case study. J. Appl. Behav. Anal. 1:201–211.

Bookbinder, L. J. 1962. Simple conditioning versus the dynamic approach to symptoms and symptom substitution: A reply to Yates. Psych. Rep. 10:71–77.

Burtle, V., Whitlock, D., and Franks, V. 1974. Modification of low self-esteem in women alcoholics: A behavior treatment approach. Psychotherapy: Theory, Research and Practice 11:36–40.

Davison, G. C. 1968. Systematic desensitization as a counter conditioning process. J. Abnorm. Psych. 73:91–99.

Dockens, W. S. 1973. Toward a behavioral ecology: A psychological systems approach to social problems. Unpublished manuscript. Uppsala.

Dockens, W. S. 1975. Operant conditioning: A general systems approach. *In* T. Thompson and W. S. Dockens, Applications of Behavior Modification, p. 425–442. Academic Press, New York.

Epstein, L. H., Doke, L. A., Sajwaj, T. E., Sorrell, S., and Rimmer, B.

1974. Generality and side effects of overcorrection. J. Appl. Behav. Anal. 7:385–390.

Eysenck, H. J. 1954. Further comment on "Relations with psychiatry." Amer. Psych. 9:157–158.

Eysenck, H. J. 1970. Behavior therapy and its critics. J. Behav. Ther. Exp. Psych. 1:5–15.

Fawcett, S. B., and Miller, L. K. 1975. Training public-speaking behavior: An experimental analysis and social validation. J. Appl. Behav. Anal. 8:125–135.

Fawl, C. L. 1963. Disturbances experienced by children in their natural habitats. In R. G. Barker (ed.), The Stream of Behavior, p. 99–126. Meredith Publishing Co., New York.

Ferster, C. B. 1961. Positive reinforcement and behavioral deficits of autistic children. Child Dev. 32:437–456.

Ferster, C. B. 1965. The repertoire of the autistic child in relation to principles of reinforcement. In L. Gottschalk and A. H. Auerback (eds.), Methods of Research in Psychotherapy, A.C.C., New York.

Franks, C. M. and Wilson, G. T. (eds.). 1975. Annual Review of Behavior Therapy, Theory and Practice, Vol. 3. Brunner/Mazel, New York.

Goldstein, G. S. 1974. Behavior modification: Some cultural factors. Psych. Record 24:89–91.

Gump, P. V. 1969. Intra-setting analysis: The third grade classroom as a special but instructive case. In E. Willems and H. L. Raush (eds.), Naturalistic Viewpoints in Psychological Research, p. 200–220. Holt, Rinehart, and Winston, New York.

Gump, P. V. 1971. Milieu, environment and behavior. Design and Environ. Spring: 49 ff.

Gump, P. V., and Kounin, J. S. 1960. Issues raised by ecological and "classical" research efforts. Merrill-Palmer Q. 6:145–152.

Hall, R. V., Lund, D., and Jackson, D. 1968. Effects of teacher attention on study behavior. J. Appl. Behav. Anal. 1:1–12.

Hardin, G. 1963. The cybernetics of competition: A biologist's view of society, In P. Shepard and D. McKinley (eds.), The Subversive Science: Essays toward an Ecology of Man, p. 275–296. 1969. Houghton Mifflin Co., New York.

Hawley, A. H. 1961. Ecology and human ecology. In G. A. Theodorson (ed.), Studies in Human Ecology, p. 144–151. Row, Peterson, and Co., Evanston, Ill.

Henderson, J. D., and Scoles, P. E. 1970. A community based behavioral operant environment for psychotic men. Behav. Ther. 1:245–251.

Herbert, E. W., Pinkston, E. M., Hayden, M. L., Sajwaj, T. E., Pinkston, S., Cordua, G., and Jackson, C. 1973. Adverse effects of differential parental attention. J. Appl. Behav. Anal. 6:15–30.

Hilts, P. J. 1974. Behavior Mod. Harper's Magazine Press, New York.

Ingham, R. J., and Andrews, G. 1973. An analysis of a token economy in stuttering therapy. J. Appl. Behav. Anal. 6:219–229.

Jordan, P. 1972. A real predicament. Science 175:977–978.

Kazdin, A. E. 1973. The failure of some patients to respond to token programs. J. Behav. Ther. Exp. Psych. 4:7–14.

Keeley, S. M., Shemberg, K. M., and Carbonell, J. 1976. Operant clinical intervention: Behavior management or beyond? Where are the data? Behav. Ther. 7:292–305.

Kirby, F. D. and Shields, F. 1972. Modification of arithmetic response rate and attending behavior in a seventh-grade student. J. Appl. Behav. Anal. 5:79–84.

Koegal, R. L., and Schreibman, L. 1974. The role of stimulus variables in teaching autistic children. In O. I. Lovaas and B. D. Bucher (eds.), Perspectives in Behavior Modification with Deviant Children, p. 537–546. Prentice-Hall, Englewood Cliffs, N.J.

Levin, Y. and Lindsmith, A. 1937. English ecology and criminology of the past century. In G. A. Theodorson, Studies in Human Ecology, p. 14–21. 1961. Row, Peterson, and Co., Evanston, Ill.

Lloyd, K. E., and Garlington, W. K. 1968. Weekly variations in performance on a token economy psychiatric ward. Behav. Res. and Ther. 6:407–410.

Lockard, R. B. 1971. Reflections on the fall of comparative psychology: Is there a message for us all? Amer. Psychologist 26:168–179.

London, P. 1972. The end of ideology in behavior modification. Amer. Psychologist 27:913–920.

Lovaas, O. I., Berberich, J. P., Perloff, B. F., and Schaeffer, B. 1966. Acquisition of imitative speech by schizophrenic children. Science 151:705–707.

Lovaas, O. I., and Simmons, J. Q. 1969. Manipulation of self-destruction in three retarded children. J. Appl. Behav. Anal. 2:143–157.

Lovitt, T. C. 1975. Applied behavior analysis and learning disabilities, Part 1: Characteristics of ABA, general recommendations and methodological limitations. J. Learn. Disabil. 8(7):432–443.

Mahoney, M. J., Kazdin, A. E., and Lesswing, N. J. 1974. Behavior modification: Delusion or deliverance. In C. M. Franks and G. T. Wilson (eds.), Annual Review of Behavior Theory, Therapy and Research, Vol. 2, pp. 11–40.

Menzel, E. W. 1969. Naturalistic and experimental approaches to primate behavior. In E. P. Willems and H. L. Raush (eds.), Naturalistic Viewpoints in Psychological Research. pp. 78–121. Holt, Rinehart, and Winston, New York.

Michaels, J. W. 1974. On the relation between human ecology and behavioral social psychology. Social Forces 52:313–321.

Minkin, N., Braukmann, C. J., Minkin, B. L., Timbers, G. D., Timbers, B. J. Fixsen, D. L., Phillips, E. L., and Wolf, M. M. 1976. The social validation and training of conversation skills. J. Appl. Behav. Anal. 9:127–140.

Miran, M., Lehrer, P. M., Koehler, R., and Miran, E. 1974. What happens when deviant behavior begins to change? The relevance of a social systems approach for behavioral programs with adolescents. J. Commun. Psych. 2:370–375.

Moos, R. H. 1973. Conceptualizations of human environment. Amer. Psychologist 28:652—665.

O'Leary, K. D., and O'Leary, S. G. (eds.). 1972. Classroom Management: The Successful Use of Behavior Modification. Pergamon Press, Inc., New York.

Orne, M. T. 1962. On the social psychology of the psychological experiment: With particular reference to demand characteristics and their implications. Amer. Psychologist 17:776—783.

Orne, M. T. 1969. Demand characteristics and the concept of quasi-controls. In R. Rosenthal and R. L. Rosnow (eds.), Artifact in Behavioral Research, pp. 143—179. Academic Press, New York.

Paul, G. L. 1966. Insight vs. desensitization in psychotherapy. Stanford University Press, Stanford.

Pendergrass, V. W. 1972. Timeout from positive reinforcement following persistent, high-rate behavior in retardates. J. Appl. Behav. Anal. 5:85—91.

Phillips, E. L. 1968. Achievement Place: Token reinforcement procedures in a home-style rehabilitation setting for "predelinquent" boys. J. Appl. Behav. Anal. 1:213—223.

Phillips, E. L., Phillips, E. A., Fixsen, D. L., and Wolf, M. M. 1972. The Teaching-Family Handbook. University of Kansas Printng Service, Lawrence, Kan.

Quinn, J. A. 1939. The nature of human ecology: Reexamination and redefinition. In G. A. Theodorson, Studies in Human Ecology, pp. 135—144. 1961. Row, Peterson, and Co., Evanston, Ill.

Quirk, D. 1974. A follow-up on the Bond-Hutchison case of systematic desensitization with an exhibitionist. Behav. Ther. 5:428—431.

Raush, H. L. 1954. Comment on Eysenck's "Further comment on relations with psychiatry." Amer. Psychologist 9:588—589.

Reppucci, N. D., and Saunders, J. T. 1974. Social psychology of behavior modification: Problems of implementation in natural settings. Amer. Psychologist 29:9.

Rimland, B. 1964. Infantile Autism: The Syndrome and its Implications for a Neural Theory of Behavior. Appleton-Century-Crofts, New York.

Risley, T. R. 1968. The effects and side effects of punishing the autistic behaviors of a deviant child. J. Appl. Behav. Anal. 1:21—24.

Rosenthal, R. 1969. Interpersonal expectations: Effects of the experimenter's hypothesis. In R. Rosenthal and R. L. Rosnow, Artifact in Behavioral Research, pp. 181—277. Academic Press, New York.

Sajwaj, T., Twardosz, S., and Burke, M. 1972. Side effects of extinction procedures in a remedial preschool. J. Appl. Behav. Anal. 5:163—175.

Schreibman, L. 1975. Effects of within-stimulus and extra-stimulus prompting on discrimination learning in autistic children. J. Appl. Behav. Anal. 8:91—112.

Schuman, H., and Duncan, O. D. 1974. Questions about attitude survey questions. In H. L. Costner (ed.), Sociological Methodology, 1973—74. Jossey-Bass, San Francisco.

Sells, S. B. 1969. Ecology and the science of psychology. In E. P. Willems and H. L. Raush (eds.) Naturalistic Viewpoints in Psychological Research, pp. 15–30. Holt, Rinehart, and Winston, New York.

Seymour, F. W., and Stokes, T. F. 1976. Self-recording in training girls to increase work and evoke staff praise in an institution for offenders. J. Appl. Behav. Anal. 9:41–54.

Sherman, J. A., and Baer, D. M. 1969. Appraisal of operant therapy techniques with children and adults. In C. M. Franks (ed.), Behavior Therapy–Appraisal and Status, pp. 192–219. McGraw-Hill, New York.

Sidman, M. 1960. Tactics of Scientific Research. Basic Books, New York.

Skinner, B. F. 1971. Beyond Freedom and Dignity. Alfred A. Knopf, New York.

Stokes, T. F., and Baer, D. M. 1977. An implicit technology of generalization. J. Appl. Behav. Anal. In press.

Taylor, G. R. 1970. The Doomsday Book. World Publishing Co., New York.

Tharp, R. G., and Wetzel, R. J. 1969. Behavior Modification in the Natural Environment. Academic Press, New York.

Theodorson, G. A. (ed.). 1961. Studies in Human Ecology. Row, Peterson, and Co., Evanston, Ill.

Wahler, R. G. 1969. Setting generality: Some specific and general effects of child behavior therapy. J. Appl. Behav. Anal. 2:239–246.

Wahler, R. G. 1972. Some ecological problems in child modification. In S. W. Bijou and E. Ribes-Inesta (eds.), Behavior Modification: Issues and Extensions, pp. 7–18. Academic Press, New York.

Wahler, R. G. 1975. Some structural aspects of deviant child behavior. J. Appl. Behav. Anal. 8:27–42.

Wahler, R. G., Sperling, K. A., Thomas, M. R., Teeter, N. C., and Luper, H. L. 1970. The modification of childhood stuttering: Some response-response relationships. J. Exp. Child Psych. 9:411–428.

Walker, H. M., and Buckley, N. 1968. The use of positive reinforcement in conditioning attending behavior. J. Appl. Behav. Anal. 1:245–252.

Wallis, W. A., and Roberts, H. V. 1956. Statistics–A New Approach. The Free Press, New York.

Ward, B., and Dubos, R. 1972. Only One Earth. W. W. Norton and Co., Inc., New York.

Wexler, D. B. 1973. Token and Taboo: Behavior modification, token economics, and the law. California Law Review 61:81–109.

Wicker, A. W. 1969. Size of church membership and members' support of church behavior settings. J. Personal. and Soc. Psych. 13:278–288.

Willems, E. P. 1965. An ecological orientation in psychology. Merrill-Palmer Q. 11:317–343.

Willems, E. P. 1973a. Behavioral ecology and experimental analysis: Courtship is not enough. In J. R. Nesselroade and H. W. Reese (eds.), Life-span Developmental Psychology Methodological Issues. Academic Press, New York.

Willems, E. P. 1973b. Go ye into all the world and modify behavior: An ecologists's view. Rep. Res. Soc. Psych. 4:93–105.

Willems, E. P. 1974. Behavioral technology and behavioral ecology. J. Appl. Behav. Anal. 7:151–165.

Wolf, M. M. 1976. Social validity: The case for subjective measurement. Paper presented as an invited address to the Division of the Experimental Analysis of Behavior, American Psychological Association, September, 1976, Washington, D.C.

Yates, A. J. 1958. Symptoms and symptom substitution. Psych. Rev. 65:371–374.

Zifferblatt, S. M., and Hendricks, C. G. 1974. Applied behavioral analysis of societal problems: Population change, a case in point. Amer. Psychologist, 29:10, 750–761.

5

Some Comments on the Structure of the Intersection* of Ecology and Applied Behavior Analysis

Donald M. Baer

Two disciplines have developed that share a common critical term. The disciplines are behavior analysis and ecology; the common term is environment.

Behavior analysis has found that the most intimate control of ongoing behavior lies in the immediate environment of behavior, and that the important aspects of the environment are themselves not difficult to control. Thus, behavior analysts simply took near-total control of small laboratory environments and thereby uncovered systematic formulae of resultant behavior control within those settings. Subsequently, *applied* behavior analysts tried those formulae on other behaviors that existed not in laboratory environments but in real-life ones, and that constituted problems for at least some of the people in those environments. The applied behavior analysts knew from the work of the behavior analysts what kinds of environmental process to control. Of practical and social necessity, they took only partial control of the real-life environments; but the soundness of the environmental principles that they used was such that they often succeeded in altering the behaviors that they meant to, in the directions that their analyses suggested would constitute solutions to problems.

Environment was an intriguing term to have in common with the

---

*Willems said that courtship was not enough. But this looks like a shotgun wedding. (Still, the side effects of a shotgun wedding can be fun.)

ecologists. Long since, ecology had found that environments can be studied as such: they have their own structure and their own laws, despite their apparent diversity. Among these laws is one that makes environments seem like behaving organisms: they react to actions applied to them, and the reaction often functions to recover the previous state of affairs—the one that held prior to the actions applied to them. Inevitably, those reactions also affected the behavior of any nonmetaphorical organisms living in those environments.

When the behavior analysts had exercised their near-total control of small laboratory environments, they hardly intercepted this ecological principle. This was probably because they had vivisected the environment, excising from it only a small, deliberately artificial segment that they could prevent from reacting to their manipulations in any ways other than those they desired. In effect, they reduced the environment to a fraction of itself, incapable of displaying its most basic characteristic of whole-environment function, which is reaction to intervention (see Baltes and Reese, 1977). The applied behavior analysts, however, unable to vivisect real-life environments to that extent, nevertheless intervene in them, merely to change a few contingencies here and there. Thereby, they operate in an environment capable of reacting in all the other ways that they either do not seek to control or are unable to control; because of that, it is argued, they will encounter that reactive principle of ecology quite often.

Thus, warning is served that although behavior analysis may well be a reasonably self-sufficient analysis of laboratory behavior, applied behavior analysis may be a seriously incomplete analysis of real-life behavior, in that it has not yet recognized ecological reaction as a principle relevant to itself. Because of that lack of recognition, applied behavior analysis has neither 1) explored the possibility of its inherent long-term ineffectiveness, nor 2) begun the development of a technology to detect and handle ecological reaction to behavioral intervention. Which of these two reactions to the intervention of the ecologists' logic is appropriate would appear to depend on some facts not yet gathered. However, upon analysis, this problem may prove to be more often a matter of assumption than of the gathering of facts. The following arguments are offered in support of that possibility.

QUESTIONS ARISING FROM THE INTERSECTION OF ECOLOGY AND APPLIED BEHAVIOR ANALYSIS

On the face of it, there are some factual questions to be answered if the principle of ecology is to be considered as an essential part of applied behavior analysis. The first and most basic question is whether that principle is true often enough to be considered a principle. That it is descriptive of so-called side effects[1] on at least some occasions seems clear enough from the everyday experience of workers in the field; but if these occasions are few in number or very specialized in nature, then perhaps the problem can be filed away as a quirk rather than a principle, and the development of applied behavior analysis may continue much as at present, unaffected by ecological logic. Thus, the first requirement is simply for a great deal of pointed observation about any side effects of behavioral interventions: how durable the programmed changes prove to be, and what sort of unprogrammed changes occur. But as Holman points out elsewhere in this volume (Chapter 4), this is not at all a simple requirement. What to look for, and how, and at the expense of doing what else instead, are exceptionally difficult questions to answer. Indeed, these questions are so difficult and so expensive that exceptional justification ought to exist before the necessary resources are committed to them. Some of that justification exists in the form of ecological observations of human behavior that is not problem behavior and into which, conse-quently, there is no intervention; some of it is based on theories of the ecology of behavior paralleling those observations; and much of it consists of truly ecological reactions to interventions, but documented only in numerous *biological* interactions. The present requirement is for new research to evaluate whether or not that is a principle for behavioral interventions as well. Commitment to pursue this new, difficult, and expensive research might flow from a prior commitment to the probable generality of the biological principle. Unfortunately, it will be a great deal easier to assume that generality rather than to evaluate it empirically, especially in the absence of pointed advice on how to pursue it empirically (see Willems, this volume).

Then it will be tempting to move on to a second question that arises, which is: what are the mechanisms of ecological reaction to behavioral intervention? However, if that move is made by assumption rather than as

---

[1] Side effects are indeed so-called. As the preceding argument was meant to imply, environmental reaction to intervention is as basic a principle as any principle on which the intervention itself might be based. Thus, that reaction is not a "side" effect; it is a basic effect. However, when neither intervener nor ecologist could have said in advance what form that environmental reaction would take, and are more or less surprised by it (at least, by its form, if not its existence), then it is likely to be called a side effect, in tribute to its surprise value (and also as an implied putdown of its worth—how dare it appear in a well planned intervention that had not anticipated it!). In the present chapter, admitting the above, the term side effect will be used simply to index any reaction to intervention that was not targeted by the interven-tion, nor exists on an easily recognizable generalization gradient from any of the stimuli or responses that were targeted in the intervention.

a result of an empirical demonstration that the question needs to be asked, then it is at least possible that we find ourselves looking for mechanisms of a phenomenon that does not occur, or does not occur often. In the past, learning theorists sometimes found themselves devoting a great deal of effort to clarifying the mechanisms of a kind of learning that later turned out to occur only in, say, paired-associate memorization. Thus, we too may find ourselves repetitively examining some particular case of applied behavior analysis, e.g., the establishment of instructional control in oppositional children, just because it happens to be rich in ecological fallout, underlying which (presumably) there are mechanisms to be uncovered. The consequences for this discipline, and perhaps for this society, of an investment of research expertise and resources into what later turns out to be a nongeneral problem is itself an interesting problem in ecology.

Suppose that the second question does arise, either by assumption or by enough empirical demonstrations of unpredicted, troublesome side effects in a sufficient variety of applied interventions. Then a particular form of the second question will recommend itself: are the mechanisms of ecological reaction to behavioral interventions the same mechanisms whereby behavior is changed through applied behavior analysis? We are very likely to ask that question—it is the only kind of question that we know that we know how to answer (sic). To put the second question more specifically: when a behavioral intervention sets up a few new contingencies or rearranges a few old ones in a real-life environment, thereby altering at least for the moment some behaviors of some inhabitants of that environment, does the environment then react to this intervention by itself introducing or rearranging a few other contingencies that lead to side effects or counter effects? Or does it use mechanisms other than reinforcement, punishment, extinction, and discrimination contingencies?

If environmental reaction to a contingency-based intervention is itself a new set of contingencies, then behavior analysts may well prove to be just the researchers to investigate the reaction. But if the reaction uses uniquely ecological rather than contingency-based mechanisms, then behavior analysts will not understand them, and if they are the only researchers pursuing this problem, the resultant analysis will be incomplete. However, as long as the side effects or counter effects are behavioral, even if not the result of reactive new contingencies, then behavior analysts at least may deal with them, no doubt by imposing ad hoc additional contingencies on them or on incompatible or remedial behaviors. (For example, if overpopulation can be solved by establishing the use of contraceptive pills, but the best of these pills sometimes cause headaches as well, which lead to their disuse, then a counter solution, riskily disregarding the biochemistry of those headaches, might be to develop aspirin-using behaviors concurrently with the contraceptive-using behaviors.)

Notice, however, that if the side effects of ecological reaction to behavioral intervention are not themselves behavioral in their manifestation, or only very indirectly so, then behavior analysts are quite likely to miss them altogether. Thus, rather than an incomplete analysis, there may be no analysis at all, and perhaps there will be a great deal of trouble as well. To whatever extent this is so, it represents a strong possibility that applied behavior analysis will prove too risky a venture to be tolerated.

If the answer to the second question is that indeed, ecological reaction to behavioral intervention consists simply of some new contingencies operating to the detriment of the intervention or the intervenees, then a very tactical question presents itself: are these new detrimental contingencies, apparently requiring additional ad hoc contingencies to deal with them, truly *reactive* to the first intervention's contingencies? Or are they merely concurrent with the contingencies that were responsible for the problem in the first place, and now have become apparent, perhaps because part of the confusion has been cleared away through the partial success of the incomplete first intervention? For if they are concurrent rather than reactive aspects of the originating problem, then they can be dealt with simply by an expansion of the program that dealt with the prior part of that problem, and in time, through this kind of experience, we shall learn to apply more complete prgrams in the first place when dealing with this type of problem. In that case, they are not truly ecological phenomena, or at least are not very elaborate examples of what an ecological reaction to intervention could be. Then we may as well proceed with the development of the discipline of applied behavior analysis, not too much troubled by an inevitable characteristic of a young discipline doing understandably partial work in its early attacks on many problems. We will learn.

If ecological reaction to behavioral intervention is indeed reactive and does consist of new contingencies, then behavior analysts will ask a fourth question: are those reactive new contingencies *predictable* from the nature and context of the originating problem, and/or from the nature of the intervention? If they are not, there is a simple recourse, the same one required when reactive mechanisms that are not contingency-based nevertheless produce side effects that are behavioral: react to these unpredictable side effects with additional contingencies, designed on a necessarily ad hoc basis to deal with them, whatever they may be this time. However, in the present context, this recourse, no matter how ad hoc it may need to be, is at least not as seriously incomplete as was that former case. Here, we are dealing with reactive new contingencies by applying counter-reactive additional contingencies of our own. What could be more appropriate? At least, we will not be accused of dealing with symptoms symptomatically. Instead, we shall be dealing with reactions reactively, and on their own principles, and with their own techniques.

That does not mean that we will succeed. But before considering that grim prospect, consider instead an even more problematic one: Suppose that research shows that side effects often are contingency-based, often are reactive to the originating problem and/or the first intervention into that problem, and often are predictable in advance on just that basis. Then there arises a mighty research problem, which is to establish the principles of that reaction. Those principles at least might explain the predictability of the ecological reactions, and, better yet, might yield more predictions, better predictions, and/or more important predictions than had been gleaned empirically up to that point. Armed with those predictions, or with their explanations, we might then know how to develop a systematic *technology* of counter-reaction to those ecological, contingency-based, predictable, and therefore systematic side effects. If the side effects are systematic, according to this logic, then we may be equally systematic in dealing with them and thereby become more effective.

On the other hand, the principles underlying the ability to predict the side effects of behavioral interventions need not accomplish any of this. They might just stand there, principled, postdictive, and useless. It all depends on what they are, as principles. Therefore, while conducting the massive research probably required to find out which is the case with them, we might also proceed in our usual fashion to try developing a systematic technology of counter-reaction, even without yet knowing why it would be systematic if we succeeded in doing so. That technology could be very useful, explainable or not. All we need to know to justify our attempting cut-and-try methods to develop a counter-reactive technology is that ecological side effects are systematic enough to be predictable. Indeed, if we succeed in any part of that, the pattern of our successes may allow some induction of the missing principles.

Developing a technology of counter-reaction, whether guided by explanatory principles or mere inductive shrewdness, implies (in this field at least) an ongoing evaluation of that technology. Since the purpose of this counter-reactive technology is to deal with systematic ecological reactions to behavior interventions, the hallmark of its validity will be some degree of success in *finally* handling those reactions. Thus, a fifth question arises: when any current side effects of a behavioral intervention have been dealt with satisfactorily, do any further side effects appear? This question should be asked, whether we are proceeding from a systematic technology of counter-reacting to predictable side effects, or are dealing with unpredictable side effects through ad hoc additional contingencies.

If no further side effects appear, then applied behavior analysis is thereby a potentially reasonable discipline, and once again, with some reassurance, we may continue with its further development as such. If, in arriving at that reassurance, we are forced to develop a systematic, counter-reactive technology, one that might even be buttressed by explanatory principles, then the discipline would be much further along in its development than would otherwise be the case, and we could thank our collision with ecological argument for the outcome (unless it cost us too much, which is a question that ecologists and cost-accountants have taught us to ask).

However, if new side effects continue to emerge whenever we handle the current side effects, there is still a sixth question to be posed, and a very realistic one: are the successive side effects, albeit present, nevertheless not as severe, numerous, widespread, generalized, or in any relevant way as troublesome as were their predecessors? If not—if dealing effectively with every ecological side effect of intervention simply presents an equally (or more) troublesome, newer side effect—then to that extent, the discipline of applied behavior analysis is probably not a viable one and may as well be discontinued in favor of nonapplied behavior analysis. Nonapplied behavior analysis will do no harm while occupying an intriguing place in Academe's collection of similar puzzles, and it ought to be kept alive against the possible discovery of some currently unpredictable new knowledge that would make its truths (it *is* an empirical science) useful after all in the world of real and everyday behavior, even if only as a highly delimited special case of a more general truth.

If the answer to the sixth question is that reactive side effects, dealt with effectively, are sometimes replaced by further side effects that are less troublesome in important ways than were their predecessors, then we have a case in which the problem can always be solved by enough successive applications of that counter-reactive technology or those ad hoc additional contingencies that we have been developing. The frequency and/or effort of successive interventions may sometimes not seem worth the value of the problem's solution, of course. But the fact that successive interventions eventually constitute a solution implies that better techniques of early interventions would obviate the number and/or effort of later ones. In short, eventual success suggests that we have only some engineering problems to solve, and although those problems can be severe, nevertheless this finding justifies the continued development of applied behavior analysis as a discipline—especially as an engineering discipline.

TECHNOLOGICAL CLARIFICATION

Six consecutive, interlocking, mutually contingent questions, in any context, probably constitute too complex an argumentative structure for usefulness, unless they can be augmented with technological clarification. Figure 1 is an attempt at technological clarification; it allows the structure of the argument to be looked at rather than listened to or paged through. Visual inspection displays a number of salient characteristics of this particular argument. First and perhaps most important, it shows the relatively few ways in which the intersection of ecological principle and the practice of applied behavior analysis can result in a sound conclusion that applied behavior analysis is not a viable discipline to pursue, either because of risk or ineffectiveness. But the same visual analysis also displays with equal force how few ways there are in which the combining of ecological analysis with applied behavior analysis can validate the conclusion that the discipline should be pursued with some assurance that it is ecologically sound. Furthermore, this picture of the argument's structure makes it uncomfortably clear how arduous are the research paths that could culminate in either of these conclusions.

For example, the simplest validation of applied behavior analysis as a viable discipline worthy of further development is to answer Question 1 with NO. Doing so requires the empirically substantiated assertion that there are not usually any side effects to behavioral interventions in applied behavior analysis. Empirical substantiation of that assertion would be tantamount to an actuarial approximation to a universal negative. There are so many ways in which applied behavior analysis intervenes, on so many behaviors, in so many settings, for so many types of subjects; worse than that, there are so many possible categories and forms of side effects of any one of these interventions. It may as well be concluded that Question 1 cannot be answered NO empirically—not even in a *single* application, let alone "usually." By the same token (as we often say in applied behavior analysis), it will also be difficult to answer Question 1 empirically with YES. Then there are three recourses, each of which involves assumption rather than fact:

1. We may assume that the answer is NO, arguing (unconvincingly) that
    a. we rarely notice any side effects in our own applied behavior analyses;

   b.   the logic of our approach suggests that behavioral techniques have effects specific to the behaviors that they actually contact;

   c.   there is no clear way to be open to the infinitude of possible side effects (cf. Holman, Chapter 4 of this volume; and Willems, Chapter 3 of this volume);

   d.   looking for them is analogous to looking for a needle in a haystack, which is so expensive that it constitutes shutting down the field, which may be antisocial (cf. Holman, Chapter 4 of this volume, and Baer, 1974) if the field in fact is producing occasional improvements in important social/personal problems;

   e.   some of the fear that applied behavior analysis is dangerous or ineffective may be politically or personally motivated, rather than objective.

2. We may assume that the answer is YES, arguing (unconvincingly) that

   a.   we think that we did notice some side effects in some applied behavior analyses;

   b.   ecological theory suggests that there usually will be side effects;

   c.   the frequent observation of clear, unpredicted side effects in biological interactions cannot be ignored, and behavioral phenomena, at root, are biological;

   d.   even in the absence of clear methods for assessing the infinitude of possible side effects, we can and should begin, and if we do, we may find something useful (we often do) (cf. Willems, Chapter 4 of this volume);

   e.   some of the defensiveness about applied behavior analysis may be politically or personally motivated, rather than objective.

3. We may assume that the answer is YES, simply to get started on finding at least one case of unpredicted side effects of a behavioral intervention so that we may move on to Question 2. After all, Question 1 is apparently unanswerable other than by assumption, but some of the other questions may be answerable, at least in given cases, and whereas Question 1 has little usefulness in given cases (it really is about the "usual" case), Question 2 can have quite interesting usefulness for some given cases. But the only logical way to get to Question 2 is to assume at least a possible YES answer to Question 1. Besides, if we look insistently for some instance of unpredicted side effects in an applied behavior analysis, we may find one. That may suggest to us how to look more efficiently for another. If we find another, the two of them together may suggest even more efficient ways of looking for a third. If we then find a third, we are well on our way to an inductive generalization, namely that there are indeed side

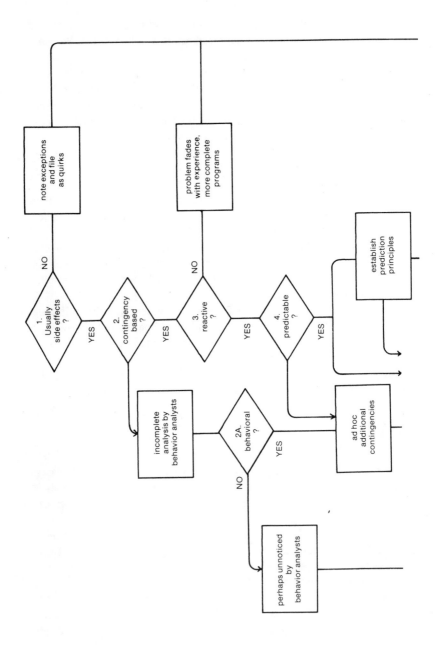

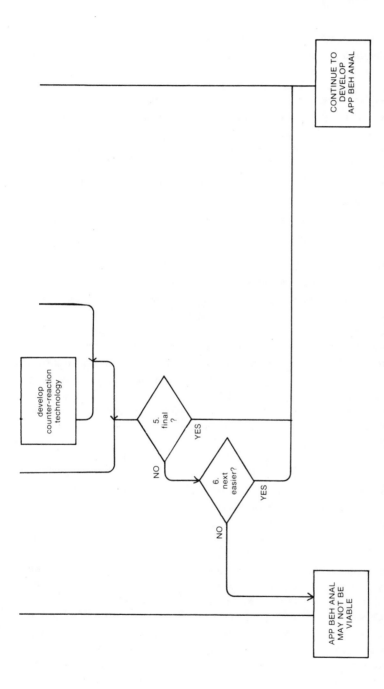

Figure 1. Visual depiction of questions arising from the intersection of ecological principle and the practice of applied behavior analysis (APP BEH ANAL—applied behavior analysis).

effects to be found, if you look for them properly. Thus, inductively, Question 1 *can* more and more powerfully suggest a YES answer, although it can hardly ever yield a similarly powerful NO answer. Then we may as well assume a YES answer to Question 1, because that is the only answer that could possibly be induced. (Thus, Question 1, for all its face appropriateness, is a set-up. Yet that, after all, is pretty much the way that we validated the generality of the reinforcement principle: we kept finding ways to make it work in application after application. We never surveyed all the possible applications that there are—the induction was strong enough without that.)

Continuing: Question 2, like Question 1, is about the usual case: if there are side effects of behavioral interventions, are their mechanisms usually contingency-based? For exactly the same sorts of reasons that apply in the case of Question 1, we can never establish NO as the usual answer. But we can find that in instance after instance, side effects, when we find them at all, are contingency-based, and if we do find that, then we may begin an induction that it will usually be so. If this research is conducted exclusively by behavior analysts, then it may be noted, wryly, that contingency-based mechanisms are the mechanisms that will be uncovered—they are the mechanisms that behavior analysts understand and are prepared to detect, even in their subtle applications. As Kuhn (1962) points out, we are all trapped by our paradigms to discover only what those paradigms are able to discover—or to discover nothing, if what there is eludes the paradigm. Thus, depending on which researchers take on Question 2, we may have to assume that the answer is YES, or else simply wait with no answer yet.

Question 3 is like Question 1: on the face of it, a NO answer to Question 3 sends us back to the ongoing development of applied behavior analysis, secure in the knowledge that whatever side effects may be seen in that discipline, they are at least not reactive to the interventions that make up the discipline so far. But, as with Question 1, there is no way to secure a NO answer to Question 3—it, too, is a set-up. It allows the discovery that reactive side effects may operate in at least some instances, even as it disallows the discovery that they never operate in any instances. So, again, we may as well assume that the answer to Question 3 occasionally will be YES, or else that we shall be waiting with no answer yet. As was the case with Question 1, we may even make this assumption cheerfully, on the grounds that doing so will send us off on the positive quest of finding, somewhere, an intervention that does create its own side effects, simply so that we may get on with Question 4 (which, like Question 2, is interesting even in the single instance, despite the fact that it is at heart a "usual" question).

Again, Question 4 will not admit to a NO answer: there is no way to discover that any reactive side effects of behavior interventions are *not* predictable from the nature and context of the problem and/or the nature of the intervention. We may fail to find anything (yet), or we may find some instances in which the prediction is possible. So again, we may as well assume that the answer will be YES, at least sometimes, and again, cheerfully and positively seek out some instance when it is, so that we may begin to examine that prediction problem.

With this much inductive mass behind them, readers will no doubt already be pointing out that Question 5 cannot be answered NO either— there is no way to establish that the handling of any side effect was the final handling that the problem required because, at any future point, research may indicate that there was a further side effect after all (if you knew where to look for it).

However, Question 6 offers a refreshing turn: in asking if the successive reactive side effects that might be observed in some cases are successively easier to deal with, it offers us a case that cannot be answered YES with any assurance—all that we could ever assert is that the successive side effects *that we have noticed so far* seem easier to handle. But that does not establish that there are not more serious, albeit more subtle, side effects occurring that have escaped our attention so far. Pessimists may always continue to look for them. In the same way, Question 2A, if it is interpreted to ask, Are all the side effects behavioral ones?, cannot be answered with a firm YES: we may be able to establish that some side effects are behavioral, but how could we prove that there are no non-behavioral side effects? Nonbehavioral pessimists may always continue to look for them.

Indeed, it can be instructive to consider what a phenomonological pessimist might hypothesize, answering NO to a Question 2A interpreted to ask, Are *all* the side effects behavioral ones? Suppose that, in fact, there are important side effects that are phenomenal. What might they be? Although specialists in phenomenal phenomena probably would consider *this* chapter an exceptionally unfavorable place for the flowering of competent hypothesis about cognitive or affective side effects, a line of hypothesis will be explored.

THREE ATTITUDINAL REACTIONS

Consider the possibility that the recipients of applied behavioral analyses are likely to display three major attitudinal reactions: 1) no attitudinal change at all, a case that may well occur, but will be put aside for now; 2) a positive reaction, consisting of the belief that good has been done to them, that they have learned new skills and gained in personal competence, and that the applied behavior analyst is a benevolent person (or at least well worth the fee); or 3) a negative reaction, consisting of the belief that they have been exploited, that they were manipulated for someone else's benefit, not their own, and that the applied behavior analyst is an enemy or at least a running dog of an enemy. These attitudinal changes need not result in behavioral consequences; sometimes attitudes, positive or negative, are simply contained for indefinite periods of time, leading only to verbal expression, and even that expressed only under skillful interrogation. Then we may say that the intervention has caused a phenomenal change, and/but also has been accepted as a *fait accompli.* No further side effects are likely in reaction to future interventions. Perhaps, however, in the case of acceptance of a *fait accompli* when the client feels manipulated, exploited, and defeated, we may well expect a residue of phenomenal resentment, resignation, or depression. Even if these attitudinal changes are not at the moment behavioral, they ought to be dealt with, on both or either of two bases: they are undesirable in their own terms and/or they may well represent a motivational base, not functional enough for the present to produce behavior, perhaps, but nonetheless enduring and available for recruiting if future events add to them in the wrong ways or if some future intervener, correctly assessing their presence and function, mounts the appropriate white horse to call them to arms. (Whether *that* intervener is seen as savior or demagogue is an exercise in values, relevant to, but apart from, the mechanics of this analysis.)

On the other hand, both the positive and negative attitudinal changes may trigger behavioral manifestations. In the case of a positive attitudinal change, the behavioral manifestations may well take the form of the client maximizing self-exposure to the intervention, helping it along in various ways. That client may even show generalized effects of the intervention, developing related responses to which the intervention had not (yet) been directed, and/or extending the newly developed behaviors to settings in which the intervention had not (yet) occurred. Such clients may seek further interventions of the same sort for other problems or for future problems, or, in idealized cases, show self-control: they may design and implement their own applied behavior analyses, generalizing from the form of their last encounter with that body of technique. It is, after all, usually a very obvious collection of technique and principle. Then the ranks of applied behavior analysts may begin to swell with unofficial, uncertified members, each of whom will begin to generate effects and side effects and have Figure 1's of their own to worry about (and be worried about— by us).

In the case of a negative attitudinal change, the behavioral manifestations may take a variety of forms. Clients may attempt to escape from the intervention or at least its agent. Or, they may display counter-control, in the form of passive aggression, active aggression, or rebellion, or in the form of systematic reinforcement of the agents of the intervention for no longer intervening—in a word, counter-control. Anyone who considered the original intervention a desirable program will consider these reactions as undesirable side effects, and ecologists, whatever their values in the case, will point to it as a classic instance of the environment reacting to an intervention so as to cancel its effects.

The key question then will be, did the behvioral manifestation of the negative attitudinal change succeed? If it did not, then probably the manifestations will diminish; if they continue to fail in escaping or undoing the intervention, they will extinguish. The residue still will be phenomenal, probably in the form of resignation or depression, as in the case of no behavioral manifestations to a negative attitudinal reaction. And again (as in that case), there are not likely to be systematic behavioral side effects to be seen in the future interventions. But the resignation or resentment remains to be dealt with because each is undesirable in its own terms, and also because they may cumulate, eventually, finally to produce sharply undesirable side effects for client and intervener alike.

When a negative attitudinal change produces successful behavioral manifestations of escape,·aggression, or counter-control, then it should be supposed that such success is reinforcing to the client and will intensify those behaviors for future occasions. Indeed, if these behaviors succeed on the future occasions as well, they are on their way to becoming systematic skills, such that this client and all similar ones will show up as a core of almost-nonintervenables—at least, not intervenable by any methods recognizable to them as the ones against which they have learned to prevail. Thus, because of these people, Question 1 in Figure 1 more and more will be answered YES, there are indeed side effects; Question 2 more and more will be answered NO, the side effects are not simply other contingencies (at least, not immediately); Question 2A will find that YES, there are plenty of behaviors to be dealt with (even though their etiology was phenomenal); and, hardest case of all, the ad hoc additional contingencies then called for will have to be very, very good indeed.

In fact, they will have to be so good that it seems unlikely that they will remain ad hoc. If it is a systematic set of effects that they must deal with, then they will of necessity become equally systematic—if they are developed successfully, and very likely they can be. This, then, might prove to be exactly the core of the counter-reaction technology that was cited as necessary in Figure 1, if it turned out that behavioral interventions had to deal with reactive, predictable side effects. It is simply that the occasion for developing that technology arises now (by hypothesis) from a nonbehavioral line of argument—an argument that the underlying nature of the side effects to be handled will be the phenomenal reality of the client rather than the behavioral reality of the intervention.

However, should not the first element of a technology for counter-reaction to side effects of behavioral interventions be the assessment of the presumably underlying phenomenal reality? A proposal to do just that usually will arouse two kinds of reaction: one, a despair of ever succeeding coupled with a refusal to abandon objectivity; the other, not unrelated to the first, a delight that a solution to any technological unemployment of psychologists now is overcome permanently. Assessment of phenomenal reality is an infinite task, like defending against "enemies." We can spend any amount of our resources on it, we will never finish, we will never solve the problem, and, if we fail eventually, we will not care much afterward anyway.

A nonphenomenal attempt to solve the same problem, based on a sense of social ethics rather than a scientific paradigm, is suggested by Holland (1975): not modifying the behavior of people who are not willing to have their behavior modified, an outcome that can be approached closely (by hypothesis) simply by not modifying anyone's behavior *for someone else.* That is, behavior modifiers usually have clients. When those clients ask that not their behavior, but someone else's behavior be modified, then the behavior modifier can accomplish the first and perhaps most important component of the counter-reaction technology by refusing. Given that, further development of the counter-reaction technology could prove to be relatively small in scope.[2]

---

[2] If the refusal to modify anyone's behavior for anyone else is the first, preventative component of the counter-reaction technology, then there arises—as a side effect, presumably—the sort of problem posed by, for instance, those parents who want their children toilet-trained but whose children manifestly do not wish to be toilet-trained, which is a small version of the sort of problem posed by the society that wants its children taught to read, write, and figure but whose children manifestly would rather learn sports, sex, and various other turn-ons. Alas, there is no guarantee that proceeding from a sense of social ethics is itself side-effect-free. Indeed, it may be argued that the application of social ethics to the current practice of behavioral intervention is itself a behavioral intervention into the side effects arising from those recent behavioral interventions; whereupon it may be argued quite convincingly that those very behavioral interventions, of the sort that trouble Willems (Chapters 2 and 3 of this volume) and Gump (Chapter 6 of this volume), were themselves interventions not into a virgin society but into the side effects of some massive and very longstanding behavioral interventions conducted long ago by the society (or its politicians) rather than by that small corps of behavioral scientists wrestling with the

None of this need be taken as a triumph of phenomenal or ethical theory over behavioral theory, or even of theory over pragmatism. Behaviorists, stubbing their toes over undesirable side effects of behavioral interventions, inevitably will classify those side effects, probably in terms of what response is required by the intervener to deal with them. In particular, a positive-negative polarity of side effects will be discerned very quickly, especially if it consists of, on the one hand, pleased acceptance, self-maximization, generalization, and self-control, and on the other hand, escape, anger, depression, aggression, and/or counter control. Remedial contingencies would be required mainly for that other hand. And, if there is a correlation between the negative pole of side effects and the fact that someone's behavior is being modified not at their own request, but for someone else, that will be noticed very quickly, too. Then, first among the remedial contingencies there should be expected the preventive one: not to intervene in the first place. Indeed, a tightly discriminated don't-intervene response may be the major target behavior that the ecologists have intended all along since they have been contemplating the efforts of behavior modifiers. (It is clear, now, that they do not intend a generalized don't-intervene response.)

Thus, Figure 1 shows merely a single process labeled "develop a counter-reaction technology;" it may well be to deal with the cases suggested by the phenomenal side effects argument that the prescribed technology will develop, and in a shape according to that analysis. Thus, Figure 2 displays both the questions, answers, and resultant processes implied by that kind of phenomenal analysis and, in the same format, outlines a possible structure of the counter-reaction technology. If the counter-reaction technology is developed well, the phenomenal quality of the analysis will disappear, one might suppose, in favor simply of the

---

last .00000000001% of the variance of their society's behavior. That is, behaviorists devise and apply marriage contracting to a microscopic fraction of the world's couples who have trouble—but the institution of marriage was devised not by them, but by their predecessors, for reasons thoroughly shrouded in prehistory, but presumably to solve some pressing problems of survival in large and small societies. Troubled marriages, then, represent a side effect of *that* intervention, and side effects of current interventions into the side effects of that intervention are just that—certainly they are nothing novel or abstruse. They may be somewhat more thoughtful than their predecessors, and a little more technological, and a great deal more carefully monitored, but otherwise, they are nothing novel or unique. Then where were the ecologists when the original—and truly large, basic, and important—interventions were being applied? (They were in the same situation as the behavioral scientists: not yet invented. But the problems of ecology had long since been invented; they did not arise with the *Journal of Applied Behavior Analysis.*)

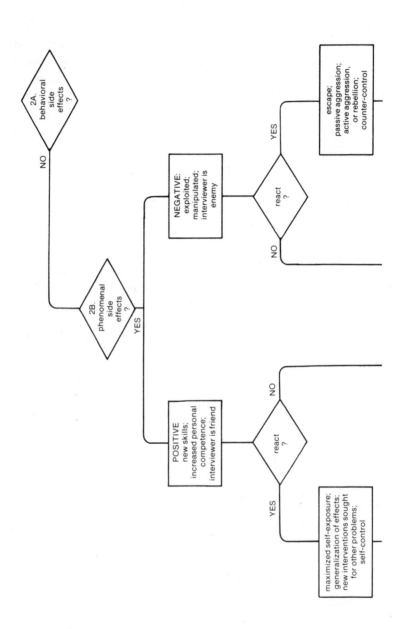

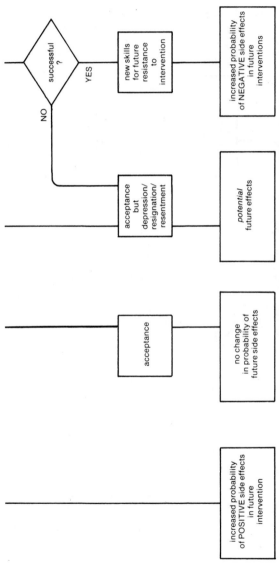

Figure 2. Outline of a possible structure for the development of the counter-reaction technology called for by the phenomenal analysis.

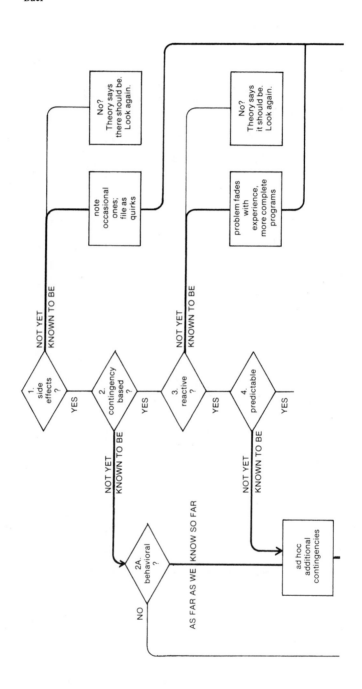

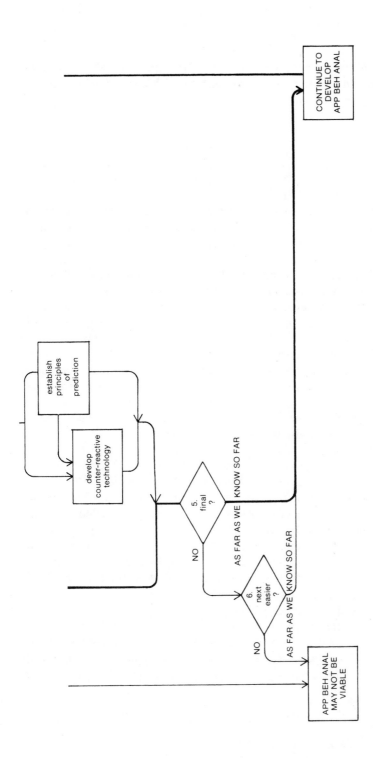

Figure 3. Readjustment of Figure 1 offering endorsement of continued development of applied behavior analysis.

structure of the adequate technology. Meanwhile, read all of Figure 2 as the contents of the process box in Figure 1 labeled "develop a counter-reaction technology."

CONCLUSIONS

Two repetitive conclusions seem to derive from this kind of analysis, especially when the analysis is considered in light of the pathways de-lineated in Figures 1 and 2.

The first conclusion is that there is less research to be done on this topic than must have seemed the case at first. Quite a lot of the question structure gets answered by assumption, rather than by confirmation. Nevertheless, there is a core of genuine empirical research still surviving in that structure. Its character may be summed up in the motto: "There are some phenomena possible, but not certain. Go look for them. And keep looking: it may be possible to find them, but it won't be possible to say they aren't there. And if they are, you're probably going to need a lot more technology." In other words, the possibility of side effects, whether contingency-based, reactive, and/or predictable, cannot be disproved: either valid instances of such phenomena will be found, or nothing conclusive may be found, yet. The necessity of that "yet" means that this is a nondisposable issue; it is neither biodegradable nor psychodegradable. In simpler terms, the ecologists can only win this argument; there is no way for them to lose it. No wonder they have persevered.

The second conclusion follows sharply on the heels of the first. It is that, after all, research scientists rarely live in logic. They, like everyone else, are more sensitive to reinforcement, punishment, and extinction than to proof or disproof.[3] Consequently, Figures 1 and 2 may be pictures of the *logical* structure of the necessity for an ecological outlook by applied behavior analysts, but they probably are not quite the pictures of the behavioral structure of our next 20 years of effort. It is not that applied behavior analysts will not respond to a logical analysis; it is simply that they will continue to do so only a little longer than they can interest other scientists (and journals) in the results of doing so. Thus, to use Figure 1 as a behavioral prescription for some partly rational, partly realistic research behavior, replace the NO answers for Questions 1, 2, 3, and 4 with the weaker but more actionable statement, NOT YET KNOWN TO BE, and you will have a map of the paths to be taken by many researchers in this field. And for Questions 2A, 5, and 6, replace the YES answers with AS

---

[3] I wish that I could find a reference to support this undoubtedly true assertion.

FAR AS WE KNOW SO FAR, and again there will result a map of highly probable actions.

If these substitutions are made, Figure 1 becomes Figure 3, a permissive rather than a prescriptive guide to research and application, with those paths that seem highly probable for applied behavior analysts to follow indicated as darker, thicker lines. Rather than requiring research in the service of ecological principles intersecting those of applied behavior analysis, it encourages it; but it also allows a fairly rational—at least, temporarily rational—endorsement of the process labeled CONTINUE TO DEVELOP APPLIED BEHAVIOR ANALYSIS. "Temporarily rational" is all that NOT YET KNOWN TO BE and AS FAR AS WE KNOW SO FAR could mean. Even so, NOT YET KNOWN TO BE is quite a reasonable, yet still negative, temporal softening of NO; similarly, AS FAR AS WE KNOW SO FAR is much more prudent, yet still affirmative version of YES.

If Figure 3 is now an invitation to do a great deal of research, much more imaginative and possibly more socially important than has been done so far in applied behavior analysis, then it is also an invitation to recruit some additional researchers other than applied behavior analysts. Those additional researchers might very well be ecologists. It would help if, in Question 2, they knew how to look for side effects that were not exclusively contingency-based, because the applied behavior analysts tend to recognize only the ones that are contingency-based. It would also be good if, in Question 2A, they knew how to look for nonbehavioral side effects (for much the same reasons). Again, in case the answer to Question 4 sometimes is YES (reactive side effects can be predictable), the additional researchers had better understand prediction technology in most of its formidabilities. Finally, if they would bring a cost-accountant along, we might establish the current worth of being ecological in given cases—AS FAR AS WE KNOW SO FAR, of course.

An alternative to inviting all this company is for applied behavior analysts to acquire all or some of those skills themselves. But when the additional researchers indicated here can state the case for inviting them, in as logical, engaging, and altogether reinforcing way as Willems has done (1974 and Chapter 3 of this volume), then it seems that the only choice is to issue the invitations—to what will surely prove to be a party, even if nothing else.

LITERATURE CITED

Baer, D. M. 1974. A note on the absence of a Santa Claus in any known ecosystem: A rejoinder to Willems. J. Appl. Behav. Anal. 7:167–170. Also reprinted as Part I comment of this volume.

Baltes, M. M., and Reese, H. W. 1977. Operant research in violation of the operant paradigm? *In* B. C. Etzel, J. M. LeBlanc, and D. M. Baer (eds.), New Developments in Behavioral Research: Theory, Method, and Application. In Honor of Sidney W. Bijou. Lawrence Erlbaum Associates, Hillsdale, N.J.

Gump, P. V. Ecological Psychologists: Critics or Contributors to Behavior Analysis. Chapter 6 of this volume.

Holland, J. G. 1975. Is institutional change necessary? Paper presented at the Conference on Behavior Analysis and Ethics, June 1975. Morgantown, W. Va.

Holman, J. The Moral Risk and High Cost of Ecological Concern in Applied Behavior Analysis. Chapter 4 of this volume.

Kuhn, T. 1962. The Structure of Scientific Revolutions. University of Chicago Press, Chicago.

Willems, E. P. 1974. Behavioral technology and behavioral ecology. J. Appl. Behav. Anal. 7:151–165. Also reprinted as Chapter 2 of this volume.

Willems, E. P. Steps Toward an Ecobehavioral Technology. Chapter 3 of this volume.

COMMENT
On Viewing with Alarm:
A Modest
Proposal

Donna M. Gelfand

There are historical reasons for behavior analysts to be more than usually sensitive to the charge that their interventions could have some negative effects. In the infancy of the behavior analysis movement, psychodynamic writers charged that a direct attack on deviant behaviors would have dire consequences. According to this view, an attempt to treat so-called symptoms would leave underlying personality conflicts to simmer undisturbed (see Cameron, 1963). In addition, symptom substitution, or the emergence of new, different, and potentially more dangerous behaviors, would result. These dynamically oriented therapists, incidentally, were not as eager to examine the possible ill effects of their own interventions as they urged behaviorists to be.

In an effort to deny these serious allegations regarding symptom substitution, behavior analysts emphasized the positive direct and indirect effects of their treatments. In most cases, only anecdotal, indirect evidence was offered, based on testimonials provided by treated individuals or their caretakers. Understandably, behavior analysts did not seek out potentially adverse effects of their programs. Their willingness to do so now is a sign of healthy self-confidence. Only the strong can engage in serious self-examination.

Willems, Holman, and Baer agree on the desirability of identifying possible negative as well as positive effects of treatment. They disagree, however, on the urgency with which this search should be conducted. Willems would have us mount such studies immediately and intensively. He urges that we refrain from large-scale application until such analyses have been completed and our procedures are certified as safe. This time, and just in case of adverse consequences, the scientists should be there ahead-of-time. Willems argues persuasively that problem behaviors do not occur in a social vacuum and that the complex nature of the human environment would lead us to expect that behaviors are interdependent. Modifying the rate or topography of one behavior may well affect many others. If we fail to appreciate this complexity, we may well overlook a variety of effects of treatment programs.

Holman suggests a much more limited attack on the problem of unexpected effects by means of consumer satisfaction interviews. Such interviews are not themselves easy to conduct, however. Polite clients usually thank professional therapists graciously and are somewhat reluctant to complain about, or even to detect, negative treatment effects. We have yet to develop an adequate technology of interviewing. Parenthetically, I would expect that, if any group can develop such a technology, the behavior analysts can. This is just to say that it is not a simple task. After all, for years client interview data were considered to indicate the effectiveness of traditional conversational therapies. One can get what one wants or expects in interviews. The trick is to elicit unexpected information. Then behavior observations can be used to evaluate the validity of the verbal reports. Such a procedure would not be prohibitively expensive or time-consuming.

Baer cautions that indirect effects may be idiosyncratic and unpredictable, and they may even be nonbehavioral. Hence, they may go undetected, should they exist. Clients and caregivers probably would not associate such changes with the intervention, and so would not report them. Certainly the evidence available to us at this point does not indicate indirect treatment effects occurring for large numbers of clients in a regular, predictable manner. Time, and systematic research (such as that outlined by Wahler et al., Chapter 10), will tell whether or not such effects will be found. As has been frequently pointed out, we lack guidelines regarding the types of undesirable reactions that might occur. Given the many settings and the many behaviors among which to choose, and given only a finite amount of time and resources, where should we look for negative reactions to behavioral interventions? To the extent that the field of behavioral ecology can suggest answers to this central question, this allied field will be of importance to applied behavior analysts. If no precise predictions can be made, then the argument resembles the original one between behavior therapists and psychodynamic therapists regarding side effects of direct treatment of deviant behavior. As Bandura (1969, Chapter 1) has characterized that exchange, the psychodynamic writers lost the battle because of their inability to specify the negative behaviors to be produced by behavioral treatments. Few novel, undesirable behaviors were reported following intervention, and there was no compelling evidence that the few observed were produced by the treatment rather than by other factors.

The case may be different in the proposed alliance between behavioral ecology and applied behavior analysis. There is some degree of intellectual confrontation, to be sure, and that can sharpen thinking and so benefit both fields. But the verbal behavior of members of both disciplines testifies to their mutual willingness to listen to each other, to exchange ideas and expertise, and to work together toward a more effective solution to human problems than was previously possible. That possibility of collaboration is encouraging.

Let us now consider how serious the side effects problem might be. Certainly we cannot afford to make new mistakes in the manipulation of human behavior in our increasingly dangerous world. The present situation is a precarious one, with more and more nations acquiring nuclear weapons, with war as a pandemic condition, with widespread famine a future probability, and with serious environmental degradation a reality. On the other hand, it strikes me as highly unlikely that we will make human behavior any more aggressive, competitive, and short-sighted than is presently the rule.

This is where the Willems analogy to the physical environment breaks down. The social and the physical situations are *not* analogous. There is no social counterpart to the earthly paradise, to the serene azure globe that astronauts have viewed from space and that is being threatened by the popularity of the internal combustion engine and the underarm deodorant in the aerosol can. The social situation is quite different and is far from benign. We believe that we have achieved something of magnitude if we do not go to war every 20 years. Chances are that behavior analysts could only improve the social climate, given its present dreadful state. Clearly, there is merit to the case for the thoughtful behavioral intervention.

It is naive, however, to believe that *any* intervention will have only positive benefits and will not be misused. Both of these assumptions will almost inevitably prove untrue in large-scale interventions involving many individuals. Some practitioners will prove inept, some will abuse positions of power. A certain degree of risk is present, whether the intervention's nature is medical, agricultural, educational, therapeutic, or scientific. The difficult part is to detect and to quantify such risks. We will not always be able to do so, as Baer points out (Chapter 5 of this volume). If undesirable side effects are delayed, if they are infrequent (on the order of one per 500 or one per 1,000 persons treated), or if they are idiosyncratic, we may, in fact, not be able to detect them, especially not in small-scale applications.

Consider the case with drug side effects. Some serious side effects cannot be detected either in practice or in principle except in large clinical trials. The rare but perhaps fatal allergic reaction, or the dangerous but infrequent synergistic reaction with other drugs or with certain foods, may only emerge after a drug has been in use for some time.

The durg example is instructive in other ways, also. Those who have an economic or professional stake in the outcome are not the best guardians of the public interest. We would do best to have our drugs evaluated by truly independent investigators rather than by pharmaceutical companies, and we would like to have the test results evaluated by an FDA that has not been dominated by the industry that it is supposed to regulate. We do not live in this idealized world, however. But as a consumer of psychological or educational services, I would like to know that some disinterested, but not antagonistic, scientists are providing checks of available programs. This is now being done for the Achievement Place program (Jones, 1976), which represents an important step forward in program evaluation. And I would like to be centrally involved in decisions on whether to and how to treat my family and myself. Perhaps we cannot provide much in the way of independent evaluations now, but we can make sure that consumer voices are heard and that their desires help determine our programs. Some programs are taking this approach very seriously. In the Ora and Reisinger Regional Intervention Program (Reisinger and Ora, in press), parents take major responsibility for determining and delivering treatment programs for their own seriously disturbed children. They evaluate the professional staff and consider the adequacy of the treatment programs. The Achievement Place Program (Wolf, Phillips, and Fixsen, 1974) offers another excellent example. Programs and procedures for training parents are carefully evaluated by consumer representatives. Paternalism is on the decline, and that benefits all of us.

To summarize, we need to keep behavioral ecology issues in mind, but in perspective. I have an old college friend, now a nuclear engineer, who likes to write short stories. After writing one in which he was sharply critical of the immense and insensitive power of behavioral psychology, he sent his story to me. I read it with interest and then reminded him that it was not behavioral psychology that gave us the nuclear bomb and other such engines of destruction. Our weapons tend to be clipboards and timers. We do not deal in explosions and toxic chemical reactions—just the familiar social influence techniques long in use. We are more persistent and systematic about it, that's all. I have not heard from my friend since then, but I sense that my point was not lost on him.

There may be dangers from behavioral interventions. We should recognize that threat, and we should inquire into possible negative effects. However, we should not be too alarmed about it. At least not yet.

LITERATURE CITED

Bandura, A. 1969. Principles of Behavior Modification. Holt, Rinehart, and Winston, New York.

Cameron, N. A. 1963. Personality Development and Psychopathology: A Dynamic Approach. Houghton Mifflin, Boston.

Jones, R. R. 1976. Achievement Place: The independent evaluator's perspective. Paper presented at the American Psychological Association Meeting, September, 1976, Washington, D.C.

Reisinger, J. J., and Ora, J. P. Parent-child clinic and home interaction during Toddler Management Training. Behav. Ther. In press.

Wolf, M. M., Phillips, E. L., and Fixsen, D. L. 1974. Achievement Place: Phase II. Final Report for Grant No. MH #20030 from the Center for Studies of Crime and Delinquency, National Institute of Mental Health, University of Kansas, Department of Human Development, Lawrence, Kan.

PART III

NATURAL ADAPTATION: THE EVOLVING RELATIONSHIP BETWEEN ECOLOGY AND BEHAVIOR ANALYSIS

6

Ecological Psychologists: Critics or Contributors to Behavior Analysis

Paul V. Gump

In order to consider an ecological perspective for behavior analysis, that consideration must take its shape from the forces or events that have prompted it. Why should there be an ecological perspective in the area of behavior modification?

A recent impetus to ecological considerations has been the contribution of Willems (1974 and Chapter 2 of this volume) who pointed out that the changes wrought by application of behavior modification, if they follow the model of other technological "improvements," could lead to unintended and undesirable effects. The direct response of behavior modification people to this specific challenge has been already offered by Holman (Chapter 4 of this volume) and Baer (Part I Comment and Chapter 5 of this volume) and I will not try to improve or to elaborate upon the unintended or side effect aspect of the discussion. There is another condition implicit in the issue requiring examination: the condition of *interdependence*. A particular target behavior must be presumed embedded in a set of behaviors which themselves may be affected by intervention. This we might refer to as the *behavior-behavior* interdependence. Another area of important interdependence is *person and environment (behavior-environment)* interdependence. Although the behavior modification approach focuses upon discriminative cues and contingency events in the environment around the person, this focus includes only a narrow and unique portion of the context in which the person and his/her behavior are embedded. If that person has certain behaviors changed, the environment may respond to that new behavior by creating changed inputs to the person or by changes in operations beyond the person.

Behavior analysis as a science has certainly not ignored person-environment interdependence; after all, the basic principle is that the environmental consequences of behavior determine that behavior. However, behavior modification has ignored the study of any parts of the environment which seem irrelevant to the targeted behavior and the associated intervention activity. But what is irrelevant at one time becomes relevant at another. We presume that knowledge—scientific knowledge—of the environmental units in which persons live would be useful to some of the interests of behavior modifiers.

Yet a third area of interdependence can be examined, an area that becomes important only when social scientists have become interested in the context around the subject and have ceased their primary focus upon individuals' behaviors. Study of the proximate environment of persons will reveal interdependencies within that environment. Among these relations, the interlocking of settings, such that events in one sustain and constrain events in the other, represents an *environment-environment* interdependence. Recognition of the three kinds of interdependencies provides a continual, implicit pressure to take an ecological perspective. Several points are important here. First, this interdependency network is not the conceptual invention of some social scientists who wish to make a field for themselves; on the contrary, the interdependency is reality given. Common experience informs us that such relations demand our respect if we wish to deal effectively with the real world. The second point flows directly from the first: wherever behavior analysis has dealt with nonlaboratory problems practical account has been taken of the interdependency. Behavior analysts know that there is an important relationship between giving tokens for desired behavior and the establishment of "an economy" or environment appropriate for such contingency management. Not only must the environment facilitate token delivery but it will be necessary to select or establish sub-environments for token spending. The obvious case of the token economy represents only a fraction of the extent to which behavior analysts have had to become concerned with an environmental context much larger than that contained in the cues and contingencies related to targeted client behaviors. As success with small scale intervention has increased, so has pressure to engage in more massive and comprehensive attempts. By now, more or less total environments come under the control of behavior analysts, as is testified to by the adventures with Achievement Place and Follow Through[1] and the development of nursery schools and day care establishments.

---

[1] The Achievement Place program and the Follow Through program are federally funded projects conducted through the Department of Human Development and the

Perhaps the most vivid delineation of the behavior analyst's concern with comprehensive environments appeared 30 years ago. B. F. Skinner described a total community in which 1,000 people lived and worked under arrangements deemed far superior to those existing for most Americans in 1945. This vision of ecological possibilities was, of course, *Walden Two* (1948, 1976). An examination of the novel reveals environmental concerns and solutions ranging far beyond contingency management; in fact, contingency management as a principle of operation in *Walden Two* does not appear early and does not dominate the novel when it is considered.

Two aspects of the *Walden Two* conception are relevant here. First, the environment, in terms of what the ecological psychologists would call behavior settings, is given close attention. Over 100 different sites or settings are alluded to; for at least 30 of these, both physical features and activity characteristics are specified. The verbal pictures of community settings illustrate ecological features designed to make life more efficient and enjoyable. For example, what might have been a mere passageway rising from the children's quarters to the dining rooms becomes, in Skinner's imagination, a multi-purpose setting providing a gallery for exhibit of inhabitants' artistic creations and a pleasant relaxation area with alcoves for rest, conversation, and the taking of tea. This passageway, the "Ladder" (p. 20), is just one of a group of settings exhibiting novel and presumed life-enriching qualities; others in this group might include the outdoor school, the pond, the walk, and the various dining rooms.

A second aspect of *Walden Two* involves hypotheses about ecological or environmental operation. One set of such hypotheses deals with the size of human groups. In his last preface to *Walden Two,* Skinner maintains that small communities not only make contingency management "more effective" but also that small communities "are optimal for recycling materials and avoiding wasteful methods of distribution" (1976, p. x). The author points out the tendency of the city to produce many one-time contacts between inhabitants that lead to indifference on their part regarding the effects of their action upon others. Still concerned with size, Skinner, through his hero, Frazier, speaks disparagingly of crowds: "What good are crowds? Are they useful? Are they interesting?" Frazier goes on to declare that his community has "much better arrangements for bringing together compatible people of common interests" (1976, p. 35). Paren-

Bureau of Child Research at the University of Kansas. The purpose of the Achievement Place project is to develop community-based treatment for delinquent and predelinquent youths. The Follow Through project provides remedial education for primary grade children. Both programs are based on behavior-analysis approaches.

thetically, it might be noted that ecological psychologists have produced considerable data bearing on size effects; some are discussed later.

A more thorough detailing of the contents and implications of the ecological features of *Walden Two* would be instructive but perhaps enough has been described to make a major point: Behavior analysis has been heavily concerned with an ecological perspective from its early days.

Why should there be an ecological perspective in behavior analysis? I would propose that such a perspective has, to varying degrees, been there all along and that the developments in the world of *action* (as opposed to the world of novels or of psychological theories) has increased this perspective. History and contemporary events have combined to require that behavior analysts employ an ecological perspective. The more basic question is whether this perspective is going to remain a matter of practical, case-by-case, improvisation of environmental arrangements—such as become necessary when behavior analysts attempt to improve behavior in institutions or communities—or whether that perspective will take on the discipline of a science. The particular question, for my discussion here, is whether or not the concepts, units, and relationships that have been developed by ecological psychologists to study the interdependencies between behaviors and environments will become part of the *research* effort of behavior analysts. We would assume that an experienced behavior analyst, one who has tried to alleviate some problems in a residential treatment home or in a ghetto community, has developed considerable practical lore about environmental arrangements that is not specifically limited to the issue of contingency management. The question is whether or not this lore can be systematized and verified so that it communicates to others; so that it implies further relationships among variables; so that, in a word, it becomes scientific.

A colleague within behavior analysis predicts that many in this field will be quite pragmatic about making ecological ideas and findings a part of their scientific resources. To the extent that applications can be improved—to this extent only—will an effort be made to understand the interdependencies mentioned above. While it would be tempting to offer some examples of how ecological psychology in its present development might assist intervention, it may be more profitable to raise this question: "Has the field of behavior modification outrun its scientific resources?" At one point, the problem was of the opposite kind. A development of operant principles expressed in *Behavior of Organisms* (Skinner, 1938) was available but, in its author's view, not ready for extension outside the laboratory. (An older Skinner reports that, as a younger man, he said at that time, "Let him extrapolate who will" (Skinner, 1976, p. vi).) However, Skinner, and many others *did* extrapolate and the scientifically developed principles supported numerous applied efforts. Although the scientific aspect of the field remained vigorous, it also remained focused upon limited aspects of subject behavior and very restricted aspects of the external context of that subject. Yet the world of action demanded efforts to improve schools, mental hospital wards, residential treatment homes, community life, and so on. There may be insufficient scientific resource within the behavior modification field available for extrapolation to these larger problems. In this sense, perhaps behavior modification has outrun its scientific base.

The remainder of this chapter becomes conditional: *If* behavior analysis seeks greater scientific command of areas of behavior and of environment beyond direct contingency management, *then* an ecological perspective, an ecological science, may offer a contribution. The ecological perspective that I want to sketch is that of ecological psychology because that is what I know the most about. (Clearly other highly related fields offer similar possibilities: behavioral ecology, parts of environmental psychology, the work of Risley's "Living Environments Group," etc.)

Communication between behavior analysis and ecological psychology may be most profitable if members of both groups try to make only realistic expectations of one another. While we might readily agree that the two disciplines "play the (scientific) game differently," a more radical statement is that "they play different games." Ecological psychology approaches a given situation with the question: "What goes on here?" Behavior analysis asks, "How may I intervene here to improve individuals' behavior?" Our game analogy would not be stretched too much to say that ecological psychologists feel that they have won points if they can investigate a previously not understood situation and develop a systematic, quantitative description of that situation. Behavior analysts would feel that they had "scored" in their game when behavior had been modified, by their interventions, in a positive direction.

A second difference relates to how scientific inferences regarding causal relationships are to be obtained. Consistent with their interventionist spirit, behavior analysts are likely to trust only those stated relationships that have been experimentally verified. ("Experimentally" means manipulation of independent variables.) Ecological psychologists have several counterpoints. First, it is often useful, even scientifically necessary, to provide accurate descriptions of "what goes on" even if cause-and-effect relationships are not derived. Second, while ecologists would admit that inference based upon experimental manipulation may be strong, inferences derived for systematic study of ecologically given contrasts can also yield trustworthy data—especially if alternative hypotheses to the one under test can be eliminated by examination of available data.

With the understanding that behavior analysis and ecological psychology play different games, attention might now be turned to samples of developments within ecological psychology which may contribute to a scientific ecological perspective within behavior analysis. The discussion can be organized with regard to the three kinds of interdependency cited earlier: *behavior-behavior, behavior-environment,* and *environment-environment.*

BEHAVIOR-BEHAVIOR INTERDEPENDENCE

If behavior analysts decided to research the issue of unintended or side effects, one very important area is that part of the subject's behavior not under modification. How does nonconsequated activity change as a result of the interventions of behavior analysts? When this "other behavior" is examined, the range of behavioral material is greatly enlarged. Ecological psychologists have invested considerable time studying comprehensive, naturally occurring, behavior spans. Rather than seeking only to relate variables, these psychologists have attempted to derive conceptual equipment to deal with behavior structure. Two aspects of this struggle with structure may be of interest to behavior analysts: *levels* of behavior and *units* of behavior.

Molar versus Molecular Levels of Behavior

If an investigator is open to all of a subject's behavior, to the "streams of behavior," levels of phenomena can be noted to vary across levels illustrated by: muscle contractions, fine motor movements, simple acts, and ordered sequences of actions. Systematic recording and analysis will require a deliberate selection of a target level within this range. Wright (1967) has offered the molar-molecular dimension for distinguishing within the various levels of behavior output. To oversimplify, it may be stated that molecular pieces of behavior (Wright calls them "actones") are performed by parts of the person dealing with elemental aspects of the environmental context, e.g., thermal conditions, sound waves, physical impacts. In contrast, molar behaviors ("episodes") are carried out by the person in relation to segments of the environment which have meaning for him, e.g., the American flag, a friend, his classroom. Wright would further insist that molar behavior usually occurs within the cognitive field of the actor and represents a "getting to" or "getting from" some part of the environment.

Finally, Wright points out that there is a relation between the molecular and molar levels: the molecular units are as media to the higher, more inclusive molar units. Put briefly, episodes tend to form the patterns of actones. Behavioral accounts rendered by ecological psychologists are centered on the molar level of behavior; molecular detail is employed to specify and fill out the molar description.

Strict behaviorists (those who resist influences about the cognitive states of subjects) may not find Wright's approach to their taste. However, rejection of Wright's solution will eliminate neither the existence of various levels of behavior nor the confusion that results when data from different levels are treated as if they are from a single level.

Unitization of Molar Behavior

When the level of behavior is selected, the identification of units upon this level can be attempted. Experimental psychologists usually by-pass the problem of discovery of units inherent in behavior structure by simply imposing arbitrary "units" that are more or less indifferent to any assumed behavioral structure. Often spans of behavior are "chopped" into time sections and the presence or absence of a target behavior in each section is tallied. Barker (1963) has described this method of partitioning the behavior stream as yielding "tessarae" (pieces) instead of units. Ecological psychologists maintain that units are inherent in the stream of behavior and that these units, properly delineated, can reveal structures of behavior.

Units in behavior sometimes operate singly, sometimes in two or more simultaneously operating epidoes, and methods are suggested for handling the overlap (Barker and Wright, 1955; Wright, 1967). The discovery of naturally occurring units provides leverage to behavior understanding not available when tessarae are employed. For example, once an episode is identified, its beginning and its end are also marked. Details of these terminal points can be examined, particularly the relation of the person to his current situation. Often it is possible to infer what initiates or closes an episode by examining these points. It is often of interest to know whether our subject's behavior episodes are begun spontaneously, are instigated, or coerced; whether episodes are ended for one of these reasons, or because environmental support has ceased.

When behavior is arbitrarily sectioned into time pieces, the location of starts and stops is difficult, and discovery of the relation of external conditions to these points becomes unlikely. Instead, the user of the arbitrary units must often relate their content to a more distal condition; for example, to a general experimental manipulation.

Ecological psychologists have provided other units applicable to the experimenter-free behavior stream: Schoggen (1963) has noted that social action in relation to the subject can also be unitized, and he labels this segment an *environmental force unit*. With application of the environmental force method, it is possible to learn the nature of the subject's "psychological situation." The units could provide literal close-ups of how the subject was dealt with before and after various interventions.

At this point, it is not certain how the behavior anlysts will use the ecologists' solutions to the problems of behavior-stream complexity, if they use them at all. However, several matters are clear: Serious concern with the "other" behavior changes that accompany those wrought by behavior modification will necessarily open up the range and difficulty of behavior to be researched. This opening will bring the behavior analysts to the same realities and problems faced by the ecological psychologists when the latter determined to study the behavior stream as a whole. Rather than immediately centering upon variables to relate, analysts might turn attention first to behavior structure. Structure delineation may not only suggest what variables to examine but where (in the behavior stream) to most profitably examine them. In any case, instead of struggling over the same behavioral ground on their own, the behavior analysts might progress more rapidly by an open-minded examination of what the ecologists have produced for behavior-stream analysis.

BEHAVIOR-ENVIRONMENT INTERDEPENDENCE

The "environment" in the label behavior-environment interdependence can be quite specific to the subject whose behavior is being analyzed. However, the "environment" can have a more general, stable, "subject-free" status. It is this second kind of environment that I want to discuss. However, ecological psychologists have worked with both types and have tried hard to keep them distinguished. The distinction is important enough to examine more closely.

The environment of the *environmental force unit* is that which an individual subject experiences; such an environment changes markedly as the actions of the subject shift. Other aspects of the behavior-stream analyses refer to the "subject's situation." When such "environments" are analyzed, it is clear that they are "inhabitant-reaction environments" not external world environments (Gump, 1975). The habitat in such systems is unique to each individual. In the case of typical behavior-stream analysis, this environment tends to be phenomenological—that is, it is described in terms of inferences made about the motives and interpretations of the subject. If one is seeking to understand relationships between subject behavior and an environment *independent of that behavior,* it is clear that use of the psychological situation or even the environmental force unit creates a kind of circularity. For example, we may note that the child receives a criticism (environmental input) from a setting leader, but we realize that the criticism may have been invited by the subject. The circularity only exists if we wish to speak of an environment which is not subject-determined. But the circularity does exist whenever subject behavior is used to define the presumed external world environment—and this kind of defining occurs in behavior analysis as well as in behavior-stream research. If reinforcement is used as an environmental concept, clearly reinforcement is based upon reactions of individuals. Even if we leave out reinforcement as an environmental concept, simple listing of inputs to the subject also yields an inhabitant reaction environment. The inputs that come to the subject represent much that he selects or invites; other inputs that "missed" the subject, but that are typical of his environmental context, cannot appear in the list.

If behavior analysts wish to study scientifically the environments they create for individuals and the relation of these environments to inhabitants, they simply cannot restrict themselves to description of stimuli related to cues or to reinforcement schedules and their impact. The child in a token economy is living in a complex context and it might be useful to learn how qualities of these contexts affect behavior of their inhabitants. Studies by Kounin and others have demonstrated that on-task behavior of children can be related to the type of setting entered, and that child glee is about 10 times more likely in one kind of setting than another (Kounin and Gump, 1974; Sherman, 1975). Variables that can be applied to settings—not to individuals' unique "environments" within settings—are involved in the behavior analysts' work, and the behavior analysts do take account of them, at least in order to carry on their behavior modification. However, as was maintained earlier, it is simply a matter of whether the effort will be made to *research* such environments or merely to handle them on a practical basis. The point to be made here is that behavior modification language cannot be used to describe these contexts any more than episodes and other psychological descriptors from ecological psychology can be used to describe external world environments.

Behavior Setting Units

These units are external to the subject and, although his behavior is coupled to them, they are not described in terms of that behavior. Examples of settings would include such diverse habitats as offices, dining rooms, hallways, classes, even meetings at conferences. These units contain both the physical *milieu* aspect of the man-made or natural environment and the action or *program* side as well. A conference meeting has a physical enclosure—tables and chairs, various presentation and refreshment gadgets—that are elements of milieu. A meeting also has a program, a "way of doing," which determines what goes on. Barker and Wright (1955) refer to this side of the behavior setting as the "standing pattern of behavior." The relation between milieu and program is one of "synomorphy," similarity of shape; for example, a geographical congruence exists between the shape of the presenting, receiving behavior in the conference and the layout of podium, tables, and chairs.

The behavior setting tends to be ubiquitous; most of our civilized existence occurs in one setting or another. From one point of view, our homes, our institutions, our communities can be understood as behavior setting clusters. The quality of our experience and behavior is much conditioned by the qualities of the settings we enter and by the setting positions we occupy once we enter.

Behavior Settings and Behavior Analysts

Barker (1968) lists the major qualities of the behavior setting as a concept. Briefly, this unit of the external world is naturally occurring (not experimenter-imposed), has temporal and spatial extent (not highly abstract), often possesses considerable durability, and is "preperceptual" (not dependent upon any one person's perception of it). The conceptual characteristics of behavior settings are not similar to those involved in the analysis of individual streams of behavior. In this sense, the thinking involved with these ecological units may be more congenial to behaviorists than the cognitive or phenomenological aspects of individual behavior units.

Scientific description of settings so far developed can be considered in two phases. First, some descriptors for setting qualities have been developed; examples are: the extent to which various *action patterns* or *behavior mechanisms* are called for by the setting program. Second, the structure of the setting has been drawn using a limited number of cybernetic concepts (Barker, 1968). Both methods of description depend upon concepts that are *not* at the same level as those of the psychology of individual behavior; ecological psychologists have become convinced that psychological concepts, including those of behaviorism, are not appropriate to describe environmental contexts.

Studies of the relations between particular settings and qualities of individual behavior have been alluded to above. There are many others, e.g., Gump, Schoggen, and Redl, 1957; Gump and Sutton-Smith, 1955; Raush, Dittman, and Taylor, 1959. However, the potential of the behavior-setting unit is realized more fully when arrays of settings are examined. For example, it is possible to describe classrooms, schools, churches, communities in setting terms and then relate the qualities of the arrays of settings to behavior of individuals. Recent developments make it possible to describe the *size* of an environment by employing settings-data (Barker and Schoggen, 1973). Further, the *size* measurement is independent of the *use* measurement. Until now, size of institutions and of communities typically has been measured by how many people use them. We speak of cities of one-million size. Of course, when size and use are mixed together we are presented with another circularity problem in environment-behavior relationships.

A simple use measurement from ecological psychology that might be of interest to behavior analysts is that of *occupancy time*. The amount of time that persons inhabit settings of given qualities can be noted; quantitative assessments can be made of the extent to which groups are exposed to given environmental qualities. In our attempts to understand behavior in naturally occurring environments, we may check: first, the *availability* of certain environmental supports or contexts; next, the extent to which these contexts are actually used; and, finally, the more specific environment-behavior transactions of particular individuals.

One of the major contributions dealing with the coercivity of settings-arrays upon individual behavior appears in the school size studies of the ecological psychologists (Barker and Gump, 1964; Wicker, 1968; Willems, 1967). These investigations demonstrated that a wide range of variables are markedly influenced by the size of an institution. What is most pertinent to present consideration is the model of relationships that proceed from the more global ecological conditions to the behaviors and experiences of individuals. The explanatory chain develops as follows: Compared to a large institution, the smaller one will have reduced environmental size and differentiation (e.g., fewer settings) but even further reduced population. With fewer persons available to sustain ongoing environmental operations, there are more pressures on the persons in the smaller (more "under-manned") institution to work hard, to assume more central setting positions. With the harder work and the more frequent taking on of responsible roles, other reactions tend to occur. Compared to persons in the larger institution, those in the smaller report more satisfaction relating to competence development, to being challenged and being valued, to pleasure in sharing group taks; they also report more feeling of obligation to the settings of the institution.

The conceptual gap between ecological factors and those of individual behavior is a difficult one. Those who wish to assess how well the gap has been bridged by ecological psychologists might consult two sources: a simple yet illuminating schematic display by Wicker (1968) or a more detailed exposition of the forces and structures that are involved by Barker (1968, pp. 178–203).

ENVIRONMENT-ENVIRONMENT INTERDEPENDENCE

Once a conception of environmental units is established, the question of relations between units and unit clusters can be approached. One set of relations between settings derives from their location in time and space. Within a setting cluster, particular settings may occur simultaneously, in immediate sequence, or at clearly separated times. Certain settings may occupy the same space (almost always at separate times), adjacent spaces, or separated ones. Doubtless, men and women who create and manage organizations have considerable practical wisdom regarding locational relationships; however, very little research has been carried out regarding the effects of setting contiguity or noncontiguity. Some information is available to show that temporal boundary areas between settings have special effects upon inhabitants. In third-grade studies, behavior of teachers at transitions was consistently more controlling than at the interiors of the settings (Gump, 1969). In a nursery school, Krantz and Risley (in press) showed that attention behavior in a "listening to stories" setting could be elevated or depressed by providing quiet or highly active preceding settings (e.g., rest periods or recesses).

In an ongoing study of open architecture schools, Rhonda Ross and I are finding that whether open programs are maintained for physically open milieus is correlated to the locational arrangement of settings. For example, shared teaching (presumably one aspect of the open program in schools) requires that the relevant teachers and groups be in adjacent places at the time when the same general subject matter is to be studied. At many schools, other priorities meant that such time, space, and subject matter adjacencies were sporadic and fragmentary. Necessarily then, meaningful program sharings between teachers and class groups were infrequent.

More investigation of variables related to the spatial and temporal location might be quite profitable to those who become interested in the assembly of setting clusters, a task that faces anyone who wishes to create new or different environments.

Settings are involved in dynamic relationships as well as in locational ones. A setting cluster either will be designed or will evolve such that some settings control others, some settings support operations in other settings, and so on. Extensive arrays of settings may be under the control of one setting, as is the case in a community where hundreds of settings are regulated by the school board. Sometimes settings may be under the control of settings outside their own cluster; the ecological psychologists would say that they lack local autonomy. Barker and Schoggen (1973) showed that settings in an English town enjoyed less local autonomy than settings in a comparable American town. Further, it appeared that that setting autonomy of the English community had decreased over the nine-year period for which before and after measures were taken.

The necessity for support settings appeared in the open school study mentioned above. It became quite clear that much cooperative staff planning was required if an open program was to occur in the open schools. Of the 19 schools we studied, only a minority were actually attempting team teaching, flexible use of space, provision of extensive student options, or other format qualities typical of open programs. However, most of the minority that did present program openness also established settings to support the program; that is, there would be weekly, school-time planning settings of teacher sub-groups, often attended by the principal. During these sessions, necessary agreements were reached, the required task assignments were made, and the assembly of necessary materials and facilities was accomplished.

In these open schools, another kind of support setting was the library or learning center. Such facilities were present in all schools; the difference arose from the relationship between this support setting and the classrooms. When teachers went with their students to use the center and when the library teacher visited the classrooms or otherwise became familiar with the teachers' curricula, flow of students from classroom to center became easy and frequent. A goal such as "individualization of instruction" became more feasible if this flow operated.

In a current study by Tina Adelberg and Herbert Wright (personal communication) a comparison between the lives of black and white children in an urban community showed that the black children were more frequently occupying positions of some responsibility in adult settings. Closer examination of the source of this superior positioning showed that the black church generated and maintained settings (nonreligious as well as religious) that made possible the black child's responsible activity. Some settings clusters, like the black church, become hosts for other settings and, thus, for the behavior and experience that these settings support.

If beneficial environments are to be created and maintained, it appears that simple presentation of the appropriate consumer settings is not sufficient. Also required are support settings and appropriate supportive relationships between settings.

I conclude by reiterating an earlier assertion: an ecological perspective is not only necessary in behavior analysis, it is already present; the unsettled issue is whether or not behavior analysis will begin *scientific* pursuit of the ecological issues with which they must deal. If that quest is undertaken, useful concepts, methods, and findings are available from ecological psychology. Many of these deal with the units and structures appearing in the behavior streams of individuals and in the settings they inhabit. The eventual outcome of that pursuit may present us with features not present at this time in either field—an exciting possibility.

LITERATURE CITED

Adelberg, T., and Wright, H. Personal communication.

Baer, D. M. Some comments on the structure of the intersection of ecology and applied behavior analysis. Chapter 5 of this volume.

Barker, R. G. 1963. The stream of behavior as an empirical problem. *In* R. G. Barker (ed.), The Stream of Behavior. Appleton-Century-Crofts, New York.

Barker, R. G. 1968. Ecological Psychology. Stanford University Press, Stanford.

Barker, R. G., and Gump, P. V. 1964. Big School, Small School. Stanford University Press, Stanford.

Barker, R. G., and Schoggen, P. 1973. Qualities of Community Life: Methods of Measuring Environment and Behavior Applied to an American and English Town. Jossey-Bass, San Francisco.

Barker, R. G., and Wright, H. F. 1955. Midwest and Its Children. Harper and Row, New York. Reprinted by Archon Books, Hamden, Conn., 1971.

Gump, P. V. 1969. Intra-setting analysis: The third grade classroom as a special but instructive case. *In* E. Willems and H. Raush (eds.), Naturalistic Viewpoints in Psychological Research. Holt, Rinehart, and Winston, New York.

Gump, P. V. 1975. Environmental psychology and the behavior setting. *In* B. Honikman (ed.), Responding to Social Change. Dowden, Hutchinson, and Ross, Stroudsberg, Pa.

Gump, P. V., Schoggen, P., and Redl, F. 1957. The camp milieu and its immediate effects. J. Soc. Iss. 13:40–46.

Gump, P. V., and Sutton-Smith, B. 1955. Activity setting and social interaction. Amer. J. Orthopsych. 25:755–760.

Holman, J. The moral risk and high cost of ecological concern in applied behavior analysis. Chapter 4 of this volume.

Kounin, J. S., and Gump, P. V. 1974. Signal systems of lesson settings and the task-related behavior of pre-school children. J. Educ. Psych. 66(4): 554–562.

Krantz, P., and Risley, T. Behavioral ecology in the classroom. J. Appl. Behav. Anal. In press.

Raush, H. L., Dittman, A. T., and Taylor, T. J. 1959. Person, setting, and change in social interaction. Human Relations 12:361–378.

Schoggen, P. 1963. Environmental forces in the everyday lives of children. *In* R. G. Barker (ed.), The Stream of Behavior. Appleton-Century-Crofts, New York.

Sherman, L. 1975. Glee in small groups of preschool children. Child Dev. 46:53–61.

Skinner, B. F. 1938. Behavior of Organisms. MacMillan, New York.

Skinner, B. F. 1976. Walden Two: Walden Two Revisited. Macmillan, New York.

Wicker, A. W. 1968. Undermanning, performances, and student's subjective experiences in behavior settings of large and small high schools. J. Personal. Soc. Psych. 10:255–261.

Willems, E. P. 1967. Sense of obligation to high school activities as related to school size and marginality of student. Child Dev. 38:1247–1260.

Willems, E. P. 1974. Behavior technology and behavior ecology. J. Appl. Behav. Anal. 7:151–165. Also reprinted as Chapter 2 of this volume.

Wright, H. F. 1967. Recording and Analyzing Child Behavior. Harper and Row, New York.

7

The Ecology of Applied Behavior Analysis

Todd R. Risley

An "ecological" perspective has evolved in applied behavior analysis as the scope of our endeavors has widened. This evolution will inevitably continue as our successes enable us to assume responsibilities for larger "ecosystems." No blandishments are needed to send us in this direction. Although discussion might provide a weathervane, it should be noted that weathervanes point to the source of the wind but do not presume to tell it which way to go.

The *external* ecology of applied behavior analysis endeavors inevitably produces prompts to expand our conceptualizations and research efforts at the ecologically appropriate time; that is, society demands larger products when we are responsible for the arena in which that product must be produced. When applied behavior analysts are responsible for a school system, a police department, a mental health center, or a retardation institution, they are faced with both the opportunity for manipulating larger variables *and* the immediate need to do so.

It is futile to propose goals for applied behavior analysis that are of greater scope than the opportunities for such analysis. Applied behavior analysis, in fact, is proceeding as rapidly as analytical opportunities permit.

We have heard applied behavior analysis criticized for so many of its past efforts being narrowly constrained: "small *n*'s," "short time spans," "no collateral measures," "repeated demonstrations of the same procedures," etc. It seems appropriate to remind ourselves (and others) to examine applied behavior analysis in terms of its total context. In other words, let us adopt an ecological perspective in evaluating applied behavior analysis.

Given the brief existence of the field and the publication lag of our journals, the most recent 10 percent of all completed, written, accepted reports of applied behavior analysts are still "in press." Even confining our inspection to the older 90 percent, it is clear that progressively increasing numbers of articles have displayed more of those features that our critics claim we are neglecting. And any single article represents only an isolated piece of a multi-year applied research and development effort. No single article from the Achievement Place project, for example, will display the massive ecological scope of that effort. To anyone familiar with the past, present, and planned concerns of the Achievement Place project—and of several dozen other applied behavior analysis efforts of similar scope—blandishments for a bigger perspective seem ludicrous.

In the 15 or so functional years of the field, one remarkable thing has occurred: there are now investigators in the field who are 15 or 20 years post-Ph.D. We are no longer exclusively young professionals, and age and a personal "track record" are prerequisites for more substantial responsibilities. Substantial responsibilities provide the opportunities, the need, *and the resources* for investigating bigger temporal, spatial, and behavioral portions of the "ecosphere." In the process, of course, more students and junior colleagues are trained to deal with larger aspects of ecospheres early in their professional lives.

I would suggest to critics of applied behavior analysis that they reread the literature (or read it) with the above statements in mind. They may find a consistent wind already blowing in their chosen direction.

Let me illustrate the development of an ecological perspective with the work of the research group with which I am associated: the Living Environments Group. As I previously stated, there are many more, and perhaps better, examples of long-range applied behavior analysis programs that have developed a broad ecological thrust through opportunity and need. I will use my own work simply as a matter of convenience.

THE LIVING ENVIRONMENTS GROUP

Earlier work in institutions, preschools, and day care centers convinced us of the need to provide more than the short-term therapeutic or educational interventions that have characterized applied research efforts. Accordingly, in 1970 I organized a team of young researchers at the University of Kansas into the Living Environments Group. The purpose of our research has been to develop pervasive environments that will serve to sustain appropriate behaviors for dependent people. The group is concerned with the description, selection, and organization of facilities, equipment, materials, and personnel, in addition to the usual behavioral intervention variables of applied psychology. This research has been conducted in various locations.

In Lawrence, Kansas, two day-care projects have been developed. At our infant day care center, we have developed a total environment for babies that incorporates the safe design of equipment, efficient methods of assigning and maintaining staff responsibilities, and the evaluation of play materials that infants prefer. In our toddler day care center, we are designing an environment in which the learning guidelines of basic self-help skills are integrated into toddler's play and daily routines.

The experimental analysis of the organization of preschool and kindergarten classrooms, a technology for operating a community recreation center and for evaluating play materials, methods of assisting residents in controlling crime, traffic, and litter in a low income housing project, and the analysis of the effects of an activity program on a pediatric ward have been part of the Living Environments Group research at locations in Kansas City.

At other locations, the development and evaluation of a living environment for retarded children and aged residents of a nursing home are part of our research effort.

These are only examples of the kind of research involved in developing comprehensive environments for the education and care of dependent people. In each setting, the program was directed by a pre- or post-doctoral professional who worked with me in developing that program. As we consider more detailed examples of some of these programs, please note the marked similarities of the applied research in each setting. Each involves environmental design, the selection of equipment and materials, job specification, training and supervision of paraprofessional staff, general measures of resident participation and staff performance, experimental demonstrations, and program packaging and dissemination. We have found that technical developments in one setting are usually immediately transferable to the others. This makes us confident that we can discover general principles of the organization of living environments that transcend particular settings and populations.

THE ECOLOGY OF GROUP CARE SETTINGS

For the past several years we have been developing systems that provide a technology for reliable care of young children and for guidance and protection of preadolescents and teenagers. This technology includes day care programs for infants, toddlers, and preschoolers, and after-school care and recreation for youth. Each program has been designed to function efficiently with staff who, except for the supervisor, are low paid, transient, and neither specifically nor extensively trained in working with children. In order to ensure quality programs with such staff, we have been attentive to many nonstaff variables, including architecture, interior design, materials selection, activity organization, development of simple "packaged" staff training procedures, self-corrective monitoring, and program evaluation techniques. In short, we have carefully considered environmental and organizational variables in order to help staff conduct quality programs. The result is a technology for operative educational programs for all the children and youth of a community, from the youngest infant through the oldest teenager. This environmental and organizational approach to child care is perhaps best depicted through the example of the infant day care center.

Infant Day Care

The infant day care center model (Cataldo and Risley, 1974; Herbert-Jackson et al., in press; Macrae and Herbert-Jackson, 1976) is designed to provide full-day care for a maximum of 20 children four weeks to twelve months of age with the equivalent of five full-time staff members. The center is based on an open environment design that facilitates both child supervision and monitoring of staff, and it is divided by low, movable partitions into a series of activity areas for diapering, feeding, play, sleep, and receiving/departing (Twardosz, Cataldo, and Risley, 1974a).

Because previous research (Doke and Risley, 1972; LeLaurin and Risley, 1972) has shown that children can be more continuously engaged with their environment when staff are assigned responsibility for specific activity areas rather than specific children, staff assignments in the infant center are defined by areas of activity, i.e., one staff member acts as the supervisor and the others are assigned on a rotating basis to specific activity areas.

In each activity area, the arrangement of the area and the staff procedures are designed to facilitate reliable child care by full- or part-time paraprofessional staff. For example, the diapering area is arranged for maximum safety and efficiency. Each child's diapers, powders, and ointments are stored in the child's individual diaper bin. Taped to each child's bin are instructions from his parents on diapering and for the use of any special medications for diaper rash. Other materials needed (paper towels, tissues) are arranged conveniently on or near the diapering table so no child is ever left unattended.

Design and selection of materials have been carefully done for all areas in the infant center. For example, cribs are bolted on top of crib stands which also serve as storage shelves for children's blankets, favorite crib toys, and pacifiers. Thus, all materials are easily accessible at nap time. The cribs have collapsible sides for convenience in placing and removing the child. Further, the cribs are at adult eye-level for maximum eye contact. In the play area, materials and activities have been selected that both engage infants in activities and promote adult-child interaction, and the environment has been designed to allow maximum exploration with a minimum of danger.

In addition to efficient organization and selecting necessary materials, simple "packaged" staff routines are also crucial for effective child care. The staff procedure for the diapering area provides an example. When a child at the infant center needs a change, the staff member in charge of the diapering area first sets out the necessary materials from the child's diaper bin. When everything is within easy reach, the infant is brought into the diapering area. Because of such efficient planning, there is time for adult-child social interaction and play. After the child is changed and placed in another area, the diapering area is cleaned and a record of why and when the child was changed is made for both the center and the parents. Each step in this routine has been described in writing, and checklists have been prepared for use in training new staff members and in regular monitoring of performance levels. As a result of this attention to organization, design, materials selection, and simple staff procedures, this infant center model provides quality care for children regardless of staff experience or previous training.

Our approach to developing this infant center technology has been to describe those procedures and designs that best facilitate reliable child care. While some aspects of this technology are explicit and just plain common sense, others required experimental investigation. For example, while the diapering area routine and design of necessary materials are straightforward and the monitoring of staff performance in the routine uncomplicated, efficient organization of diapering involves more than just replacing wet with dry. We found that the average staff member assigned to diapering spent more than a quarter of his/her time just checking diapers to determine whether or not the well considered and efficient diapering procedures needed to be put into effect. A study was therefore designed to determine how the diaper-checking procedure could be made more efficient without significantly altering the frequency of diaper changes. As a result of this study, we can recommend that a child's diapers be checked in the normal course of moving him/her from one activity area to another, such as from play to feeding, and that a supplemental check be made every hour for those children who have not changed activity areas during the hour (LeLaurin, 1974).

Similarly, we have conducted research demonstrations in other areas of the center to substantiate particular elements of our procedures and design. In the sleep area, for example, we have shown that the recommended open environment design, with no walls or visual partitions between areas, does not hinder children's sleep even though their cribs are open to the sights and sounds of the rest of the center (Twardosz, Cataldo, and Risley, 1974a). Another study in this area showed that when toys are present in cribs, children do play with them, but that neither the onset nor the duration of sleep is affected by the additional stimulation (Twardosz, Cataldo, and Risley, 1974b).

In a study in the feeding area, we found that children's individual schedules are more closely adhered to, even by new and substitute staff, when a large feeding-schedule board is displayed within view of the entire infant center (LeLaurin, 1973). Thus, a simple architectural device which publicly displays each child's schedule and his status vis-a-vis that schedule may enable children to receive individual care in group settings. In another feeding area study, we compared the procedure of holding children while feeding them with that of having children eat while seated in high chairs or infant seats. Since no difference was found in the amount children eat or the time they spend eating, it can be recommended that children be fed in infant seats or high chairs, a procedure that makes feeding several children at the same time possible, often a necessary procedure for ensuring that all children are fed at their scheduled time (Valdivieso-Cedeno, 1972).

A primary concern of infant day care is providing a high level of adult-child social interaction. At first, it might be thought that increasing the number of staff, although expensive both in terms of using paid staff or valuable volunteer time, would be effective in increasing social interaction. However, our observations, substantiated by our research demonstrations (Haskins, 1974), indicate that an increase in staff actually decreases each person's level of interaction with the children. Our technology, therefore, recommends an alternative method for increasing staff-child interaction: assigning staff responsibility for conducting specific play area activities.

Once the infant center technology was developed, the descriptions of materials, simple staff routines, and environmental designs were developed into a series of training manuals suitable for use by persons with less than a high school education. Tests employing these training manuals have shown that a high degree of accuracy in performing staff routines could be achieved simply by training staff through the use of the manuals and that this high level of adherence to routines was not lost over successive "generations" of staff turnover, as is often the case when training is conducted verbally (Sheppard, 1974).

Toddler and Preschool Day Care

Similar considerations as in the infant center have been applied to the design and operation of day care programs for toddlers (one to two years) and preschoolers (three to five years). While in the selection of materials and components of environmental design the infant center model had to be altered to suit the age and developmental level of toddlers and preschoolers, the requirement of developing a technology to be implemented by a relatively small number of nonprofessional staff remained the same.

The toddler center technology employs an open environment design, similar in concept to that employed in the infant center, because it provides for efficient use of both space and personnel without interfering with children's sleep or small group activities (Twardosz, Cataldo, and Risley, 1974a). As in the infant center, toddler center staff responsibilities are organized by areas of activity, and again we found that increasing the number of staff was not as effective in increasing personal attention to children as was the provision of specified activity assignments (Cataldo and Risley, 1974; Haskins, 1974).

Because children of toddler age are expected to gain certain skills, e.g., self-toileting, self-feeding, and following adult instructions, these skills must be considered in providing a group care technology for one- and two-year-olds. However, day care staff can attend to these issues only in the context of efficient daily operation. For example, regardless of whether children can or cannot feed themselves, or are in the process of learning to do so, food must be prepared and set out for the children, children must be gathered in a feeding area for their meal, they must eat, and the area must be cleaned after the meal. While many approaches to self-feeding are known to be successful, only a procedure that can be incorporated into the normal sequence of mealtime and that can be implemented by staff not highly skilled or experienced in training children is appropriate in a day care setting.

In working to make mealtime successful, we used a simple food weighing procedure to establish a set of menus composed of nutritious foods that toddlers will eat (see Twardosz, Cataldo, and Risley, 1975). At the same time, we found that certain preferred foods, because they are "mushy," tend to promote spoon use. Therefore, our recommended procedure for training self-feeding relies heavily on the selection of nutritious, preferred foods that promote spoon use so that relatively untrained staff need employ only simple prompting and, on occasion, contingent attention procedures. The supervisor, who is well trained, can then vary menus, depending upon the level of skill of the children. In asking the simple question, "How much of various foods do children normally eat?" we discovered that no one really knew for sure. This has led us into a program of research to "Provide an Empirical Basis for Child Nutrition Counseling" (Maternal and Child Health) to determine the quantity of various foods young children will normally eat and to construct menus for day care centers that will result in adequate nutrients "in the child" rather than just "on the child's plate." (See Herbert-Jackson, Cross, and Risley, in press; Herbert-Jackson and Risley, in press.)

In our work with preschoolers, we have found that some ecological variables that are very easy to implement have significant effects on children's play behavior and can be used to reduce disruptions in group settings. For example, we found that when a group of children are evenly spaced around a teacher who is reading a story or demonstrating the use of materials, their visual attention is markedly higher than when the children follow the more usual procedure of crowding around the teacher (Krantz, 1974). Likewise, inappropriate behavior can be effectively reduced through activity scheduling that avoids following an active play period with a sedentary one; instead, the intermediary step of relatively inactive play before sedentary activities produces fewer disruptions and a higher rate of attention during the sedentary period (Krantz, 1974).

Another example is found in our studies of how the type of play materials presented and the way they are presented affect children's play. Children provided with the type of toys that are commonly played with by one child at a time ("isolate" toys) show much lower rates of social play than do children presented with the type of toys commonly used in groups ("social" toys), thereby suggesting that the encouragement of social learning through play can be facilitated by the provision of appropriate toys (Quilitch and Risley, 1973). Storage of toys—whether scrambled in toy boxes or arranged on shelves—also can affect children's play significantly, and whether children have direct access to materials or must request one toy at a time from a teacher can increase the interactions that can be used by preschool teachers as learning situations (Montes and Risley, 1975).

After-School Day Care and Recreation

As children grow older, they no longer need care; instead, they need guidance in establishing the skills necessary for successful and appropriate adult behavior and protection from being seriously affected by official consequences for their occasional acts of social deviance. We have considered two technologies for achieving these goals. One, suitable for pre-adolescents who are more readily amenable to adult direction than are teenagers, is "survival training" in academic, achievement, and job-related skills. The second is a "safe passage" program to provide older youth with an alternative to the activities of the street and of irresponsible peers and to increase adolescents' contacts with and socialization to responsible adults. The focus for both programs is organized recreation, a setting that can provide both consequences for youths' activity and maximum contact with responsible adults.

In designing a technology for the safe and trouble-free operation of a recreation center as an environment free from social deviance, we have developed toy and activity evaluation procedures to insure that the center's programs are attractive and engaging for youth. Furthermore, we have developed a technology that uses the availability of recreation activities as a consequence for youths' behavior. As with our other programs, these technologies can be implemented by nonprofessional, low paid, transient staff.

Our recreation technology can best be described by two examples of research demonstrations: one, which is particularly important to the safe passage program, dealing with a method for increasing youth participation in center activities and socialization to adults, and a second describing a method of efficiently employing community staff resources.

Crucial to the success of recreation center-based youth programs are attendance and contacts with adults that involve cooperation rather than confrontation. We found that new members could be recruited by providing additional access to recreation activities for those youth who bring new members to the center (Pierce and Risley, 1974a). A second problem of many recreation centers is the high level of fights, broken equipment, and littered floors which create recurrent cost, safety, and health problems requiring immediate action. Frequently, recreation center staff deal with such disruptions by trying to determine and confront the individual responsible for maintaining order. However, we have found that disruptive behavior can be reduced without confrontation by using peer-established rules and sanctions enforced by a youth or adult supervisor on a group contingency basis. In a research demonstration when rules were enforced by the supervisor's closing the center one or 15 minutes earlier per infraction depending upon the severity of the offense, disruptive behavior was effectively decreased (Pierce and Risley, 1974a).

Once the technology for operating a good recreation program is available, recreation center directors still need some method for ensuring that their staff actually employ the technology. In many youth programs that are partially subsidized by federal, state, or local funds, staff pay is not contingent on employees' job performance but rather upon their physical presence, a situation which is not conducive to high performance levels. In an effort to increase the job performance of seven Neighborhood Youth Corps workers being paid on hourly wage for serving as aides in an urban recreation program, we first drew up thorough job descriptions and then threatened termination of employment, but neither was sufficient to maintain adequate job performance. However, when the hourly wage (required by the Neighborhood Youth Corps program) was made contingent on job performance by crediting the workers with working time proportional to their rating on a simple checklist of job performance, their job performance was maintained at near-perfect levels. Thus, while this simple semantic shift in emphasis—from *"hours* worked" to "hours *worked"*—was still interpreted as meeting the Neighborhood Youth Corps requirements for hourly pay, its behavioral effects were substantial (Pierce and Risley, 1974b).

Much of the technology for designing group-care settings so as to provide an ecology for behavioral development has been developed over the past several years as we have worked to develop quality infant, toddler, preschool, and after-school day care and recreation programs. The primary work that remains is to make this technology readily available through comprehensive training, management, and monitoring software, including quality control procedures.

The Infant Day Care Center program represents the most complete example of how these latter steps may be undertaken successfully. Software packages on tested staff training procedures (Sheppard, 1974), detailed management plans, environmental design, and monitoring procedures have been completed. The specified quality control procedures that are included can be used by state licensing and other regulatory bodies or funding agencies, and monitoring can be conducted in cooperation with program developers. This technology is viable and available (Herbert-Jackson et al., in press). To realize a comprehensive system, similar software for toddler (Porterfield et al., in preparation), preschool, and after-school care are being completed now for dissemination to intervention programs for children from depriving environments.

Although there are occasions for formal educational instruction in each of these models, we have emphasized the informal interactions between adult and child as the most important opportunities for child development. We have worked to increase such interactions by selecting proper materials (O'Brien, Hamad, Herbert-Jackson, and Risley, in press; Quilitch, Christoperhsen, and Risley, in press; Quilitch and Risley, 1973), by displaying materials correctly (Eck, Herbert-Jackson, and Risley, in press; Montes and Risley, 1975), by carefully sequencing activities and providing proper physical arrangements for children (Eck, 1975; Krantz, 1974), by increasing the general quality of such interactions by simple training manuals focused upon the caregivers interacting with children who were *engaged* in doing something appropriate (Jenkins, 1975; May et al., 1975), and by analyzing the opportunities for adult-child interactions into a small number of natural categories in order to effectively instruct adults to maximize the developmental impact of each interaction.

For example, we have developed the strategy of *incidental teaching,* which systematically uses naturally occurring occasions throughout the day for language instruction (Hart and Risley, 1974; Risley, 1972; Risley and Twardosz, 1976). An opportunity for incidental teaching occurs whenever a child initiates conversation; these child-selected, naturally occurring, one-to-one interactions are ideal "micro-teaching" occasions in which the child learns new ways of working with language and, more importantly, learns to *use* more elaborate language features throughout his day. Our research has demonstrated not only that children's abilities to use variety in their descriptive language can be increased (Hart and Risley, 1968, 1974), but that children prefer incidental teaching to its absence (Montes, 1974), and that once children have learned to work with elaborated languate at high rates, use will generalize to other people (Hart and Risley, 1975).

We have found that a program of incidental teaching of language-use (conducted throughout a three-hour-a-day, four-day-a-week preschool program) can produce changes in rate and content of the spontaneous language of disadvantaged children from the level of a matched group of Head Start children to the level of a comparison group of college faculty children—within approximately three months (Risley, 1972).

Although we are still in the process of testing the distinctiveness of each category and the completeness of the categories in covering all adult-child interaction opportunities, the following classification system seems to be holding up:

1. When a child initiates conversation with an adult an opportunity for incidental teaching of productive language occurs. The procedures for converting these opportunities into quality developmental interactions have been detailed (Hart and Risley, 1975, 1976).
2. When a child is engaged in interaction with materials or with another child, an opportunity to further his motor, cognitive, or social skills presents itself. The procedure here is to keep the child's attention focused upon the interaction (the relevant reinforcer for that child at

that moment) while suggesting a variation in behavior or while contributing another material that will both increase the complexity of the interaction and make it more reinforcing.

3. When a child is engaged in appropriate interaction but must be directed to change his activity, an opportunity for teaching receptive language and instruction-following occurs. The procedure in this case is to comment on the child's current interaction, but then direct his attention to you and give the instruction of what you wish him to do next. This should be done only from a proximate position at first so that additional prompts for following the instruction can be given, if necessary. When the child follows the instruction, the adult continues the interaction until he/she has engaged the child in interaction in the new activity.

4. When the child is engaged in inappropriate interaction and must be stopped, an opportunity for teaching the appropriate interaction occurs. The procedures for converting these opportunities into incidental teaching episodes—involving observational learning—have been detailed (Porterfield, Herbert-Jackson, and Risley, 1976; May et al., 1975).

The process of developing and testing simple instructional materials for caregivers, now underway, will determine whether some of these four categories in fact contain more than one natural type of developmental interaction. And the process of observing the implementation of complete incidental teaching for all categories of opportunities will reveal simultaneously any interaction opportunities that are not contained within these four categories.

In any case, our goal is to classify all opportunities for adult-child interactions into a finite (and hopefully small) number of natural classes and to develop simple instructional materials for adults that will improve the frequency and developmental quality, i.e., the behavioral effectiveness, of adult-child interactions.

This last example illustrates the interplay between the methodologies of ecological psychology and applied behavior analysis. We must passively observe and describe the various adult-child interactions that occur naturally in order to develop a conceptual framework for classification. *But,* our next step will be to systematically manipulate the adult side of each interaction to test the importance of the conceptualization in influencing the development of behaviors. And in the process we will have developed practical procedures for enhancing the ecology of social settings for children. The difference between passive observation alone and observation followed by systematic intervention is not simply a matter of research tactics. The results are strategically different.

Although observation can give us—indeed, is necessary for—new conceptualizations of the world, experimental intervention gives us the methodology to change the world.

The *internal* ecology of applied behavior analysis is absolutely consistent with respect to one feature: an insistence on experimental analysis. No amount of observation or description alone will suffice. Thus, I predict that the observational methodology of ecological psychology will not be the text of our future marriage contract. I suggest that the family name will be the experimental analysis of environments rather than the ecological analysis of behavior. Ecological procedures will be the offspring of our marriage, not ecological observations. Although new kinds of independent variables will lead to new dependent variables, the converse will not occur. We will gain from ecologists' ideas and concepts of the features of the ecosystem that are potent, and we will be fruitful and multiply; and the external ecology of applied behavior analysis—the simple fact that responsibility is a prerequisite to power—will continue to determine and correct the direction of our growth.

LITERATURE CITED

Cataldo, M. F., and Risley, T. R. 1974. Infant day care. *In* R. Ulrich, T. Stachnik, and J. Mabry (eds.), Control of Human Behavior, Vol. III, pp. 44–50. Scott, Foresman, and Co., Glenview, Ill.

Doke, L. A., and Risley, T. R. 1972. The organization of day care environments: Required versus optional activities. J. Appl. Behav. Anal. 5:405–420.

Eck, R. 1975. Removing the time wasting aspects of nap time for young children. Unpublished masters thesis, University of Kansas,

Eck, R., Herbert-Jackson, E., and Risley, T. R. Placement of pictures and TV in child-care centers. Environment and Behavior. In press.

Hart, B. M., and Risley, T. R. 1968. Establishing use of descriptive adjectives in the spontaneous speech of disadvantaged preschool children. J. Appl. Behav. Anal. 1:109–120.

Hart, B. M., and Risley, T. R. 1974. Using preschool materials to modify the language of disadvantaged children. J. Appl. Behav. Anal. 7: 243–256.

Hart, B. M., and Risley, T. R. 1975. Incidental teaching of language in the preschool. J. Appl. Behav. Anal. 8:411–420.

Hart, B. M., and Risley, T. R. 1976. Community-based language training. *In* T. D. Tjossem (ed.), Intervention Strategies for High Risk Infants and Young Children, pp. 187–198. University Park Press, Baltimore.

Haskins, L. K. 1974. The organization of day care environments: Increasing staff-child interaction in an infant day care center. Unpublished masters thesis, University of Kansas, Lawrence, Kan.

Herbert-Jackson, E., Cross, M. Z., and Risley, T. R. Milk types and temperatures—What will young children drink? J. Nutr. Educ. In press.

Herbert-Jackson, E., O'Brien, M., Porterfield, J., and Risley, T. R. The Infant Center. University Park Press, Baltimore. In press.

Herbert-Jackson, E., and Risley, T. R. Behavioral nutrition: Consumption of foods of the future by toddlers. J. Appl. Behav. Anal. In press.

Jenkins, J. A. 1975. Changing the patterns of staff-child interactions in group care situations: An evaluation of training materials. Unpublished masters thesis, University of Kansas, Lawrence, Kan.

Krantz, P. J. 1974. Ecological arrangements in the classroom. Unpublished doctoral dissertation, University of Kansas, Lawrence, Kan.

LeLaurin, K. 1973. The organization of day care environments: An examination of the duties of supervisor in a day care center for children under walking age. Unpublished doctoral dissertation, University of Kansas, Lawrence, Kan.

LeLaurin, K., and Risley, T. R. 1972. The organization of day care environments: "Zone" versus "man-to-man" staff assignments. J. Appl. Behav. Anal. 5:225–232.

Macrae, J. W., and Herbert-Jackson, E. 1976. Are behavioral effects of infant day care program specific? Dev. Psych., 12:269–270.

May, J. G., Risley, T. R., Twardosz, S., Friedman, P., Bijou, S., Wexler, D., et al. 1975. Guidelines for the use of behavioral procedures in state programs for retarded persons. NARC Monograph, M. R. Research 1:73 pp.

Montes, F. 1974. Incidental teaching of beginning reading in a day care center. Unpublished doctoral dissertation, University of Kansas, Lawrence, Kan.

Montes, F., and Risley, T. R. 1975. Evaluating traditional day care practices: An empirical approach. Child Care Q. 4:208–215.

O'Brien, M., Hamad, C., Herbert-Jackson, E., and Risley, T. R. Toys for toddlers: What you choose does make a difference. Young Children. In press.

Pierce, C. H., and Risley, T. R. 1974a. Recreation as a reinforcer: Increasing membership and decreasing disruptions in an urban recreation program. J. Appl. Behav. Anal. 7:403–411.

Pierce, C. H., and Risley, T. R. 1974b. Improving job performance of neighborhood youth corps aides in an urban recreation program. J. Appl. Behav. Anal. 7:207–215.

Porterfield, J. K., Herbert-Jackson, E., and Risley, T. R. 1976. Contingent observation: An effective and acceptable procedure for reducing disruptive behaviors of young children in group settings. J. Appl. Behav. Anal. 9:55–64.

Quilitch, H. R., Christoperhsen, E. R., and Risley, T. R. The evaluation of children's play materials. J. Appl. Behav. Anal. In press.

Quilitch, H. R., and Risley, T. R. 1973. The effects of play materials on social play. J. Appl. Behav. Anal. 6:573–578.

Risley, T. R. 1972. Spontaneous language and the preschool environment. *In* J. C. Stanley (ed.), Preschool Programs for the Disadvantaged: Five Experimental Approaches to Early Childhood Education. Johns Hopkins University Press, Baltimore.

Risley, T. R., and Twardosz, S. 1976. The preschool as a setting for behavioral intervention. *In* H. Leitenberg (ed.), Handbook of Behavior Modification and Behavior Therapy, pp. 453–474. Prentice-Hall, Englewood Cliffs, N.J.

Sheppard, J. 1974. The evaluation of the adequacy of training procedures for transmitting job skills from one staff member to another across successive generations of day care workers. Unpublished honors thesis, Department of Human Development, University of Kansas, Lawrence, Kan.

Twardosz, S., Cataldo, M. F., and Risley, T. R. 1974a. Open environment design for infant and toddler day care. J. Appl. Behav. Anal., 7: 529–546.

Twardosz, S., Cataldo, M. F., and Risley, T. R. 1974b. Infants' use of crib toys. Young Child. 29:271–276.

Twardosz, S., Cataldo, M. F., and Risley, T. R. 1975. Menus for toddler day care: Food preference and spoon use. Young Child. 30:129–144.

Valdivieso-Cedeno, L. 1972. The relative effects of seating versus being held on the feeding behavior of infants in a day care setting. Unpublished masters thesis, University of Kansas, Lawrence, Kan.

COMMENT

Arguments for an Expansion of Behavior Change Concepts

David E. Campbell

Gump's message (as stated in Chapter 6 of this volume) may be summarized as follows: Applied behavior analysts are moving into areas in which they are dealing with whole, intact environments. In doing so, they are confronted with ecological issues. In the past, they have dealt with these issues in a nonscientific manner that prevents any cumulative understanding. If a scientific approach is taken toward the ecological issues in the manipulation of whole environments, then potential mistakes may be avoided by attention to the concepts and findings of ecological psychology. With regard to behavior-behavior interdependency, applied behavior analysts should note that behavior occurs in discrete, naturally occurring units. Events occurring at the temporal boundaries of these units may influence the success of an intervention effort. At the level of behavior-environment interdependence, behavior can be considered partly a function of the quality and structure of the behavior settings in which it occurs. Setting arrays have important effects on behavior, some of which depend on setting size. Finally, with regard to environment-environment interdependence, temporal boundaries between settings and the locational arrangement of different settings have important effects on inhabitants. Gump concludes that applied behavior analysts should make use of the concepts, methods, and findings from ecological psychology so that the ecological issues in behavior modification will be approached in a more scientific manner.

Gump has suggested that applied behavior analysis could benefit from the incorporation of new concepts and methods. This case could be made even stronger. Program developers in applied behavior analysis put considerable faith in the efficacy of appropriately applied reinforcement and punishment techniques; however, they acknowledge that these techniques are sometimes difficult to apply effectively (Reppuci and Saunders, 1974) and undesirable consequences may accompany their use (Levine and Fasnacht, 1974; Sajwaj, Twardosz and Burke, 1972; Wahler, 1972; Willems, 1974, Chapter 3 of this volume). Applied behavior analysts rarely find fault with their techniques or concepts when an intervention effort does not go as expected. Rather, they tend to blame individual persons involved in the intervention. When a parent does not apply contingent reinforcement to a child as directed by the behavior analyst, the latter is likely to ask: "What is wrong with this parent?" The parent may get blamed for being unable to follow straightforward directions on how and when to reinforce for any extended period of time. Perhaps *nothing* is wrong with the parent. Perhaps the behavior analyst should consider another question: "What is wrong with my theory?" (See Eisenberg (1972) for a discussion of overly narrow conceptions of human problems and interventions).

If one suspects that the success of behavioral interventions is limited by too narrow an approach, in what direction should the approach be expanded? Gump points in the direction of ecological psychology, and suggests a methodological expansion of applied behavior analysis. If time sampling methods miss important temporal boundaries of activities, methods of gathering specimen records might be considered. These methods are available for both direct observation (Wright, 1967) and for self-recording (Michelson, 1975). Perhaps behavior analysts should also consider expanding the conceptual base of their intervention strategies by taking advantage of previous efforts to classify environments in terms of setting qualities and structure. Possibly setting-treatment interactions may be discovered that will enable them to predict when an intervention will be successful. Barker (1968), and Indik and Berrien (1968) provide examples of such classification efforts. Such conceptual expansion might also lead behavior analysts to consider the locational arrangement of settings and the occurrence of necessary support settings. Attention could be directed toward the temporal boundaries between settings.

By attending to the environment of target individuals whose behavior is to be modified, behavior analysts might become more sensitive to the notion of ecological diagnosis (Willems, 1974). An ecological diagnosis of human problem behavior takes account of the environmental context of that behavior, particularly the physical setting. One example of synomorphy between physical arrangement of a setting and the behavioral "program" that occurs within the setting was found by Gump and Ross (1975).

They reported that when there was poor fit between the environmental features of a school and the program of behavior, the performance of teachers and students was less adequate than when a good fit was evident. Other studies have shown aspects of the physical design of settings to be related to a variety of behaviors such as social interaction (Sommer, 1969), crime (Newman, 1973), friendship formation (Festinger, Schacter, and Back, 1950), and accident behavior (Neutra and McFarland, 1972). Where aspects of the physical environment are related to the targeted problem behavior, behavior analysts might incorporate the scientific findings of ecological and environmental psychology into the design of interventions.

There are other directions, in addition to strictly ecological ones, in which behavior analysts might expand conceptually. Applied behavior analysts stand to improve their modification efforts if attention is given to several other areas of scientific literature addressing the context of their intervention efforts. The operant equation may be insufficient to guide intervention involving whole person-environment systems. Addition of concepts and methods in the directions outlined above can lead to a valuable expansion of the repertoire of change strategies available to applied behavior analysts. For example, when the target of intervention is a group of persons, simple efforts to apply contingent control to reinforcers and punishers may prove insufficient. Concepts from the area of organizational psychology may enhance the behavior analyst's control over the instigation of a treatment effort. The literature on participative decision-making suggests strategies for eliciting cooperation from persons who must directly run the intervention program (Lowin, 1968). Research in equity theory suggests that, in some situations, people do not act so as to maximize their reinforcements (Adams, 1965; Lawler, 1971). Research in program evaluation shows clearly that the success of an intervention requires close attention to factors external to the design of the intervention strategy itself (Suchman, 1967; Weiss, 1972).

Risley (Chapter 7 of this volume) argues that there is no need for ecologists to criticize behavior analysts for lack of an ecological perspective. He feels that behavior analysts can only be as ecological as their research situations permit and that these situations are permitting such a perspective with greater frequency all the time. Risley's work with the Living Environments Group illustrates a comprehensive research program that involves the development of environments that sustain desirable behaviors for dependent people. Such development requires concern for architectural design, equipment selection, job specification, and staff selection and training, as well as for measures of the behavioral performance of staff and clients. This research effort has addressed questions of environmental design, staff assignment, food choice, activity scheduling, toy use, member recruiting, disruptive behavior, and language development. The work with language development is particularly interesting because it involves observational as well as experimental research approaches, a combination of methods attributed to ecological psychology and applied behavior analysis. Risley emphasizes that applied behavior analysis will remain essentially an experimental field. It will borrow concepts from ecological psychology as opportunities for an ecological orientation arise, but it will never emphasize descriptive methods.

Risley states that applied behavior analysts are as ecological in method and perspective as their current opportunities and responsibilities permit. He seems to believe that measurement of many aspects of a setting should occur only when the researcher has control over the whole setting. Ecological psychologists have shown that this need not be true. The latter rarely have control over an environment; yet, they manage to monitor many facets of behavior within the environment. For example, Ittelson, Proshansky, and Rivlin (1970) had no control over the activities within a mental institution, yet they managed to monitor the changes in how behavior was distributed throughout the institution when remodeling occurred to one of the rooms. Ecologists argue that one does not need control, in fact is often better off without it, in learning about behavior-environment relationships in a setting.

In his closing comments, Risley points to a methodological distinction between applied behavior analysis and ecological psychology. He says behavior analysts insist on experimental analysis while ecologists limit themselves to observational techniques. Gump appears to accept this distinction. It is quite acceptable for behavior analysts to insist on experimental demonstrations—for an obvious reason. A fundamental goal of applied behavior analysis is to develop techniques for changing human problem behavior in desired directions. If the goal is to *change* behavior, the preferred research strategy must be to modify, change, or manipulate whatever necessary to create the desired change. It must be recognized that ecological psychology has a different goal: to understand behavior in everyday settings. A first step in understanding is to describe "what goes on." The ecologists accept that naturally occurring behavior has many determinants that vary in relative weights at different times. An experimental manipulation would show whether a given set of determinants *can* influence dependent variables of interest under specified conditions. However, to understand whether or not such causal relationships normally occur in everyday settings, noninterventionist research strategies are necessary. A variety of methods are available for making causal inferences from nonexperimental research, including quasi-experimental designs (Campbell and Stanley, 1963), cross-lagged correlational analyses (Yee and Gage, 1968), time-series designs (Glass, Willson, and Gottman, 1975), natural experiments (Campbell, 1969), and path analysis (Blalock, 1971). The ecologists, because of their chosen research goal, have no choice but to emphasize naturalistic research strategies. They resort to experimental manipulation only as necessary to answer their research questions (Willems and Raush, 1969). The price they pay is less certainty as to how to alleviate human problems. Applied behavior analysts, on the other hand, are more certain about the results of their programs but can say little about how the target problems arose in the first place. The fact that reinforcement procedures increase desirable behavior provides little evidence that reinforcement strategies are responsible for the problem. To make such an assertion would be to make the same logical error as that illustrated by the belief that headaches are caused by an insufficiency of aspirin in the body.

Gump has argued that applied behavior analysts should expand their concepts so as to better develop effective intervention strategies. Risley has shown one route for such an expansion. It is this author's hope that Gump's and Risley's papers give no one peace of mind. Rather, it is hoped that their arguments may make both ecological psychologists and applied behavior analysts less certain of their positions.

LITERATURE CITED

Adams, J. S. 1965. Injustice in social exchange. In L. Berkowitz (ed.), Advances in Experimental Social Psychology, Vol. 2, pp. 267–299. Academic Press, New York.

Barker, R. G. 1968. Ecological Psychology. Stanford University Press, Stanford.

Blalock, H. M. (ed.). 1971. Causal Models in the Social Sciences. Aldine-Atherton, Chicago.

Campbell, D. T. 1969. Reforms as experiments. Amer. Psychologist 24: 409–429.

Campbell, D. T., and Stanley, J. 1963. Experimental and Quasi-experimental Designs for Research. Rand-McNally, Chicago.

Eisenberg, L. 1972. The human nature of human nature. Science 176: 123–128.

Festinger, L., Schachter, S., and Back, K. 1950. Social Pressures in Informal Groups. Stanford University Press, Stanford.

Glass, G. V., Willson, V. L., and Gottman, J. M. 1975. Design and Analysis of Time-series Experiments. Colorado University Press, Boulder, Col.

Gump, P., and Ross, R. 1975. Problems and possibilities in measurements of school environments. Paper presented at the Third Biennial Conference of the International Society for the Study of Behavioral Development, July, 1975. University of Surrey, Guilford, England.

Indik, B. P., and Berrien, F. K. (eds.). 1968. People, Groups, and Organizations. Teachers College Press, New York.

Ittelson, W. H., Proshansky, H. M., and Rivlin, L. G. 1970. The environmental psychology of the psychiatric ward. *In* H. M. Proshansky, Ittelson, W. H., and Rivlin, L. G. (eds.), Environmental Psychology: Man and his Physical Setting, pp. 419–439. Holt, New York.

Lawler, E. E. 1971. Pay and Organizational Effectiveness: A Psychological View. McGraw-Hill, New York.

Levine, F. M., and Fasnacht, G. 1974. Token rewards may lead to token learning. Amer. Psychologist 29:816–820.

Lowin, A. 1968. Participative decision making: A model, literature critique, and prescriptions for research. Organiz. Behav. Hum. Perform. 3:68–106.

Michelson, W., and Reed, P. 1975. The time budget. *In* W. Michelson (ed.), Behavioral Research Methods in Environmental Design. Dowden, Hutchinson, and Ross, Stroudsburg, Pa.

Neutra, R., and McFarland, R. A. 1972. Accident epidemiology and the design of the residential environment. Hum. Factors 14:405–420.

Newman, O. 1973. Defensible Space. Collier, New York.

Reppuci, N. D., and Saunders, J. T. 1974. Social psychology of behavior modification: Problems of implementation in natural settings. Amer. Psychologist 29:649–660.

Sajwaj, T., Twardosz, S., and Burke, M. 1972. Side effects of extinction procedures in a remedial preschool. J. Appl. Behav. Anal. 5:163–175.

Sommer, R. 1969. Personal Space. Prentice-Hall, Englewood Cliffs, N.J.

Suchman, E. A. 1967. Evaluative Research. Russell Sage Foundation, New York.

Wahler, R. G. 1972. Some ecological problems in child behavior modification. *In* S. W. Bijou and E. Ribes-Inesta (eds.), Behavior Modification: Issues and Extensions, pp. 7–18. Academic Press, New York.

Weiss, C. H. 1972. Evaluation Research: Methods of Assessing Program Effectiveness. Prentice-Hall, Englewood Cliffs, N.J.

Willems, E. P. 1974. Behavioral technology and behavioral ecology. J. Appl. Behav. Anal. 7:151–165. Also reprinted as Chapter 3 of this volume.

Willems, E. P. Steps toward an ecobehavioral technology. Chapter 3 of this volume.

Willems, E. P., and Raush, H. L. (eds.). 1969. Naturalistic Viewpoints in Psychological Research. Holt, New York.

Wright, H. F. 1967. Recording and Analyzing Child Behavior. Harper and Row, New York.

Yee, A. H., and Gage, N. L. 1968. Techniques of estimating and source and direction of influence in panel data. Psych. Bull. 70:115–126.

PART IV

APPLICATIONS OF AN ECOLOGICAL PERSPECTIVE

8

A Useful Ecobehavioral Perspective for Applied Behavior Analysis

Steven F. Warren

An ecological perspective of human behavior has been defined in a variety of ways within psychology (Holman, Chapter 4 of this volume). For example, Barker (1963, 1968) characteristically focuses on the interdependencies of the organism and the environment in specific behavior *settings*. By contrast, Willems (1974, Chapter 2 of this volume) focuses on interrelationships of *individual behaviors* within a given environment (behavior covariations, stimulus, and response classes). Auerswald (1969) is concerned about the transactions taking place between separate but identifiable behavior *systems* within a larger environment.

Each of these different perspectives lends itself to different goals. The work of Barker and his colleagues has centered on developing an understanding of the naturalistic workings of different behavior settings compared by means of molar behavior patterns. Willems' perspective evokes a concern for side effects in the form of unpredicted behavior covariations of purposeful manipulations of other behaviors. Basing his approach on Auerswald's theories, Dockens (1975) argues that the primary goal is to program the generalization of therapeutic gains.

Despite these differences, there is a general thrust common to all approaches. Bronfenbrenner (1975) characterized this as a "focus upon the dynamic relations between the organism and its surround, with both the persons and the environment engaged in reciprocal tensions and activities, and undergoing progressive changes over time." Specifically, then, an ecological orientation is one that focuses on environmental reactions to responses that alter the environment. With the exception of general areas of agreement, ecological approaches to date have varied across disciplines, creating confusion and ambiguity over what constitutes a valid ecological perspective. Holman (Chapter 4 of this volume) contended that even "armed with the same basic tenets, researchers working toward totally different goals might all achieve success (according to their own criteria) yet be regarded by each other as somewhat misguided." She went on to conclude that "being ecological" was an ambiguous entity because "to know and understand the elements of an ecological perspective does not define the actions that may result from such a knowledge."

Although an ecological perspective may be defined reliably only in very general terms, Willems (1974) offered a serious challenge to the field of behavior analysis to adopt an ecological perspective, as he defined it. In Willems' approach, the environment may be conceptualized as reacting to a response change imposed on it by a behavior modifier (or by any other agent) so as to recover baseline. This reaction may be manifested in the form of potentially serious behavioral side effects. To counter these potential dangers, Willems urged that behavior analysts place greater emphasis on the detection and control of side effects resulting from behavioral interventions. Baer (1974, Part I Comment of this volume), in a rejoinder to Willems, agreed that an ecological perspective might be a good thing for behaviorists, but in the absence of a behavioral remedy prescribed by Willems, he was uncertain what useful ecological procedures might be.

Whether or not a useful ecological perspective exists in the field of applied behavior analysis ultimately is up to behavior analysts themselves. Certainly, there are many ways by which behavioral interventions can facilitate better short- and long-term results. Indeed, behavior analysts who currently design and apply their interventions, responsive to the natural environment, may already possess an ecological perspective appropriate to the tenets and goals of applied behavior analysis (as set forth by Baer, Wolf, and Risley, 1968)—a case in point of Holman's thesis.

If any better orientation is to improve the practice of behavior modification, it must be pragmatically useful, not simply popular or intellectually appealing. This chapter proposes that a useful "eco-behavioral" orientation for behavior analysis can be derived from five already existing criteria of successful behavioral interventions. The orientation is somewhat ecological in that it is directed toward monitoring the interactions of subjects and their environments; it is not ecological in that it fails to analyze mechanisms of environmental reaction to interventions.

The criteria emphasize the durability, generality, and appropriate rate and form of a therapeutic intervention, as well as consumer satisfaction with it. They are meant to measure the outcome of a behavioral intervention. If the information they provide indicates that a therapeutic intervention has been successful, then it can be tentatively concluded that the reactions of the natural environment have been offset. If results indicate less than success, then this suggests that the intervener must change something in the treatment. Thus, an ecobehavioral approach alerts the intervener to the existence of mechanisms of environmental reactivity but does not investigate the nature of the mechanisms (as it would if it were truly ecological).

The approach is labeled as "ecobehavioral" because it is somewhat ecological but also encompasses the tenets and goals of applied behavior analysis. It represents a continuance of the strong scientific tradition of precise measurement and validation of interventive manipulations. This perspective, then, represents a union of the outcome-oriented applied behavioral treatment approach with the ecological premise that the environment is reactive to all changes, whether systematically or unsystematically imposed upon it.

These ecobehavioral criteria are proposed as a means of assessing quantitatively some aspects of the desirability of a behavior change. Thus, measurement and demonstration of changes in the target behavior remain the foremost tasks of the behavior analyst, but, now, measurement of the *appropriateness* of that change is argued as an essential allied activity.

The ecobehavioral criteria proposed here are not a set of values, but a way of building in already agreed upon values. In this case, the desirability and appropriateness of a behavior change is determined by how well a therapeutic intervention worked, not by whether the procedures used or modifications made were "good" or "bad," either morally or ethically. The values underlying the criteria are those inherent to the field of applied behavior analysis. The criteria merely provide a way to focus those values.

The criteria proposed here are designed to improve the desirability of the ultimate effects (and side effects?) of any behavioral intervention. They are applicable across five dimensions of these interventions: response *rate,* stimulus and response *generalization,* response *durability,* response *diversity,* and *consumer satisfaction.* It is this author's contention that these criteria represent an appropriate ecobehavioral perspective for applied behavior analysts because each of them is applicable, behavioral, and analytical.

The first criterion is the final rate of the behavior being changed: do the consequences of this behavior depend on its rate? For example, children's offers to share, when pursued at rates that are too high, are increasingly refused; encountering high rates of refusal may lead to undesirable social learnings by the offerer. A second criterion is the range of stimulus control of the newly changed behavior: under what stimulus conditions is this change manifest, and under what conditions is it not? Depending on the behavior, too much generalization, or too little, may constitute an undesirable effect. Third, was the main effect of the intervention shown to be durable? That is, when systematic reinforcement was discontinued, did the effect maintain independently? Fourth (if applicable), were different forms of the target behavior(s) taught to ensure diversity and prevent stereotypic responding? Or is stereotypic responding desirable? For example, there may be numerous ways to share, praise, or to respond to other's social behaviors while stereotypic forms of these behaviors could lead to their punishment and/or extinction in the natural environment. Conversely, in training a child to use inhalation therapy equipment (Renne and Creer, 1976), a specific stereotypic response is essential. Finally, did some form of consumer satisfaction survey reveal any side effects, positive or negative, as a result of the intervention?

It is this author's contention that the five criteria described here provide a readily available foundation by which to analyze both completed and ongoing behavioral research from a useful ecobehavioral perspective. This perspective is useful in that it may directly contribute to the long-term success of behavioral technology.

Three specific issues are examined in this chapter with respect to each criterion. First, an effort is made to establish the importance of each criterion. Second, the general acceptance and use of each in a sample of recent applied literature is examined and analyzed. Specifically, this author has reviewed 13 recent issues of the *Journal of Applied Behavior Analysis*, selected those articles in which ecological considerations seemed important (94), and assessed the overt attention given to each criterion. Third, behavioral recommendations are made concerning the productive future use of each criterion by applied practitioners, including suggestions for research. The general methodology used in sampling the literature is discussed first. Then a separate section is devoted to each proposed criterion. Finally, the paper concludes with a summary discussion.

METHODOLOGY

The *Journal of Applied Behavior Analysis* (JABA) was selected as the source for the literature review on the general use and acceptance of the five proposed criteria. Of the applied behavioral journals, it is the least practitioner-oriented and has the strictest peer-review procedures (Risley,

1975). Although its primary audience are the scientists who develop behavioral technology (as opposed to full-time therapists and clinicians who may only implement it), in behavior analysis the real world is often the laboratory. Thus, those who develop behavioral technology often field-test it as well. This unique characteristic of applied behavior analysis places an unusually heavy responsibility on its individual scientists, but also assures that the technology is easily applicable to nonlaboratory problems. In this instance, evidence of an ecological orientation in the lab may support (to some extent) its usefulness in behavioral technology in general. Thus, JABA seems an appropriate sample source and its audience an appropriate target for an ecobehavioral orientation.

All recent issues of JABA were reviewed, beginning with Volume 6, No. 1, and continuing through Volume 9, No. 1. The 159 research articles contained in these issues were divided into applicable and nonapplicable studies. Ninety-four of the 159 studies reviewed (59%) were applicable, 65 (41%) were nonapplicable.[1]

Applicable studies were defined as those concerning the development and application of techniques and procedures to solve problems without further extensive experimental work. These are studies that contribute to a working behavioral technology. They range from research on a "procedure for increasing oral reading rate in hard-of-hearing children" (Wilson and McReynolds, 1973), to "training a community board to problem solve" (Briscoe, Hoffman, and Bailey, 1975), to a procedure for the "elimination of thumbsucking" (Knight and McKenzie, 1974). In short, these are studies that directly and immediately contribute to an applied behavioral technology. They were conducted in real-life settings on real-life problems for immediate use.

Nonapplicable studies are basically concerned with pilot work, examining side effects or secondary variables associated with a procedure, refining or comparing different techniques, or dealing with orthogonal issues (such as observation procedures, the effects of different variables on test outcomes, etc.).

The purpose of the applicable and nonapplicable dichotomy is to isolate those studies from which this analysis can produce the most useful assessment of the results of using the five criteria outlined above. In many studies, these criteria are irrelevant to the issue at hand, in that they reveal nothing about those situations in which the criteria can facilitate the improvement of the project.

The applicable-nonapplicable classification has been employed con-

---

[1] The article by article results of this analysis are available in tabular form from the author on request.

servatively. As a rule, any study that in any way stretched the definition of applicable was classified as nonapplicable, thereby resulting in the conservative size (59%) of the applicable sample.

Each study classified as applicable was evaluated across the five criteria by answering a series of questions about the study. The questions, representing each criterion area, are presented below. The evaluation results for each of the 94 studies reviewed are presented in an appendix available from the author upon request.

Response Rate

1. Was a goal of the treatment intervention to produce a specific target response rate?

Stimulus and Response Generalization

2. Were stimulus or response generalization measurements (either as formal or anecdotal data) reported in the results?

Response Durability

3. Was treatment faded out toward the end of the study?
4. Was another specific maintenance procedure installed to maintain the treatment effects in the natural environment after the intervention?
5. Were follow-up measurements (as formal or anecdotal data) reported in the results?

Response Diversity

6. Was diversity of the target response programmed? (Defined as at least two ways of performing the target response.)

Consumer Satisfaction

7. Was feedback from any form of specific consumer satisfaction survey presented in the results?

EXAMPLES OF THE FIVE CRITERIA

Response Rate

Rate is the primary response measure of most behavioral interventions. Straightforward increases or decreases in rates of behavior are a primary component in experimental demonstrations of control. The simple productions of increases or decreases in behavior rate may be sufficient and appropriate, if the treatment goal is to demonstrate a source of control.

But when the goal of treatment is to produce a long-term and/or generalized behavior change, a particular response rate may become critically important.

It is possible that the durability and generality of a response is dependent on the appropriateness of the response rate. If the rate is too high or too low, the behavior may not be maintained by the surround. Functionally, then, an *appropriate* rate is defined as the one that the environment supports best. The environment consists both of sociocultural contingencies arbitrarily defined by society and of physical contingencies. If the rate of a response is appropriate, then these contingencies will aid in its generalization and maintenance. This conceptualization is merely a restatement of basic reinforcement theory: the future probability of a response will be dependent on how it is consequated in the present.

When behavior modifiers intervene to increase or decrease a response, they run the risk of producing artifically high or low response rates that the natural environment will not maintain independently of the treatment. Thus, when treatment is withdrawn, its effects eventually cease. However, since the appropriateness of a response rate is determined by what the environment will support, it cannot be determined whether a response is being reinforced at an artificially high or at an artifically low level by simply observing that response. However, this information can be attained in at least two ways: 1) by observing how the relevant stimuli in the surrounding environment react to the response rate, or 2) by observing "normal" rates of the target behavior as displayed by the target subject's peers. Either one or both of these approaches may be appropriate depending on the given situation.

If the behavior modifier chooses to determine appropriate rate by measuring the reaction of the surrounding environment, the major task is to select the relevant variables to observe. Once observed and isolated, these variables may show what the optimal rate of the target behavior is in terms of what the environment will maintain naturally. This task may not be as difficult as it sounds. Frequently, in fact, it may involve little more than a well educated, intuitive guess by the investigator.

For example, Warren, Rogers-Warren, and Baer (1976) taught preschool children to make offers-to-share to one another during a five-minute play period. They observed that as rates of share-offers increased, the percentage of offers accepted decreased correspondingly. Therefore, they reinforced share-offers only if they occurred at a rate of once or twice during the play period. At this rate, they observed that a high percentage of offers was accepted (75%). Previously the subjects had made many more offers, but a much smaller proportion of them had been accepted. Thus, by observing the effects of different rates of the target behaviors (share-offers) on what was guessed to be a critical environmental consequence (offer-acceptances), this study produced a possibly optimal rate of the behavior.

In a more informal example, Horton (1975) asked two fourth-grade teachers to raise their rates of behavior-specific praise to one statement per minute. This response rate was selected on the basis of previous work with teachers in which higher rates of performance had been rejected as too high a response cost. In this case, the critical environmental variable appeared to be the teachers' ability to maintain their behavior over a long period of time.

Walker and Hops (1976) provided an example of the use of normative data to determine an appropriate target response rate in terms of what the environment might be expected to support. They compared 24 subjects with relatively low appropriate behavior rates to several "normal" peers. They then made the criterion behavior levels for the inappropriate subjects correspond with the appropriate behavior levels of the normal classroom peers and intervened to increase the proportion of their appropriate behaviors to these levels.

While neither the Horton nor the Warren et al. studies attempted to show a direct relationship between a response rate and its durability, the Walker and Hops study, and a study by Lovibond and Caddy (1970), strongly suggested such a relationship.

Lovibond and Caddy conditioned a group of alcoholics to drink at moderate rates rather than to eliminate drinking entirely. They reported significantly better results *over the long term* with this moderate approach than with a group subjected to a traditional conditioning procedure designed to make them nondrinkers.

Walker and Hops took long-term follow-ups on the 24 subjects whose appropriate classroom behaviors they had attempted to increase to "normal" levels. Their follow-ups indicated that, in general, the effects of the intervention maintained in the classroom. This long-term maintenance strongly suggested a relationship between rate and durability.

Despite the fact that specific response rate appears to be an important issue, it was largely ignored in the 94 applicable studies reviewed. In 13 of the studies (14% of the sample), the target response rate was clearly specified. In these cases, the rate invariably was zero. That is, the goal of treatment was to eliminate completely the target behavior(s) from the subject's repertoire. Thus, a specific response rate was an inherent goal of the treatment. In 79 other studies (84% of the sample), no specific response rate was targeted; the goal was simply a large general increase or decrease in the target behavior(s). Finally, in two of the studies, the issue of response rate was judged to be nonapplicable.[2]

These results do not imply that researchers and applied practitioners ignore response rate when they intervene. On the contrary, it is likely that they try intuitively to avoid rates that are higher or lower than the environment can maintain. Nevertheless, the results suggest that behavior analysts are not systematically attempting to facilitate optimal therapeutic outcomes through the evaluation of specific response rates in terms of their maintenance after treatment.

Thus, the actual importance of response rate to long-term durability and generality remains unclear. The topic is largely ignored by researchers; yet, a small sample of research suggests that response rates may be used to affect the terminal outcome of treatment interventions.

Two general behavioral recommendations seem appropriate at this point:

1. Intensive research is warranted on the relationship between response rates and therapeutic outcomes—specifically, if, and under what conditions, different response rates facilitate different outcomes. Perhaps the effects of specific response rates vary unsystematically across settings, populations, and problems. However, if it can be generally determined that regardless of the situation, specific response rate is of critical importance, then measures of optimal rates should become part of all relevant interventions.

2. For the present, researchers and practitioners are advised to measure the effects of different response rates on what they judge to be critical environmental variables. This may have to be done intuitively at first. In the Warren et al. (1976) example, the investigators directly correlated share-acceptance rates with share-offer rates using a block-analysis format. Horton (1975) informally correlated what his teachers reported about his environmental procedure with the rate at which he asked them to perform it. It was less complicated than the Warren et al. approach; nevertheless, it was functional. In both of these examples, the investigators selected an obvious environmental variable and gained considerable feedback from their measures of it concerning the appropriateness of their target response rates.

---

[2] The studies judged nonapplicable were Horner and Keilitz (1975) and Clark, Boyd, and Macrae (1975). The goal of the Horner and Keilitz study was to teach retarded children how to correctly brush their teeth. Topography, not rate, was the primary target. Clark et al. examined a classroom program to teach disadvantaged youth to write biographic information. Again, topography, not rate, was the primary target.

Alternatively, researchers and practitioners can collect data on so-called natural rates of a given target response and set the criterion level for their target subject's behavior in correspondence with these rates. The assumption made in this approach is that "normative" data provide a good indicator of what the environment will support (as is) over the long term.

Generalization

Generalization might be defined pragmatically as the "occurrence of relevant behavior under different, nontraining conditions without the scheduling of the same events in those conditions as had been scheduled in the training conditions" (Stokes and Baer, 1977). This definition does not make reference to the durability of a given behavior change over time. It is the intent of this author to separate the issue of generalization from that of durability; thus, the Stokes and Baer definition is especially useful here. (Nevertheless, these two issues are closely related, and their interrelationship is discussed in the latter portions of this chapter.)

Generalization is considered here only in a short-term sense, as a process that occurs parallel or subsequent to training in time, but in nontraining situations. After an intervention has been stopped, the question of durability of all treatment effects, including generalized ones, arises. This distinction between durability and generalization is not inherent to either term but is merely a convenient and useful distinction to make in the present argument.

The issue of generalization and how to get it has become a fundamental concern of applied behavior analysts. Stokes and Baer (1977) pointed out that a "therapeutic behavior change, to be effective, often (not always) must occur over time, persons, and settings, and the effects of the change sometimes should spread to a variety of related behaviors." Ultimately, some type of generalization is desirable as a result of most behavioral interventions. Failure to get generalization naturally, or to program for it, may pose a serious limitation in terms of the actual usefulness of any behavioral procedure.

In their recent review, Stokes and Baer (1977) found 275 behavioral studies relevant to the problem of generalization. Of these, 125 studies made up a central core of literature directly contributing to a technology of generalization. In the majority of these 125 studies, generalization was measured in one way or another, but not programmed. The assessment of generalization is important because it is a means of documenting the extent and the limits of the effects of any given operant intervention technique. Furthermore, it reveals when and under what conditions it may be necessary to program for it, if it should occur.

Despite the obvious importance of generalization, many writers have noted a neglect of the issue in much of the applied literature (Kazdin and Bootzin, 1972; Keeley, Shemberg, and Carbonell, 1976; O'Leary and Drabman, 1971). Unfortunately, this neglect was confirmed in the 94 applicable studies reviewed for this chapter. Of these 94 studies, only 28 (30% of the sample) were prepared to directly measure the occurence of generalization. Thirteen additional studies (14% of the sample) reported some form of generalization but only anecdotally. Fifty-three of the studies (56% of the sample) failed in any way to address the issue of generalization.

In sum, the majority of studies reviewed included no measures, or even anecdotal reports, of generalization. In all of these studies, information on generalization, whether positive or negative, would have been beneficial to other researchers, and *especially* to practitioners who might consider using the prescribed techniques.

Baer, Wolf, and Risley (1968) advised that "generalization should be programmed, rather than expected or lamented." Many researchers have taken this advice to heart, as evidenced by the Stokes and Baer review (1977) as well as by the fact that 30 percent of the studies reviewed in this author's sample did specifically measure for generalization. Nevertheless, it appears that the majority of behavioral research still ignores the issue. Therefore, a prime behavioral recommendation to applied behavior analysts is, by all means, *measure for generalization!*

Recommending to behavior analysts that they measure for generalization is not a novel recommendation. But the discovery of how little they appear to be doing it, even in the most applied situation, is disheartening. It suggests that need for new professional contingencies (perhaps controlled by the journals) for the inclusion of at least some form of generalization data in reports of relevant applied research. While the costs of generalization assessments can be quite high, their value to the field should make them worth the expense.

Durability

Extensive research shows that operant techniques can alter diverse behaviors across a variety of settings and populations (e.g., Graziano, 1971; Lovaas and Bucher, 1974; O'Leary and O'Leary, 1972; Sherman and Baer, 1969; Tharp and Wetzel, 1969). However, whether or not these changes will have long-term durability is another issue. Lindsley (1964) and Yates (1970) challenged behavioral researchers to determine if they could actually provide "therapeutic" environments, or if they were limited to providing "prosthetic" environments. Therapeutic environments show changes that are maintained beyond the treatment conditions themselves; prosthetic environments show changes *only* during treatment conditions. The issue of long-term durability is perhaps the most crucial one facing behavioral researchers and practitioners. If durability of treatment effects proves elusive, and no pragmatic technology is developed to insure it, then the ultimate value of a behavioral technology is highly questionable. There is little to be gained from investing large amounts of time and money developing a technology that produces only short-term effects only under highly controlled conditions.[3]

A limited amount of research has reported that the maintenance of modified behaviors does not occur automatically when treatment procedures are withdrawn abruptly. (Birnbauer et al., 1965; Kuypers, Becker, and O'Leary, 1968; Walker and Buckley, 1968; Walker and Buckley, 1972; Walker, Mattson, and Buckley, 1971). These findings parallel a large body of experimental research showing that the abrupt cessation of high-rate reinforcement (vs. intermittent reinforcement) frequently results in the quick extinction of the target response. They suggest that unless systematic fading procedures are used (O'Leary et al., 1969) or efforts are made to reprogram the environment in which maintenance is expected (Walker and Buckley, 1972; Walker, Hops, and Johnson, 1975), the probability is substantially reduced that the modified behavior will be maintained.

The obvious importance of the durability issue suggests three questions to ask of any applicable behavioral intervention:

1. Were post-treatment follow-up checks taken to establish the durability (or nondurability) of the treatment results?
2. Was reinforcement (or punishment) faded out (or reduced) toward the end of treatment to facilitate maintenance?
3. Was another specific maintenance procedure implemented after the formal intervention was discontinued?

Of the 94 applicable studies reviewed, only 20 (21% of sample) made any form of data-based follow-up. Ten other studies reported anecdotal follow-ups (reports by parents, subjects, etc.). Sixty-four (68% of the

---

[3]There may be some situations where long-term durability is not desirable. For example, a behavior therapist might instruct an obese person in the use of a self-control procedure to control his/her food intake. However, if this procedure proved too durable, and the person continued to lose weight after he/she had obtained his/her proper level, *serious* problems could result (such as starvation). Thus, in this case long-term durability is obviously undesirable. On the other hand, if, when the person reached the desired weight level, a procedure was introduced that was designed to keep the individual at that level, then long-term maintenance obviously would be desirable.

sample) of the studies failed to report any type of follow-up, data-based or anecdotal.

In terms of fading out treatment, only seven studies (8% of the sample) reported having used any type of fading procedure. Nine studies (10% of the sample) reported having used some type of maintenance procedure.

These results reflect a lack of emphasis, possibly only by JABA authors, on the durability of treatment effects. This is particularly disheartening in view of the critical importance of the issue. It is noteworthy, however, that durability may receive greater emphasis in journals more clinically oriented than JABA. It is a standard policy, for example, of the Journal of Behavior Therapy and Experimental Psychiatry that "in all instances, baseline and follow-up quantitative data of no less than six months duration (12 months in the case of addictive behaviors) should be presented" (Vol. 6, 1975). However, this does not lessen the responsibility of authors in JABA, a journal dedicated to the significant advancement of applied behavior analysis, to collect and present data on durability. Like generalization, durability may occasionally be very costly to measure. Nevertheless, it seems particularly important in developing a technology that durability, as a parameter of the effects of the procedure, be carefully assessed.

In the studies in which follow-ups were taken, generalization was often assessed. Of the 94 applicable studies reviewed, 21 of them combined some type of generalization measure (data-based or anecdotal) with some type of follow-up (data-based and anecdotal). In two-thirds of these studies, the follow-ups showed maintenance of the treatment effects. However, in examining just those studies in which generalization occurred and was quantitatively measured, and in which maintenance was quantitatively assessed at least one month after treatment, complete maintenance was reported in only half (four of eight qualified studies). Thus, the safest estimate (from this sample) of the probability of generalization in facilitating durability, is that in some situations it does and in some it does not. This strongly suggests the need to program for maintenance just as one programs for generalization. A recent review of the durability issue by Keeley, Shemberg, and Carbonell (1976) also supports this conclusion.

Although some limited research has been done (Walker and Buckley, 1972; Walker and Hops, 1976; Walker, Hops, and Johnson, 1975), pragmatically, a technology for maintenance is still nonexistent. General standards defining valid follow-up procedures need to be established. In the studies reviewed here, follow-ups ranged from incidental parent reports (Foxx and Azrin, 1973) to sophisticated covert assessments taken a full 15 months after treatment (Ingham and Andrews, 1973). Minimum time periods and assessment techniques need to be established. Follow-ups, taken at least two to six months after the termination of the intervention (depending on the situation) that include some form of covert assessment (if at all possible), seem to represent a sufficiently rigorous yet reasonable standard.

The development of specific procedures for assuring maintenance deserves even more emphasis. Two basic approaches are available to researchers and practitioners: 1) fading out treatment over time to a point at which natural environmental contingencies may maintain the behavior; and/or 2) programming the natural environment in such a way as to facilitate the continued maintenance of treatment effects.

Liberman, Teigen, and Patterson (1973) provide only a potential example of an applicable reinforcement-fading procedure. They used systematic adult social attention to reduce the delusional speech of four chronic paranoid schizophrenics. After establishing impressive treatment effects in all four, they simply reduced the use of contingent attention by one-half. Unfortunately, no post-treatment follow-up data were provided! Thus, the effects of this fade-out procedure are unknown.

In an example of a simple maintenance procedure, Quilitch (1975) used assigned staff activity leaders and performance feedback to motivate staff members to provide daily activities for 95 retarded persons in an institution. Maintenance, in this case, was programmed simply by having the institution administrators continue the intervention procedure as a matter of permanent policy. This policy—continuing treatment indefinitely—represents the extreme case of programming maintenance. In another example, Walker and Buckley (1972) report successfully programming the peer group of an experimental target subject to support the target's attempts at appropriate social and academic behavior, and to ignore his incompatible behavior. This strategy was designed specifically to maintain the subject's post-treatment appropriate behavior in the regular classroom setting.

Fade-out and maintenance techniques, and covert data-based follow-up assessments appear to be feasible, even relatively simple procedures, and their pay-off in terms of the future of applied behavior analysis appears quite high. However, this author's review of 94 recent applicable studies published in JABA suggests that these aspects of behavioral interventions are largely ignored by applied researchers.

Behavioral researchers and practitioners are strongly urged to incorporate some form of fade-out and maintenance procedures in their interventions and to begin assessing the long-term durability of treatment effects. Furthermore, specific research is needed to examine optimal fade-out and maintenance techniques, as well as to determine how programmed generalization can be used to facilitate long-term durability. Finally, the validity and the usefulness of various types and forms of follow-up assessments need to be established.

Response Diversity

Response diversity is a subject that has received considerable attention in the literature of the experimental analysis of behavior, usually under the heading of response variability and differentiation. Keller and Schoenfeld (1950) reviewed a large amount of operant laboratory research dealing with the issue of response variability and stereotypy. They concluded that even when the goal of an investigator is to produce a totally stereotypic response, "some degree of response variabilty survives—complete stereotypy is never achieved."

The process of natural selection favors the occurrence of response diversity as an adaptive mechanism and works against the process of response stereotypy (Skinner, 1953). In a capricious environment, response variability should function to increase the probability of some form of the response being reinforced. Stokes and Baer (1977) pointed out that "diversity of exemplars seems to be the rule to follow in the pursuit of the maximum generalization."

In a topographical analysis of generalized imitation, Garcia, Baer, and Firestone (1971) trained four retarded children to imitate three different topographical types of response: small motor, large motor, and short vocal. Generalized imitation was observed with each subject to probes of other unreinforced responses in the same response classes (short motor, long motor, short vocal). That is, this generalization was limited to the particular dimensions of the topographical response currently being trained or having previously received training. Garcia et al. suggested that these results point out the need to train response exemplars that will reflect adequately the *diversity* of the generalization desired.

In an intervention to modify a behavior, it is conceivable that only one specific form of a target response might be programmed and reinforced by a behavior modifier. Although some response variability should occur anyway (Keller and Schoenfeld, 1950), this amount might be insufficient, and the response, because of its limited form, would then extinguish. A purely hypothesized example of this possibility is presented below:

A young child is taught to praise other children using the format "I like what you are (doing, wearing, making, ____)." Only praise statements of the form "I like _____" are reinforced by the subject's teacher. After the response is firmly established, the intervention is discontinued and the response quickly extinguishes. It appears that the subject's peer group found the "I like _____" format repetitious and boring, and therefore failed to reinforce it (perhaps even occasionally punishing its occurrence), although the target subject always used it contingently and in appropriate situations. In this case, it appears likely that if a diversity of praise-statement formats had been programmed and reinforced, the subject's peer group might not have become satiated and the response would have been maintained.

Occasionally response diversity may be undesirable. For example, Renne and Creer (1976) taught four children with severe asthma to use an inhalation therapy apparatus. Proper use of the apparatus necessitated repeated stereotypic responding from the children. Diverse responding could cause the machine to function improperly. Thus, in this case, a stereotypic form was the appropriate response, while response diversity was undesirable.

The 94 applicable studies reviewed here were assessed to determine if at least two acceptable ways of performing the target response(s) were specified by the behavioral definition(s). The assumption was that if some diversity and flexibility was clearly evident in the target response definition, then there was some likelihood that suitable diversity was programmed also. An example of a suitably diverse target-response definition might be one used by Cossairt, Hall, and Hopkins (1973). They defined teacher praise for attending behavior as "any positive or praise statement about student attending behavior." On the other hand, a response definition used by Scott and Bushell (1974) for on-task behavior may have been too narrow. They defined student on-task behavior as "children being in their seats, looking directly at their math books or the teacher, with at least one hand above their desk."

Of the 94 applicable studies, only four (4% of the sample) appear to have used too narrow target-response definitions, i.e., definitions that might have hampered maintenance. Sixty-three (67% of the sample) appeared to have suitably diverse definitions. Finally, in 27 of the studies (29% of the sample) the issue of response diversity either appeared to be an inherent feature, or, conversely, undesirable. For example, the target behavior in a study by Lahey, McNees, and Brown (1973) was reading comprehension. Kohlenberg (1973) targeted on human anal sphincter pressure. Neither target behavior lends itself to diverse response definitions.

The above data suggest that behavior analysts *may* be doing a good job of programming response diversity. But, at best, this analysis is speculative. Furthermore, this is not to say that behavior analysts would not gain from added emphasis on this issue.

Response diversity appears to be an important issue to the extent that it may facilitate generalization and durability. Extensive research is needed to define this relationship and to determine how response diversity occurs in the natural environment. As has been noted, extensive laboratory research has been done, but the issue has seldom been directly examined in the natural environment.

Behavioral researchers and practitioners are advised to program suitable response diversity when they make behavior alterations in the natural environment. Careful adherence to this criterion may facilitate the long-term durability and adaptiveness of a given target response.

Consumer Satisfaction

Holman (Chapter 4 of this volume) pointed out that "a behavior modifier interested in effecting widespread social change should be willing to engage in some independent assessment of the technology being implemented and to be sensitive to unanticipated ecological fallout." Further, she suggested that the "assessment of consumer satisfaction with the procedures and results of any behavioral program" might be a useful tactic in the detection and loose specification of undesirable ecological outcomes."

The potential seriousness of side effects resulting from behavioral interventions is a point well made by Willems (1974). But the best means to detect them is less clear. Willems proposed the analysis of behavior convariations and natural stimulus and response classes (similar to Patterson, 1974; Wahler, 1975). However, this approach has two flaws: it is extremely costly and complex, and it allows the experimenter to monitor only a few specific, preselected behaviors for side effects. In contrast, consumer satisfaction surveys might be feasible because they can be simple, cheap, easy to administer, and, most importantly, can provide maximal "openness" for detecting unanticipated side effects (Holman, Chapter 4 of this volume).

With a maximally "open" assessment, any side effect of consequence to a treatment-consumer should be revealed. Wallis and Roberts (1956) have suggested using a technique in which a question such as, "What did you think of this technique?" is posed. Then, depending on the response, a probe is made of some index of an opposite opinion (for example, "Ok, if you liked everything, what did you like the least?"). Properly designed well conducted, consumer satisfaction surveys may reveal considerably more about side effects than sampling random behaviors for covariations as Willems has proposed. Since it queries the person affected by the intervention, it should indicate only those side effects that were perceived as detrimental rather than displaying statistically significant interactions that may not be truly problematic. On the other hand, such a survey may detect infrequent but problematic events before they reach the level of statistical significance. For example, increases in intensity of physical aggression (coinciding with the beginning of treatment) might not be detected by an observation system based on number of occurrences (from which frequency and duration of aggression are calculated); thus, no covariation of behaviors might be derived. However, a sibling's report, especially if corroborated by a parental report, would quickly establish the existence of such a negative side effect.

The assessment of consumer satisfaction is proposed here as the fifth criterion to be incorporated into an appropriate ecobehavioral perspective. This criterion has a distinctively different purpose from the other four. The goal of the first four criteria is to promote the long-term generality and durability of a target response, but the purpose of a consumer satisfaction survey is to detect negative (as well as positive) side effects of the treatment. Together, the five criteria define, in this author's opinion, the parameters of a well rounded perspective for maximizing the positive treatment effects of an intervention and for assessing any undesirable side effects.

Despite the potential importance of consumer satisfaction surveys, only one of the 94 applicable studies report using such an assessment. Fawcett and Miller (1975), in an experimental analysis and social validation of a program to train public-speaking behaviors, reported that all trainees indicated that they were "very happy" with the program (as indicated by an average score of 7.0 on an assessment scale of 7). A few other nonsample studies have assessed consumer satisfaction in some form (Minken et al., 1976; Phillips et al., 1972). Generally, however, this approach has been almost completely shunned by applied behavior analysts.

Behavior analysts are strongly urged to begin incorporating consumer satisfaction surveys into their treatment interventions. These surveys can be relatively simple and easily administered. Yet, careful attention to their results may allow behavior analysts to identify and correct any negative side effects of their interventions. Furthermore, these surveys provide an important form of social validation and therefore may promote the social acceptability of behavioral technology as a whole.

Behavior analysts should be cautioned against the potential misuse of consumer satisfaction surveys. Results could be easily influenced by experimenter bias. In such cases, information from a survey could be dangerously misrepresentative. As Holman (Chapter 4 of this volume) points out, "the technique has some value for program assessment if the pursuit of openness is maximized."[4]

SUMMARY

The criteria proposed here share five qualities that make them particularly suitable for use by applied behavior analysts:

1. They Incorporate Already Existing Values into Treatment Interventions, Not a New or Orthogonal Set

The issue of whether or not particular behaviors should be modified systematically using behavioral technology still is determined by the involved individuals' ethical values. It then becomes important to make that intervention work as optimally as possible, in terms of those values. The criteria proposed here assume an already existing set of values; their use is to facilitate the optimal expression of those values.

2. They are Analytical

Given the precepts and characteristics of applied behavior analysis, no perspective can be useful unless it is analytical, i.e., unless its usefulness can be proved, not simply deduced. The five criteria proposed here lend themselves to such use. They can be incorporated into current behavioral practices without altering the existing framework of those practices. Furthermore, they are empirically based and the validity of each can be experimentally verified.

The analysis of the interrelationships of the criteria may open a critical new area of research. That is, it may be conceptualized that response rate, diversity, and generalization interact to facilitate durability in the manner diagrammed below.

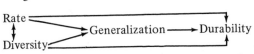

In this diagram, an interaction of rate and diversity is seen as influencing durability. Further, this interaction may facilitate generalization that in turn also may influence durability.

The accuracy of this conceptualization is untested and awaits experi-

---

[4] Holman has discussed the use and potential value of consumer satisfaction assessments at length in Chapter 4 of this volume.

mental verification. However, if durability does result from such an inter-action, then rate, diversity, and generality are critical to the future development of a socially useful behavioral technology. Sophisticated research is necessary to determine the extent of these relationships and to determine how they can be used to affect the long-term outcomes of behavioral interventions. If these relationships are found to be functional, then the above conceptualization represents a rough formula for programming durability. As noted previously, durability may well be the most critical issue facing the development of a socially useful behavioral technology in the future.

3. They Can be Immediately Beneficial

Despite a lack of emphasis in the past, all five criteria are presently applicable to behavioral interventions. Behavior analysts who apply the criteria may encounter immediate benefits. For example, a follow-up may reveal that a treatment effect has not maintained. A behavior analyst might intervene again using specific procedures (such as adjusting rate or diversity) to facilitate maintenance. A more efficient use may be for the behavior analyst to examine diversity, rate, and generality during the initial intervention, manipulate them as necessary, and thereby succeed in programming durability without waiting for failure to spur such action. A consumer satisfaction survey conducted during the intervention might reveal a serious, unanticipated side effect and thus allow the behavior analyst to correct the problem before it damages the positive treatment effects or forces the client to leave the program prematurely.

4. They are Easily Applicable

All of these criteria require considerable effort to implement; nevertheless, they all can be applied within the framework of current behavioral applications. They do not necessitate any basic technology changes nor do they require the development of a special expertise on the part of behavior analysts.

5. Within the Field of Applied Behavior Analysis, the Technology Exists to Ameliorate Most Problems that Assessment Based on the Five Criteria Might Reveal

For example, if assessment reveals insufficient generality, generalization techniques such as those outlined by Stokes and Baer (1977) can be applied. If durability is a problem, it may be programmed by facilitating contact with natural communities of reinforcement or by implementing specific maintenance techniques. Insufficient diversity can be corrected by redefining the response definition in order to program more diverse responses. Rate may be controlled through the use of different schedules of reinforcement. The ability of behavior analysts to alter their techniques in response to consumer feedback provides a means of ameliorating most consumer satisfaction problems. In sum, it is apparent that behavior analysts possess sufficient techniques to correct most types of problems that the criteria are likely to reveal.

Measures of response rate, diversity, generality, durability, and consumer satisfaction represent what this author believes to be an ecobehavioral perspective suitable for the goals of an applied behavior analyst. They are somewhat ecological in that they are oriented toward measuring specific interactions between subjects and environments; however, they are not ecological in that they are not meant to analyze the mechanisms of environmental reactivity. They are behavioral in that they represent a continuance of the strong scientific tradition of precise measurement and validation of interventive manipulations. This perspective, then, represents a union of the outcome-oriented applied behavioral treatment approach with the ecological premise that the environment is reactive (in some form) to all changes, whether systematically or unsystematically imposed upon it.

Whether or not the criteria proposed here represent an ecologically oriented perspective may not be pragmatically important in the end. Ultimately, the important pragmatic outcome will be the results of their use. The question of what constitutes an appropriate ecological perspective for behavior analysis may simply prove irrelevant, like many other conceptual issues in the past.

In conclusion, two basic behavioral recommendations are suggested as a result of this review:

First, behavior analysts are urged to extend their now occasional empirical examinations of the relationships among rate, diversity, generality, and durability.

Second, behavior analysts are urged to assess each of their applied interventions along the five dimensions expressed as criteria for determining the effectiveness of an intervention and, when necessary, program accordingly: 1) response rate, 2) response diversity, 3) generality, 4) durability, and 5) consumer satisfaction.

LITERATURE CITED

Auerswald, E. H. 1969. Interdisciplinary versus ecological approach. *In* W. Gray, F. J. Duhl, and N. D. Rizzo (eds.), General Systems Theory and Psychiatry, pp. 373–386. Little, Brown and Co., Boston.

Baer, D. M. 1974. A note on the absence of a Santa Claus in any known ecosystem: A rejoinder to Willems. J. Appl. Behav. Anal. 7:167—170. Also reprinted as Part I Comment of this volume.

Baer, D. M., Wolf, M. M., and Risley, T. R. 1968. Some current dimensions of applied behavior analysis. J. Appl. Behav. Anal. 1:91—97.

Barker, R. G., 1963. The stream of behavior as an empirical problem. In R. G. Barker (ed.), The Stream of Behavior, pp. 1—22. Meredith Publishing Co., New York.

Barker, R. G. 1968. Ecological Psychology. Stanford University Press, Stanford.

Birnbrauer, J. S., Wolf, M. M., Kidder, J., and Tague, C. E. 1965. Classroom behavior of retarded pupils with token reinforcement. J. Exp. Child Psych. 2:219—235.

Briscoe, R. V., Hoffman, D. B., and Bailey, J. S. 1975. Behavioral community psychology: Training a community board to problem solve. J. Appl. Behav. Anal. 8:157—168.

Bronfenbrenner, U. 1975. The ecology of human development in retrospect and prospect. Paper presented at the Conference on Ecological Factors in Human Development. University of Surrey, Guildford, England.

Clark, H. B., Boyd, S. B., and Macrae, J. W. 1975. A classroom program teaching disadvantaged youths to write biographic information. J. Appl. Behav. Anal. 8:67—76.

Cossairt, A., Hall, R. V., and Hopkins, B. L. 1973. The effects of experimenter's instructions, feedback, and praise on teacher praise and student attending behavior. J. Appl. Behav. Anal. 6:89—100.

Dockens, W. S. 1975. Operant conditioning: A general systems approach. In T. Thompson and W. S. Dockens, Applications of Behavior Modification, pp. 425—442. Academic Press, New York.

Fawcett, S. B., and Miller, I. K. 1975. Training public-speaking behavior: An experimental analysis and social validation. J. Appl. Behav. Anal. 8:125—135.

Foxx, R. M., and Azrin, N. H. 1973. The elimination of autistic self-stimulatory behavior by overcorrection. J. Appl. Behav. Anal. 6:1—14.

Garcia, E., Baer, D. M., and Firestone, I. 1971. The development of generalized imitation within topographically determined boundaries. J. Appl. Behav. Anal. 4:101—112.

Graziano, A. M. (ed.), 1971. Behavior Therapy with Children. Aldine, Chicago.

Holman, J. 1977. The moral risk and high cost of ecological concern in applied behavior analysis. Chapter 4 of this volume.

Horner, R. D., and Keilitz, I. 1975. Training mentally retarded adolescents to brush their teeth. J. Appl. Behav. Anal. 8:301—309.

Horton, G. O. 1975. Generalization of teacher behavior as a function of subject matter specific discrimination training. J. Appl. Behav. Anal. 8:311—319.

Ingham, R. J., and Andrews, G. 1973. An analysis of a token economy in stuttering therapy. J. Appl. Behav. Anal. 6:219—229.

Kazdin, A. E., and Bootzin, R. R. 1972. The token economy: An evaluative review. J. Appl. Behav. Anal. 5:343—371.

Keeley, S. M., Shemberg, K. M. and Carbonell, I. 1976. Operant clinical intervention: Behavior management or beyond? Where are the data? Behav. Ther. 7:292–305.

Keller, F. S., and Schoenfeld, W. N. 1950. Principles of Psychology. Appleton-Century-Crofts, New York.

Knight, M. F., and McKenzie, H. S. 1974. Elimination of bedtime thumb-sucking in home settings through contingent reading. J. Appl. Behav. Anal. 7:33–38.

Kohlenberg, R. M. 1973. Operant conditioning of human anal sphincter pressure. J. Appl. Behav. Anal. 6:201–208.

Kuypers, D. S., Becker, W. C., and O'Leary, K. D. 1968. How to make a token system fail. Exceptional Child. 35:101–109.

Lahey, B. B., McNees, M. P., and Brown, C. C. 1973. Modification of deficits in reading comprehension. J. Appl. Behav. Anal. 6:475–480.

Liberman, R. P., Teigen, J., Patterson, R., and Baker, V. 1973. Reducing delusional speech in chronic, paranoid schizophrenics. J. Appl. Behav. Anal. 6:57–64.

Lindsley, O. R. 1964. Direct measurement and prosthesis of retarded behavior. J. Educ. 147:62–81.

Lovaas, O. I., and Bucher, B. D. (eds.) 1974. Perspectives in Behavior Modification with Deviant Children. Prentice-Hall, Englewood Cliffs, N.J.

Lovibond, S. H., and Caddy, G. 1970. Discriminated aversive control in the moderation of alcoholics' drinking behavior. Behav. Ther. 1:437–444.

Minkin, N., Braukmann, C. J., Minkin, B. L., Timbers, G. D., Timbers, B. J., Fixen, D. L., Phillips, E. L., and Wolf, M. M. 1976. The social validation and training of conversational skills. J. Appl. Behav. Anal. 9:127–140.

O'Leary, K. D., Becker, W. C., Evans, M. B., and Saudargas, R. A. 1969. A token reinforcement program in a public school: A replication and systematic analysis. J. Appl. Behav. Anal. 2:3–13.

O'Leary, K. D., and Drabman, R. 1971. Token reinforcement programs in the classroom. Psych. Bull. 75:379–398.

O'Leary, K. D., and O'Leary, S. G. (eds.), 1972. Classroom Management: The Successful Use of Behavior Modification. Pergammon Press, Inc., New York.

Patterson, G. R. 1974. A basis for identifying stimuli which control behavior in natural settings. Child Dev. 45:900–911.

Phillips, E. L., Phillips, E. A., Fixen, D. L., and Wolf, M. M. 1972. The Teaching-Family Handbook. University of Kansas Printing Service, Lawrence, Kan.

Quilitch, R. H. 1975. A comparison of three staff-management procedures. J. Appl. Behav. Anal. 8:59–66.

Renne, C. M., and Creer, T. L. 1976. Training children with asthma to use inhalation therapy equipment. J. Appl. Behav. Anal. 9:1–11.

Risley, T. R. 1975. Certify procedures not people. In W. S. Wood (ed.), Issues in Evaluating Behavior Modification. Research Press, Champaign, Ill.

Scott, J. W., and Bushell, D. 1974. The length of teacher contacts and student off-task behavior. J. Appl. Behav. Anal. 7:39–44.

Sherman, J. A., and Baer, D. M. 1969. Appraisal of operant therapy techniques with children and adults. In C. M. Franks (ed.), Behavior Therapy-Appraisal and Status, pp. 192–219. McGraw-Hill, New York.

Skinner, B. F. 1953. Science and Human Behavior. MacMillan Co., London.

Stokes, T. F., and Baer, D. M. An implicit technology of generalization. J. Appl. Behav. Anal. In press.

Tharp, R. G., and Wetzel, R. J. 1969. Behavior Modification in the Natural Environment. Academic Press, New York.

Wahler, R. G. 1975. Some structural aspects of deviant child behavior. J. Appl. Behav. Anal. 8:27–42.

Walker, H. M., and Buckley, N. K. 1968. The use of positive reinforcement in conditioning attending behavior. J. Appl. Behav. Anal. 1:245–250.

Walker, H. M., and Buckley, N. K. 1972. Programming generalization and maintenance of treatment effects across time and across settings. J. Appl. Behav. Anal. 5:209–224.

Walker, H. M., and Hops, H. 1976. Use of normative peer data as a standard for evaluating classroom treatment effects. J. Appl. Behav. Anal. 9:159–168.

Walker, H. M., Hops, H., and Johnson, S. M. 1975. Generalization and maintenance of classroom treatment effects. Behav. Ther. 6:188–200.

Walker, H. M., Mattson, R. H., and Buckley, N. K. 1971. The functional analysis of behavior within an experimental classroom setting. In W. C. Becker (ed.), An Empirical Basis for Change in Education, pp. 236–263. Science Research Associates, Chicago.

Wallis, W. A., and Roberts, H. V. 1956. Statistics—A New Approach. The Free Press, New York.

Warren, S. F., Rogers-Warren, A., and Baer, D. M. 1976. The role of offer rates in controlling sharing by young children. J. Appl. Behav. Anal. 9:491–497.

Willems, E. P. 1974. Behavioral technology and behavioral ecology. J. Appl. Behav. Anal. 7:151–165.

Wilson, M. D., and McReynolds, L. V. 1973. A procedure for increasing oral reading rate in hard of hearing children. J. Appl. Behav. Anal. 6:231–239.

Yates, A. J. 1970. Behavior Therapy. John Wiley and Sons, Inc., New York.

9
Planned Change:
Ecobehaviorally Based
Interventions

Planned change is a lot like planned parenthood. Both change and babies can, and do, occur without planning. (Some would argue that the best interventions, and babies, have been unplanned.) Planning the time, place, and number of blessed events does not ensure that they will be successful, but it does help ensure that they will be welcome.

Planning change is the business of behavior analysts. We arrange and rearrange the contingent relationships between behaviors and their consequences for the purpose of changing behaviors. But as behavior analysis is extended to more settings and more clients, it is becoming apparent that behavior change procedures do not always yield the same results with each application. It is not that the principles of behavior are not applicable, but rather that their application must take into account individual circumstances. Often, adaptation is accomplished in an informal manner. Intuitively or objectively, the intervener assesses the setting and the behavior, adjusts the intervention strategy to fit both, and thereby successfully modifies the behavior. Sometimes, though, behavior modification efforts are not entirely successful, perhaps because the practitioner has failed to evaluate the setting in which the intervention is planned. Consideration of individual setting differences may be critical in the design and application of behavior change strategies.

When considerations of the setting in which an intervention is planned are included, planned change takes on new connotations. Planned change occurs when the setting has been carefully evaluated and the behavioral intervention tailored to fit the characteristics of that setting. Planning includes an examination of the physical environment and a detailed evaluation of the contingency environments.

Procedures for planning change may be grouped together to form an "ecobehavioral assessment" package. The procedures incorporate the expertise of ecologists in determining ecological variables, but the assessment is behavioral and therapeutic in orientation and purpose. Ecobehavioral assessment is a preliminary step in planning for change: it is the examination of behavior in the physical and contingency contexts in which it occurs in order to formulate optimal strategies for behavior change.

GUIDELINES FOR PLANNING CHANGE

In this chapter, a set of guidelines is proposed to be used in assessing behavior settings as a basis for planning change. Implicit in the choice and application of these guidelines are the assumptions that durable, generalized change is a goal of an intervention and that durable change can occur only when the setting supports the change in behavior.

The guidelines are a possible set of instructions for persons intervening into a natural (nonlaboratory) setting. Ideally, the guidelines will aid in formulating an effective intervention compatible with the existing behavior patterns and setting. Some of them may not be new to the experienced researcher. Many of the suggestions will have been included implicitly in the careful design of research by such persons. They are intended for the practitioner in the natural setting, who may not have an extensive research repertoire, but who wishes to conscientiously and effectively modify behavior. However, the guidelines may be useful reminders about the importance of setting events for all interveners, and they may be a necessary first step toward adopting an ecological perspective in behavior analysis.

I. Identify the Target Behavior

Ecobehavioral analysis begins with identification of the target behavior. Many behaviors occur in the same setting; the ecology, i.e., the physical and contingency milieu, for each behavior is different. Different environmental components and contingencies are relevant depending on whether a child is being taught to walk or to talk. Thus, it is necessary to identify the behavior before evaluating the setting. In the tradition of behavior analysis, the identification of the behavior should include a succinct, but comprehensive, definition of the behavior and its topography.

In addition to identifying the behavior by name and topography, assessment of its function for the subject in the target setting is recommended. If the behavior is functional, there will be opportunities to use the behavior. The behavior will aid the subject in controlling the environment. Useful behaviors will probably be maintained by natural contingencies. Some behaviors will be functional in almost any setting. However, even behaviors *assumed* to be highly functional (such as walking) can be rendered nonfunctional by the specific contingencies operating within a setting. An adult, who finds a nonambulatory child easier to manage in a wheelchair, may not provide contingent support for the acquisition of walking skills.

The analysis of function is relevant to durability of behavior change. If there is already unprogrammed support for the new behavior, or if the behavior is sufficiently functional to elicit support from persons in the setting, then it is likely that the behavior will maintain. Measurement of functionality, before the initial intervention, provides the practitioner with information about the need to program contingencies to maintain changed behavior. If there is no natural support, an evaluation of possible support systems can be made and implemented concurrent with the teaching of the new behavior.

II. Assess the Physical Setting

Next, an assessment of the physical setting for the behavior is made. Assessment of the setting is made with regard to the specific behavior. This may result in the omission of some variables, but it limits the amount of information required and tailors the gathering of information to a specific need. Generally, this evaluation might seek the following information:

1. Who Populates the Behavior Setting?   One may begin by compiling a list of persons frequently present in the target setting, noting their general role or function in relation to the target behavior and to the subject. More specific measurements (such as number of times each person has contact with the subject, the nature of these contacts, the subject's preference for any of these persons, and the reinforcers these persons can potentially provide for the new behavior) can be made if they appear necessary.

2. What Are the Important Elements of the Physical Setting?   Selecting important elements may necessarily begin with a listing of all the physical elements of the setting (furniture, room design, materials available, scheduling of activities, space available to the subjects and others in the setting) and by observing subjects as they interact with the environment, noting what areas they spend time in, what materials are preferred, and how they respond to shifts in activity. Observing who exhibits the target behavior will provide additional information about environmental components integral to the behavior.

If the target behavior does not occur, the analysis of relevant setting elements is more difficult. One must determine if any elements of the setting impede or preclude the display of the target response, as well as which elements are critical to this response. Begin by examining the target behavior and listing objects or events that might interfere with the behavior; then, examine the setting for evidence of these components.

In all phases of the environmental evaluation, it may be helpful to ask assistance from persons familiar with the setting. Within reasonable limits, increasing the number of persons involved in the evaluation will increase the likelihood that the important variables have been discovered.

3. What are the Physical Cues for the Target Behavior? Identification of important persons and physical components of the environment may provide this information. If not, it may be gained by observing the target behavior and noting the foregoing events. Stimulus cues for behavior may be complex and therefore difficult to monitor. If the target behavior does not occur, it will be impossible to monitor these cues. Analysis of events that precede the target behavior in other settings (particularly a training setting, if one is included as part of the intervention) may be useful. As in the case of important physical components (which might be subsumed under the heading of cues), it may not be possible to establish fully the exact nature of the relationship between cues and behavior through observational analysis. An experimental analysis of cue-behavior relationships is always the optimal (but costly) method for defining it.

Almost all effective contingency management depends on appropriate physical cues from the surrounding environment. A lack of environmental support, or an environmental arrangement that interferes with the contingency system, is likely to result in the breakdown of the latter system. Though assessing environmental cues is difficult, it is probably a valuable use of time.

III. Evaluate the Contingency Environment

1. Determine What the Consequences for the Target Behavior Are If the desired behavior occurs, its consequences may be observed. If the primary subject does not display the behavior, other persons may be observed as they perform the behavior, and the consequences noted. Consequences might be grouped as positive, negative, and neutral; however, it may be necessary to determine (by observation or functional analysis) if such consequences have the same perceived value to the subject. Some quantitative measure of rate of reinforcing consequences for the target behavior should be made also. Reinforcers may be present, but if the rate of reinforcement is too low, or the contingencies unclear, the behavior will not be maintained at the desired level. Appropriate rates of behavior and levels of reinforcement are intervention-specific. However, it may be possible to determine a desirable target rate by monitoring a person who performs the behavior appropriately. Necessary levels of reinforcement must be determined by observation of specific subjects. Selection of reinforcement rates and schedules may be arranged by monitoring during the actual intervention.

2. Already Existing Contingencies Should be Considered Programmed contingencies overlap with natural ones, forming a sort of ongoing contingency milieu. For example, when a teacher programs reinforcement for on-task behavior, there are still pictures to paint (when children ask for a turn and put on a painting smock), snacks to eat (if children ask for them), games to be played (providing children have gone outside when told to do so), and paychecks to be gotten (if the teacher continues to demonstrate that she is fulfilling her contract). The newly programmed contingency makes up a relatively small portion of the ongoing stream of behaviors and consequences, but the ongoing contingencies are important to the programmed contingency because they occupy the same spaces and approximate times. In a high-demand setting (one with many contingencies that require much time and effort to fulfill), a new contingency instituted as part of an intervention may fail because it simply cannot compete with the already existing (and apparently more powerful) contingencies. Assessing the ongoing contingencies will acquaint the intervener with the practical limits the new procedure will encounter. If the intervention strategy is formulated within these limits, or if the environment is restructured to change the competing contingencies, the probability of success in changing the target behavior increases.

IV. Determine What Constraints the Environment Places on an Intervention

Knowledge of constraints will aid the behavior analyst in formulating a practical intervention for the specific setting. If the setting is understaffed, interventions requiring frequent one-to-one contact may be impossible. If the persons in the setting do not have control over high-potency reinforcers or punishers, certain behavioral treatments may not be a possibility. Unless the practitioners are well trained and/or highly motivated (or can be shaped into such behaviors), many complex interventions are precluded. Staff time and training, as well as the physical arrangement of the setting, should be reviewed judiciously before selecting an intervention strategy. Asking the in-setting practitioner(s) about the practicality of a particular strategy before it is implemented also may aid in avoiding failures.

Further, look for physical arrangements in the setting that preclude the occurrence or the notice of the target behavior. Identify the specific elements or events that make it unlikely that the behavior will occur, or that make it unlikely that it will be reinforced when it does occur. In a home where there are no stairs, a child cannot exhibit newly learned stair-climbing skills. Children's vocalizations cannot be responded to if staff members spend most of their time in a glassed-in, soundproof area on the ward.

Persons in the setting may preclude the target response in much the same way that physical arrangements limit behavior. An overly solicitous staff may preempt desired child verbalizations by anticipating the children's needs and providing services before the children verbalize them.

V.   Determine if There are Environmental Arrangements that Might Facilitate the Behavioral Intervention

Planning for change also requires assessing the existing environmental support for the target behavior. Supporting cues and contingencies may already exist that will make an intervention easier and more likely to succeed. It is possible that the appropriate cues for a behavior occur but that the subject does not notice them. Reinforcement contingencies may be operating, but the reinforcement may occur too infrequently or too irregularly to allow change. Compile a list of supporting events (cues and reinforcement) and of arrangements from the observations of the setting, subject, and target behavior. Then, determine if other events or arrangements can be introduced into the setting. Consider the environment as a system of supportive and constraining arrangements and events. If the constraints outnumber the supportive events in a setting, environmental rearrangement is called for.

Many behavioral settings are not open to extensive environmental alterations, but all settings have both physical and behavioral-contingency elements available for analysis and some degree of integration into the planned intervention. Planning for change necessitates a realistic approach: environments will be changed when it is necessary and possible, but other adaptations (contingencies) must be considered when environmental changes are not likely. A planned change evaluates both physical and contingency components in a setting and then includes them in the proposed intervention.

The analysis of necessary cues may suggest changes in the training environment (if it is separate from the natural environment) when generalized usage of a new behavior is desired. The cues programmed during training may be matched to those in the natural setting. If the assessment of the natural setting and its implicit cues for the behavior is made before beginning a teaching program, the natural cues may be programmed into training. Perhaps no alterations of the natural environment will then be needed.

In programming cues which are not yet present, three additional guidelines may be suggested. First, select cues that are functionally related to the behavior and that already occur in conjunction with the behavior (as in training) or that are likely to occur (cues that have been observed to precede the behavior in other settings). Second, select cues that prompt both the target subject and the practitioner of the intervention. Third, consider environmental cues, behavioral prompts, and reinforcement as a cue-complex. By making the consequences of behavior discriminable to the subject, an additional supportive cue for the target behavior may be provided. Descriptive verbal reinforcement is an example of a reinforcer that is likely to have a cueing function as well.

If no reinforcement for the target behavior is present, then it must be programmed. Ideally, its programming should derive from the ecobehavioral analysis.

Again, three guidelines apply. First, select reinforcers that are functionally related to the behavior and that are likely to occur in the setting. Second, select reinforcers that can be easily managed by the intervention practitioner. (Functional reinforcers may be the easiest to administer because they will be present in the environment and/or in the practitioner's repertoire.) Third, incorporate cues for the behavior into the reinforcer complex whenever possible.

APPLICATION OF THE GUIDELINES FOR PLANNING CHANGE

To illustrate how the guidelines may be applied in planning an intervention, a hypothetical example with two parallel target behaviors follows: Teachers in a preschool classroom wish to increase sharing among children in that setting.' One teacher suggests that on-task behavior should be increased as well. With two problems, a consultant seems justified. A behavior analyst is called in and asked to design an intervention to modify each of the behaviors.

Procedure

The analyst proceeds in the following way:

1. Identifying Probable Target Behaviors In the case of sharing, the behavior analyst queries the teachers about what they accept as sharing, discusses possible alternative definitions, and finally writes a clear and concise behavioral code for defining and recording sharing. The teachers are polled to determine which children are likely to be subjects of a sharing modification procedure and which children already exhibit appropriate sharing. The behavior analyst makes anecdotal and time-sampling observations of both sharers and nonsharers to verify the teachers' reports about the children's behavior.

A similar procedure is followed in regard to on-task behavior. A definition is developed, samples of appropriate and inappropriate task-related behaviors are taken, and an anecdotal account of the cues and responses to on-task behavior are noted.

2. Evaluating the Setting in Which Intervention is Proposed by Assessing Physical and Contingency Variables Setting evaluation has already begun with the initial rate and anecdotal observations, but it is useful to include more specific information. The foci of environmental assessments for two behaviors may be quite different, although interventions for both behaviors are proposed in the same setting.

The same basic procedures are used in assessing setting variables for each behavior. The behavior analyst will want to know: 1) who populates the setting and what each person (or group of persons) does in the setting relevant to the behavior, 2) what the important elements of the physical setting are, 3) what the cues are for the target behavior, and 4) what the reinforcers are for the target behavior. With sharing and on-task behaviors, the only overlap may be in who populates the setting. Even then, teachers and peers have different functions for each of the behaviors.

Different physical events are critical to sharing and on-task behaviors. The two behaviors are appropriate at different times in the preschool schedule and in the presence of different materials. Sharing is most appropriate during freeplay and outside times when there are toys to be exchanged and things to be done cooperatively. It is less desirable when children are working on individual preacademic skills or when they are performing large group activities such as listening to a story or singing. On-task behavior is most desirable during preacademic time but, by definition, impossible during snacks (unless the task is eating cookies, in which case very high rates are already displayed and no intervention is needed). Physical variables that support one behavior may impede the other behavior. For example, having children in close proximity with a few choice materials is likely to encourage sharing but makes on-task behavior less likely.

For both behaviors, the number of adults present and their behavior will be important. Adult presence may maintain on-task behavior but limit sharing (if the adult interferes with ongoing social interactions among children). In terms of the intervention strategy, noting that there are three adults with 15 children during preacademics indicates that high-rate teacher-child contact procedures can be recommended to increase on-task behavior. If sharing is most likely when adult participation is limited, a delayed reinforcement or peer-administered reinforcement procedure would be a good choice for increasing sharing.

Specific cues for on-task behavior and sharing are different (although their general nature is similar). Peer verbalizations, teacher instructions, and materials are cues for both behaviors; however, the *content* of the verbalization and the particular materials that have a cue-function are behavior-specific.

In some instances, reinforcers for sharing and on-task behavior will be similar (teacher praise, tokens, or edibles) although, again, content and contingency will vary. It is likely that peers will reinforce sharing more frequently than on-task behavior. The natural communities of reinforcement available to children who exhibit the two behaviors are diverse. If on-task behavior leads to academic accomplishment and learning, children may gain parent attention or be introduced to new and interesting academic information. Sharing, on the other hand, brings children into social contact with each other and may provide an entry to other peer reinforcers.

From the initial observations of the rate of the behavior, and the accompanying anecdotal information, it may be possible to determine the rate and type of reinforcement available for the target behavior. If positive consequences available in the classroom are provided, contingent upon display of the target behaviors, then only an increase in rate is called for. If no reinforcement is occurring following the behavior, an assessment of potential reinforcers is needed.

As the behavior analyst compiles information about the physical and contingency environments, information about constraining events or arrangements in the setting will be considered. The assessment of the physical arrangement and cues for sharing may suggest that sharing will be limited when many materials of the same type are accessible or when the children are seated at separate tables and working on individual projects. On-task behavior is precluded during snacks and outside times because the materials that define the behavior are not present.

Suppose that, in this example, an assessment of ongoing setting contingencies reveals two existing demands that may compete with newly programmed contingencies. There are three minimally skilled children who require physical assistance with most tasks and who take up a large portion of the teachers' time; in addition, teachers already use a prompting and praising procedure to increase child verbalizations.

Designing an Intervention Based on the Information About the Setting and the Target Behavior   This intervention is structured around the physical and contingency arrangements that observations have suggested facilitate the occurrence of the behavior. To encourage sharing, children are seated around one large table with a moderate supply of materials placed in the center of the table during some freeplay activities. During preacademic time, when high rates of on-task behavior are desired, the children work at individual tables clustered around a resource area or around a teacher's desk. High-rate off-task children are dispersed throughout the room rather than being seated next to each other.

Whenever possible, the natural contingencies evident in the setting are utilized as reinforcers. Children primed into sharing are allowed to continue their social interaction without teacher interruption. Nonsharers are seated near children who already share to provide exposure to appropriate models and to "trap" nonsharers into, at least, occasional shares. Papers and projects completed during preacademic time are posted near the door where parents will see them and hopefully will comment on them.

Cues are programmed to support the teaching staff as well as the child population. The same physical arrangement of children at individual desks around the teaching area will help to direct the teachers' attention to children who are on-task. A tape recorded signal might be used to prompt the teacher to scan the children for on-task behavior when setting demands are high. Tokens are used as reinforcers for on-task behavior because they are discriminable to both students and staff. The supply is kept in a prominent place where both teachers and children can see them. Appropriate child behavior (both sharing and on-task) are descriptively praised and pointed out to adjacent persons (parents, peers, other teachers) who might comprise a potential source of unprogrammed reinforcement.

During both assessment and intervention periods, the teachers are asked about specific aspects of the environment or the target behaviors. This information is used as an indicant of consumer satisfaction throughout the intervention. Teachers in this example were already somewhat skilled as behavior modifiers, and it was possible to add two new contingencies to the environment. Teacher feedback, as well as the data collected during the intervention, indicated that the environmental support was sufficient to successfully increase the target behaviors.

SUMMARY

A set of guidelines for assessing environments in which an intervention is proposed has been presented. These guidelines focus on optimizing intervention strategies by tailoring change procedures to fit the specific characteristics of the setting and the target behavior. The active use of ecological information might be integrated into the design of an intervention by following a decision making process such as the one shown in Figure 1.

After the subject, setting, and target behavior have been selected, the intervener asks a series of questions about the support that the setting offers for behavior change. As long as one receives positive answers to the questions in the right-hand column, the planning for the intervention may proceed with some confidence that the intervention will be effective. If the answer is negative, indicating that some supporting element is not currently available for incorporation into the intervention, there are two clear choices: 1) fix the trouble, thereby changing a negative answer to a positive one, or 2) if the difficulty is serious, do not intervene. A third alternative is implicit: ignore the negative feedback and continue with the intervention. In some instances it may be possible to compensate for the lack of support in one area by arranging additional support from another. By taking into account the limitations of the setting, the intervener, at the very least, should have a good idea of what needs to be changed if the intervention is not succeeding.

Any recommendation that assumes that important variables can be identified by observation must be made with caution, and certainly the identification of variables would bear experimental validation. However, since the aim is to make a rather general, global evaluation of which environmental elements can be used to support new behavior, the dangers are not as great as those occurring when one relies on a single physical event or contingency to explain or maintain behavior. Where time, skill, and interest permit, the use of more sophisticated tools is always an option. However, the use of complex measurement techniques carries an implicit danger: if the response cost of the assessment is too high, it will not be done, or the information may be disregarded without sufficient analysis to make it useful. The goal of these general suggestions is to obtain useful information, relevant to a specific problem, at minimal cost to the practitioner. If these three conditions (usefulness, relevancy, and

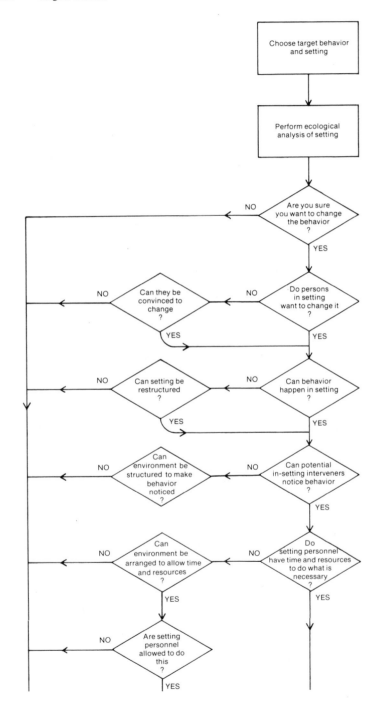

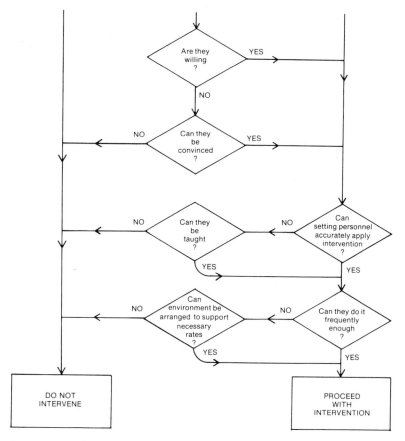

Figure 1. Preintervention assessment strategy.

minimal cost) can be met, it is likely that the information will be used in formulating the intervention.

The procedures for evaluating settings before an intervention may already be implicit in the practice of successful behavior modification. In a sense, these procedures are the art portion of the "art and science" of behavior analysis. The skilled practitioner applies the guidelines and asks the appropriate questions of the setting. The success of that practitioner's application of science may exceed that of the practitioner who fails to assess systematically the environment because the former has fit the intervention to the setting. Yet, these procedures are neither taught to new students of the science nor reported in journals along with the methods for carrying out a research program. They are implicit, and in a science that focuses only on observables, they may be unobservable.

If these procedures are already being used, then behavior analysts may know much more about environments than they readily admit. The intervener, who assesses the setting before intervening, is attending to the important ecological variables. Given, the practitioner is not attending to as global a set of ecological variables as the traditional ecologist might, but he/she is attending to the variables that are critical to the immediate behavioral objectives.

Finally, given the goals of behavior analysts, these procedures may be as ecological as we need ever be in prescribing behavior change techniques. They are highly functional procedures and therefore likely to be applied regularly and conscientiously (if this is not already being done). The feedback from their application is likely to be noticed. Changes in intervention strategy are likely to be made when the importance of such changes is evident. Certainly, the guidelines presented in this chapter are a kind of ecological perspective, but one that is uniquely and integrally related to the goals and methods of behavior analysis. While they may appear narrow to the traditional ecologist whose interests are descriptive, they are sufficiently broad to provide necessary environmental information for the behavior analyst.

10

Social Systems Analysis: Implementing an Alternative Behavioral Model

Robert G. Wahler, Robert M. Berland, Thomas D. Coe, and George Leske

In helping troubled children, the prevalent method of behavioral technology is based on what might be termed the "reeducation" model. This model assumes that a reprogramming of stimulus contingencies in social environments can be accomplished, behavior consequently can be changed, and these changes can be maintained by equipping the people who live in these environments with the tools of operant psychology. Since the classic statement of Bijou and Baer (1965), this notion has been the bedrock model of the field. As a therapeutic technique, it has enjoyed a seductive success and its underlying suppositions form the foundation of motivation behind the efforts of clinicians and researchers in applied behavior analysis. When aimed at troubled children, the reeducation assumptions include:

1. Caregivers are used as therapeutic agents.
2. The therapeutic intervention is designed for the natural setting of the child.
3. The caregivers are trained in the technology of operant conditioning.
   a. These operant techniques are to be used to solve present-day problems.
   b. These operant techniques are also to be retained by the caregivers for use in the event of future problems.

Much of the research presented in this chapter was funded by research grant MH 18516 through the National Institute of Mental Health, Crime, and Delinquency section.

4. The behavior change will be maintained by positive reinforcement processes, i.e., the caregivers and the client will be so pleased with all the positive reinforcement they receive for their new behavior that they will continue such behavior.

In general, the assumption of the reeducation model is that the professional helper (e.g., psychologist, social worker, etc.) can give the tools of behavior change to the caretakers of the client. These tools, the techniques of operant behavior modification, can be easily taught to the caregivers who can use them in applied settings now and in the future. The model asserts it will be self-perpetuating by way of positive reinforcement processes.

The difficulties with the reeducation model center on the issue of generalization, which may be conceptualized as extending across three dimensions: time, settings, and behaviors. O'Leary and Kent (1973) have documented the widespread failure of behavior modification to produce results that generalize over time. Inseparable from this issue is the point that behaviors fail to generalize across settings. Wahler, Berland, and Leske (1977) showed convincingly that behavior changes made in a highly regarded residential treatment facility for children did not generalize over time and across settings. When the children left the residential facility, their behavior reverted (in 82% of the cases) to the presenting complaint behaviors responsible for sending them into treatment originally. Furthermore, behavioral technologists have concentrated, in their allegiance to the operant conditioning model, on single behaviors and their direct consequences or antecedents. A growing body of research, however, tends to contradict the notion that single responses operate without altering other behaviors. These "side effects" can be desirable or undesirable, but their distinguishing characteristic is the difficulty involved in their prediction. Wahler et al. (1970), Risley (1968), Sajwaj, Twardosz, and Burke (1972), and Wahler and Nordquist (1973) all discovered unexpected changes in nontargeted behaviors when contingency management was used on a single response. In studies by Wahler (1975) and by Kara (1975), it was found that some side effects could be predicted. The explanation, according to the operant paradigm, is that these behaviors ought to be under the control of some common stimulus that would explain the covariation of these behaviors. However, a search for such stimulus control has proved fruitless.

The difficulties of the reeducation model do not call for its wholesale rejection but instead summon its expansion. Such a broadening of the model's focus would attempt to deal with the generalization problems posed by an operant-based behavior technology while retaining many features of the model such as the use of caregivers as "therapists," the natural setting approach, and the use of operant techniques to produce initial behavior changes. The problems with the model center on its narrow scope, that is to say, on its predilection toward the measurement of only a few responses and their dyadic or two-person settings. Wahler and Coe (1975) assert that the stumbling block of generalization may be attributable, in part, to the fact that while our intervention strategies may concentrate on dyadic interchanges, the sources of stimuli may indirectly form a network, known as a social system. The usual strategy for applied behavior analysis is to concentrate on teacher-child or parent-child interactions. Figure 1 shows that other forces can directly or indirectly impinge on the child's behavior and that a focus on any single dyad may delete vital data. Behavior modification studies have shown that changes in teacher behavior can have effects on student behavior (see Madsen, Becker, and Thomas, 1968), that students can influence changes in teacher behavior (see Sherman and Cormier, 1974), that students can affect each other's behavior (see Solomon and Wahler, 1973), and that teacher reinforcement of a target child's behavior can have a vicarious reinforcement effect on peers (see Kazdin, 1973). Looking at these studies as a group, it seems logical to assert that no perspective that accounts for a single pair of interacting variables (e.g., teacher-child) can explain the functioning of what is essentially a social system—such as a classroom or a family. Our reeducation model does not readily permit the grasping of such complex data. In its place we propose an expansion of the model.

THE SOCIAL SYSTEMS APPROACH

As an alternative to reeducation, we propose a model of behavior that appreciates a systems view of phenomena. This approach should not be

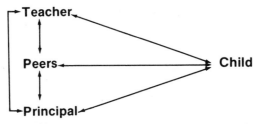

Figure 1. A schematic protrayal of stimulus contingencies likely to affect the behavior of a single child in a public school setting. Notice that some contingencies directly affect the child, while others serve an indirect function.

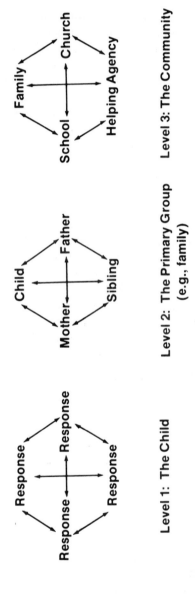

Level 1: The Child

Level 2: The Primary Group (e.g., family)

Level 3: The Community

Figure 1. A schematic portrayal of interdependencies governing behavior at three levels. Level 1 considers the child as a system of covarying behaviors. Level 2 views the primary group (in this case the family) as a system of covarying people. Level 3 reaches the community level of system operation. Here, groups of people are seen as covarying units comprising a community.

confused with the discipline "systems analysis" (Huse, 1975), but should be seen as an heuristic tool for looking at behavioral data in a new way. The systems approach, as we define it, understands the world as comprised of systems and subsystems that function as wholes and must be understood as wholes. Borrowing a bit from the Gestalt psychologists, this systems model argues that the parts never explain the wholes, borrowing from Roger Barker (1968), the approach argues that behavior must be studied in its context to be understood.

Behavior seems to be determined by subsystems that always form the components of other systems. At the first level is the covarying system of behaviors within a child's repertoire of responses (sometimes known as a response class). At the next level is the interacting behavior system of the child's primary group, such as the family. At the third level, the family subsystem serves as a component of the community system. When portrayed in simple fashion, these levels look something like Figure 2. As can be seen, each level is a subsystem that forms a component of other systems of increasing complexity. It is essential to note that in higher level systems, whose components are themselves subsystems, the subsystems operate simultaneously. This staggering complexity only underscores a need to expand the reeducation model of therapeutic behavior change. Let us now turn to a detailed examination of the multi-level systems approach to this endeavor.

Level 1: The Child as a Behavioral System

Reference has been made above to findings indicating that changes in rates of target behaviors have impact on other behaviors in the child's repertoire. These side effects are manifested by correlated changes in other behaviors that have not been tied to changes in external controlling stimuli. These groups of covarying behaviors have been called "response classes" (Sajwaj et al., 1972; Wahler, 1975) and suggest limitations in operant explanations of human behavior.

The previously reviewed response class findings suggest a view of the child as a behavioral system, responding predictably (although not simply) to stimulus input according to as yet unspecified principles. As such, the child's repertoire must be dealt with as a complex, interdependent network of behaviors. Tampering with one behavior would be expected to have impact on other behaviors in the system, and problem behaviors therefore cannot be modified in isolation from the rest of the child's repertoire.

This systems model, then, describes interrelationships among the child's behaviors in terms of correlations among them in their day-to-day occurrences. Aside from indicating the presence of a complex behavioral system, these correlations have direct clinical applications that are discussed later in this chapter. Implications of the model deserve mention now, however. One is the possibility of correlational or response class differences among children—particularly between deviant and nondeviant children. One such difference has been confirmed already by several investigators. DelFini, Bernal, and Rosen (1974), Lobitz and Johnson (1974), and Moore (1975) found a larger number of significant correlations among behaviors in deviant than in nondeviant children. This has been interpreted as greater predictability within the repertoires of deviant children than those of nondeviant children (Moore, 1975). Such a finding has implications for the possible detection of children in need of psychological help.

A second possibility is that specific correlational relationships could be held in common by troubled children. Wahler and Moore (1975) report indications of such common correlations for a sample of deviant children in home and school classroom settings. In essence, these investigators discovered that the children's serious problem behaviors could be predicted on the basis of their *appropriate* social behaviors. On days when these children were particularly gregarious, they were also likely to engage in deviant activities such as stealing, fighting, truancy, and property destruction. The possibility of changing such children's problem behaviors *indirectly* is suggested by these correlations.

Level 2: The Primary Group as a Behavioral System

Children do appear to locate themselves in a fairly common and limited set of environments. As Barker and Wright (1954) demonstrated, these environments, such as the home, school classroom, and playground, call forth different but predictable styles of behavior. The people making up these environments might well be referred to as the child's "primary" group—"primary" in the sense that most children seem to become members of these groups at various points in their lives. Response class phenomena are probably evident in a similar form at this group level.

Berland (1976) extended individual response class findings to whole families as behavioral systems. A family response class is derived from the intercorrelations of daily behavior totals, within and among persons, for all family members. This requires that each family member's behavior be sampled during each observation session, and that the behaviors then be correlated across sessions. Response classes in the sample families included more than one behavior from a given individual, and behaviors from several different persons. As with the individual response classes, the family response classes included both deviant and nondeviant, and social and nonsocial behaviors.

The family response classes were "well knit" (Morgan et al., 1976) in that there were numerous intercorrelations among the behaviors in a given response class. Response classes could be derived that included multiple problem behaviors from several different family members. This suggests a notion of the family as a complexly interdependent behavioral system. This interdependency clearly is not limited to behaviors intrinsic to social exchanges. Interrelationships among isolate behaviors, across family members, exist in families as groups. Family members affect one another's day-to-day output of social and nonsocial behaviors.

As with individual deviant children, deviant families were found to have significantly more intercorrelations than nondeviant families. This difference was not simply the result of more correlations within deviant individuals' repertoires than those of nondeviants. There were more correlations *between* deviant family members than between nondeviant family members, thus truly extending response class findings to families as behavioral systems. The correlational model can be said, then, to provide a means for describing individuals and families in comparable terms. It also provides a means for demonstrating the interdependent and contextual relationship among behaviors within an individual's repertoire and among individuals' behaviors in the family setting. Assessment can be made of the impact of change in an individual's behavior on others around him/her. The context (supportive or destructive) of such a change also can be assessed—and dealt with.

Level 3: The Community as a Behavioral System

While the primary group can be viewed as an immediate context for children, it also is apparent that the members of such groups interact with one another. This sort of group-group interchange constitutes another level of behavioral interdependency—a level that any change agent must consider seriously. Data to verify the correlational or systems model for higher level systems such as the community are scarce. As we noted, the model would view a larger system like the community as being comprised of interdependent behavioral units such as families, schools, public agencies, businesses, etc. Assessing the impact of these elements on one another need not pose an extraordinarily difficult task. Behavioral outputs of these units (toward one another and independent of one another) could be intercorrelated to describe relationships existing among them. This type of analysis is part of the authors' continuing work with the social systems model.

We are currently collecting data that at least may reflect community system operation and its impact on families and individuals, as suggested by the social systems model. These data stem from a notion we refer to as the "insularity hypothesis." Insular families show less "functionality" in their interactions. While there may be greater predictability among deviant family members' behaviors, their interactions with one another have little impact on the participants and do not lead to alterations as a result of the exchange. Such families also may have contact with other elements in the community, but these contacts have less effect on the family members, individually or interactively, than do those for noninsular families. It is speculated that family insularity bolsters the development and maintenance of deviancy by eliminating self-correction in the family in response to input from within, and from outside, the family (see Hoffman, 1971).

Our development of the insularity hypothesis actually began some time ago through research by colleagues at the Oregon Research Institute (Patterson and Reid, 1970) and through out own efforts (Wahler, 1969). The Patterson group marshalled data to show that deviant families appear to be "locked" into stylized manding interchanges (e.g., command or instructional interchanges) between parent and child. As such, other forms of parent-child interchange (e.g., affection) are unlikely to be functional—a speculation supported by Wahler (1969). Thus, deviant family operations were expected to be more predictable than those of nondeviant families because the former are characterized by a more limited communication network. Stated another way, the minimal social exchange options available to the deviant family "insulates" the members from one another.

The next step in developing the insularity hypothesis came from a series of treatment failures by the authors (Wahler and Moore, 1975). These authors discovered that families living in community areas marked by poverty, broken families, and high crime incidence were particularly resistant to change. Repeated contacts between these families and other subsystems of the community (e.g., helping agency, school) had little sustained impact on the ways in which these families operated. Thus, at the community level, some families might be expected to display insularity in reference to their subsystem context. From a correlational viewpoint, the operations of such families should not interrelate with the operations of other subsystems in the community.

The data taken to help reflect family insularity in the community are daily records of the number and nature of parent contacts with people outside the immediate family. The nature of parent contacts include such factors as distance of the contact from home, relationship of the interaction associate to the parent, quality of the interaction (positive, negative, etc.), duration of the interaction, etc. If these data were correlated with family members' behaviors, the amount of impact that outside contacts were having on the family might be partially assessed. More correlation would imply less insularity. The kinds of impact outside contacts were having also might be assessed by: 1) the type of behaviors correlating with the contact measure, and 2) the direction (positive or negative) of the correlations.

The presence of such correlations and differences between deviant and nondeviant families, beyond verifying the insularity notion, would confirm the contextual effect of the community on family and individual behavior as suggested by the social systems model. This would further verify the importance of looking at factors at various levels of behavioral systems when designing and implementing treatment strategies.

Practical Derivations of Subsystem Analysis

As indicated above, the social systems view, in general, and the correlational model, in particular, have some direct clinical applications. To begin with, reliable behavior covariations across treatment conditions suggest the possibility of indirect modification procedures. These procedures would be particularly useful when the target response is not very amenable to immediate consequation. For instance, imagine a child whose referral problems include excessive approaches to his parents when he is home, and petty thievery from local stores. Petty thievery is an example of the low-rate problems many parents have with oppositional children. Many of these problems occur when the child is beyond the parents' range of monitoring, which makes dealing with them very difficult. If this child's petty thievery rates correlated positively with his rates of approach to his parents, a contingency reducing parent approaches might reduce his rates of petty thievery. From another point of view, Wahler (1975) and Kara (1975) have shown that various "side effects" from treatment (desirable and undesirable) could be predicted from baseline correlations among behaviors. Wahler (1976) reported that additional contingency management procedures readily corrected undesirable "side effects." The important factor was the multiple behavior measurememt and response class assessment to detect them in the first place.

The within-child behavior correlations found common to a sample of children (Wahler and Moore, 1975) have suggested their own new approach to indirect modification. Nonsocial toy play in the home and nonsocial schoolwork in school were found to be inversely related to low-rate problem behaviors in their respective settings. These relationships are not considered to be just the result of mutual incompatibility of the behaviors. The sampling periods for the nonsocial activities ("productive solitude") were quite different from those for the low-rate problems. The rate and duration of periods of nonsocial toy play by deviant children have been increased in the homes with positive reinforcement contracts. In these contracts, the children are rewarded for producing continuous periods of isolate toy play for a required amount of time each day. This is an enjoyable procedure for the children and easy for parents to administer. Preliminary findings indicate that beside reductions in low-rate problems, other unexpected but desirable changes have occurred. Parent-child interactions and parent attitudes toward the children have markedly improved in some previously intractable families and high-rate problems have also shown declinés. Even if these findings were not to be borne out in further research, the toy play contracts have turned out to be a useful means of training a population of families in contracting that found traditional contracts almost impossible to implement and maintain.

The family response class data suggest that indirect modification across family members also might be explored. Intervention with multiple deviant family members might be simplified if deviant behaviors covaried across them and if indirect strategies were utilized. If target behaviors for two children were positively correlated, the parent might punish only one of these children, but more effectively, and change both. This is, of course, ultimately an empirical question. Furthermore, the presence of family and individual behavior patterns (in particular settings) suggested by the response class findings indicates the possibility of identifying family and individual patterns likely to lead to future, more severe problems. Such families might be picked up as referrals by social agencies, be identified in terms of these patterns, and be offered the option of being put on some type of preventative follow-up program.

A final clinical strategy was suggested by the insularity hypothesis, which itself was the result of a broadened social systems orientation. If family members were insular (nonfunctional) in their intra- and extrafamilial interactions, effective feedback might be restored and deviancy decreased if insularity were reduced. By forming these people into weekly meeting groups, we hope to promote their positive interchange and thus increase the likelihood that they will reinforce one another outside the group meetings. If so, family insularity would be reduced and a means of sustaining therapeutic family change could be offered.

As the preceding section has shown, there can be some practical benefits of a systems approach in applied behavior analysis. Large scale research programs with such an orientation might well offer new tools to the community helping agent. "Productive solitude" and "insularity" could mark the initial products of this model.

TECHNOLOGICAL FEATURES OF THE SOCIAL SYSTEMS MODEL

Thus far we have limited our discussion of the social systems approach to a rather abstract presentation. We now intend to get down to the practical specifics of this orientation—specifics of use to the research worker interested in pursuing the approach.

In essence, the defining feature of a social systems model is *assessment*. Concepts outlining stimulus networks require assessment or measurement techniques that encompass multiple rather than singular sets of data. Our concern with multiple measurement was deemed necessary for three reasons: 1) assessment validity can be evaluated through concurrent validation among measures; 2) a single measurement is rarely capable of detecting all important aspects of child behavior interactions (for example, direct observational techniques are unlikely to detect low-rate behaviors such as stealing or setting fires, nor can they adequately sample the feelings and attitudes of the caretakers); 3) it often is not feasible to set therapeutic contingencies directly for difficult-to-detect behaviors. Behavior modifiers attempt to deal with these problems *indirectly* through the setting of contingencies for the accessible high-rate behaviors. This response class model has been a central feature of our investigations. Multiple measurement systems allow the clearest empirical identification of these potential behavioral covariates.

Ecological Interview

The first stage in the implementation of any treatment and measurement procedure involves, of course, interviewing the principals involved. Foremost among the three main purposes of the ecological interview is the educational experience it provides for both parent and interviewer. As such, it involves the interviewer in the perceptual and ethnic biases of the caregiver and thus gives a better perspective of the behavior within the family. Initially, few caregivers are able to adequately describe their children's behavior, its consequences, and its immediate environmental context. Most report vague developmental factors, cite personality traits, or characterize their child with some nebulous behavioral description (e.g., "hyperactive"). Some rudiments of social learning theory are taught to the caregiver to facilitate communication between consultant and caregiver and to aid in the later implementation of intervention procedures.

Second, the interview permits the initial specification of reinforcement traps and their situational descriptions. This procedure involves the "mapping" of the child's behavior through the course of a typical day. This serves the additional purposes of specifying the best times for direct observations with a standardized coding system (Wahler, House, and Stambaugh, 1976) and of pinpointing those low-rate problem behaviors not sampled by direct observations (e.g., stealing). These latter behaviors are typically monitored by daily parent report.

A third and often overlooked function is gathering contextual data for the target child, sibling, parents, and community on actual living conditions that may have a profound impact on the success or failure of an intervention procedure. In particular, such contextual variables might influence the generalization of changes produced in the target child over time, across settings, and across behaviors.

Direct Observational Procedures

Conditions for an acceptable observation usually are set during the ecological interview. Common criteria for setting an observation time generally include: 1) most family members should be present, and 2) they should not be engaged in some distracting individual activity, e.g., TV watching, eating. There are of course a variety of environmental conditions that occur in any valid observation period which may result in significant change in the incidence of behavior detected by direct observation. Common factors include a parent leaving or entering the observational area, the number of children present, etc. These conditions are reported along with the targeted child's interactions as reported by the standard observational coding system. The standard observation codes (SOC) (Wahler, House, and Stambaugh, 1976) permit the recording of 20 child behavior categories, six social environment categories of adult and peer behavior, and the interval-by-interval coding of the visual presence of the mother or father. As can be seen in Table 1, a wide range of behaviors can be measured. These include social and nonsocial, deviant and nondeviant, active and passive sorts of behavior. Social event categories include nonaversive and aversive attention provided by adults and peers, and aversive and nonaversive instructions by adults.

Each observer carries a portable tape player that announces by earphone consecutive 10-second observation intervals and alternating 5-second record intervals. Observers watch the child subject and his adult and child interaction associates for 10 seconds and then record in the next 5 seconds all categories that occurred in the preceding 10-second interval. Since observation sessions are restricted to half-hour periods, a maximum

Table 1. Brief descriptions of standardized observational codes (SOC) categories[a]

A. Target child behaviors
  1. *Compliance (C).*[b] Any instance of compliance with an adult instruction (except those instructions forbidding some activity).
  2. *Rule violation (RV).* Any instance of noncompliance with a permanent rule or temporary rule (see Nonaversive Adult Instruction—IA+).
  3. *Opposition (O).* Any full 10-sec interval of noncompliance with an instruction.
  4. *Aversive opposition (O—).* Valence quality of a Rule Violation or Opposition that is also scored if an occurrence of either of these has an aversive quality (see Aversive Adult Instruction).
  5. *Complaint (CP).* Any instance of whining, crying, or any verbal or nonverbal act of protest.
  6. *Self-stimulation (S).* Any rubbing of any body part against the body or some other surface at least three times during an interval, e.g., foot-tapping, finger-dumming, scratching, etc.
  7. *Object play (OP).* Idle, or nonpurposive manipulation of an object (three of the same movements within an interval), e.g., rocking a chair, pencil tapping, etc.
  8. *Self-talk (T).* Any instance of recognizable language spoken by the child to himself/herself.
  9. *Sustained noninteraction (NI).* A full interval of no meaningful interaction with person or object.
  10. *Sustained school work (SS).* A full 10-sec of any school-related work.
  11. *Sustained toy play (ST).* A full interval of appropriate play with some object, with or without other children, e.g., 1) running a car around on the rug, 2) pushing a stick in the dirt, 3) riding a bicycle, 4) reading a comic book, 5) playing with a doll, 6) pushing a pencil around on the table.
  12. *Sustained work (SW).* A full 10-sec of adult-approved work, e.g., cleaning his or her room, washing dishes, taking out the garbage.
  13. *Sustained attending (SA).* A full 10-sec of directing visual or auditory attention toward a single person or event.
  14. *Approach child (AC).* Any initiation of an interaction with another child during the interval by the target child. May be verbal or nonverbal.
  15. *Approach adult (AA).* Same as Approach Child, only to an adult.
  16. *Social interaction child (SIC).* Social behavior by the target child (toward another child) that is either part of an interaction in progress when the interval began, or in response to initiation by another child. May be verbal or nonverbal.
  17. *Social interaction adult (SIA).* The same as Social Interaction Child, only toward an adult.
  18. *Mand child (Mc).* Any instance of the target child commanding or giving an instruction to another child.

19. *Mand adult (MA)*. Same as Mand Child, only toward an adult.
20. *Slash (SL)*. Any target child behavior that is not covered by any of the other categories.

B. Behaviors by other people toward the target child

21. *Nonaversive adult instruction (IA+ or IAP)*. Instructions to the target child by an adult. May command the child to engage in some activity, or may forbid the child from engaging in some activity. In the latter case, it is scored like a rule until the setting changes and is called a "temporary rule."

22. *Aversive adult instruction (IA− or IAM)*. Same as Nonaversive Adult Instruction, only judged aversive in delivery because of: 1) content (threat, ridicule), 2) tone (loud, angry), or 3) assertiveness (e.g., gesture, posture).

23. *Nonaversive adult social attention (SA+ or SAP)*. Any noninstructional contact by an adult with the target child. May be verbal or nonverbal.

24. *Aversive adult social attention (SA− or SAM)*. Same as Nonaversive Adult Social Attention, only aversive (see Aversive Adult Instruction).

25. *Nonaversive child social attention (SC+ or SCP)*. Any contact by another child with the target child. May be instructional or not, and verbal or nonverbal.

26. *Aversive child social attention (SC− or SCM)*. Same as Nonaversive Child Attention, only aversive (see Aversive Adult Instruction).

27. *Visually present (FP, MP)*. These categories are scored respectively for the visual presence to the target child, for any instance of the father (FP), or the mother (MP). "Visually present" means that the child could look up from his/her current position (swiveling $360°$, if necessary) and see the other person. If the child would have to get up to look over or around an obstacle, the other person is not considered visually present.

---

[a]See Wahler, House, and Stambaugh (1976) for complete definitions, with examples.
[b]Note that these categories are not mutually exclusive. One behavior may be scored as several categories at the same time.

of 120 units of a category occurrence can be scored. The observational sessions are generally scheduled two to three times per week in most school classrooms and homes.

Caregiver Reports: Episodes, Attitudes, and Community Interactions

Often, families report behaviors not likely to be detected by SOC observations. These low-rate behaviors are tracked and reported as frequencies, or in an occurrence-nonoccurrence manner (e.g., Did the child steal today?; How many times did the child fight today?). These reports are prompted at the conclusion of a SOC observation by the SOC observer. The observer is also responsible for obtaining a caregiver attitude report on the target child after each SOC session. Wahler, Leske, and Berland (1977) conceptualized these as summary reports at least partly determined by public events. Often, caregivers can only vaguely specify these public events. The attitudes or summary reports are usually one aspect of the presenting complaints about most referred children. In these summary reports, caregivers may characterize the child as *mean, distractible,* or some other general, descriptive term. The function of the attitude assessment is to specify those public events that covary with the attitudinal reports. If public referents for these reports can be specified, there is a greater hope for change by focusing on these public events. The caregiver attitude dimension is constructed from the earlier attitude statement. This dimension is presented to the caregiver at the end of each observation. That person is then asked to rate the behavior of the child as it occurred during the observational period. The dimension is a 7-point scale with the most negative aspect (e.g., very mean) anchored by the 7 and the most positive aspect of the attitude (e.g., not at all mean) anchored by the 1. The chosen value reflects the caregiver's summary judgment of the child on that dimension during the SOC session.

The recording of the interactions of caregivers with members of their communities is designed to yield information that will reflect family insularity. These exchanges are qualified along four dimensions: 1) *functional characteristics* of the parents' interaction associates (e.g., friend, helping agency, stranger); 2) *distance* of interaction from home (e.g., in home, outside neighborhood); 3) *duration* of interaction (e.g., minutes, hours); 4) *valence* of interaction (e.g. positive, negative, neutral). This information is recorded for each outside interaction that the caregiver has had that day. This information will be correlated with the behavioral measures taken in the home to assess insularity.

Data Processing

Integrating and analyzing the measures described above can quickly become a very cumbersome process when done by hand. A computer-based data management process was devleoped to ease this burden and to provide for almost immediate utilization of data as well as easy application of statistical analyses. A crucial feature of this process was the design of computer scan forms that could be hand coded rapidly and machine scored. After the scan forms are machine scored, computer programs summarize the data and store them for application of packaged statistical analyses.

A flexible retrieval program that allows the recall of any single observation or aggregate of variables for inspection or future calculation is an important feature. The retrieval system is augmented enormously by the availability of a variety of statistical packages. These combined features allow the retrieval and analysis of almost limitless combinations of variables. The statistical procedures include reliability calculations of both trial and session data. This feature allows detailed reliability checks during all experimental conditions. The availability of ANOVA models makes practical the application of rather elegant procedures for the evaluation of behavioral measures (Cronbach et al., 1972). For example, Jones, Reid and Patterson (1974) have suggested a procedure for calculating the reliability of observational data that allows for the isolation of components of variance attributable to subjects, occasions, coders, and their interactions.

OVERVIEW

We have presented a methodological strategy reaching beyond the guidelines of reinforcement theory. As such, it is important to note that the strategy does not bear allegiance to theory. Social systems analysis carries no assumptions concerning *why* or *how* child and caregiver behaviors are interrelated. Rather, the analytic strategy argues for the broadest possible scope of measurement—a scope constrained only by the usual psychometric requirements of reliability.

The measurement of multi-level systems will undoubtedly have future impact on the assumptions behind reinforcement theory. Already, some products of such analyses have been of a type not readily sorted out or made understandable through the present assumptions (e.g., side effects). One might view systems analysis as an inductive means of adding to or altering these assumptions. It is our guess that continued use of this strategy eventually will yield some fruitful modifications of the reinforcement paradigm.

Finally, we think it is important to note that social systems analysis can provide the clinical practitioner with new tools. As we outlined earlier, this expensive and cumbersome strategy has led to the discovery of some potentially useful intervention techniques. Generalization problems—the thorn in applied behavior analysis—might well be solved by a more complete understanding of the social context in which child problem behaviors are maintained.

LITERATURE CITED

Barker, R. G. 1968. Ecological Psychology. Stanford University Press, Stanford.

Barker, R. G., and Wright, H. F. 1954. Midwest and its Children: The Psychological Ecology of an American Town. Row, Peterson Publishers, Evanston, Ill.

Berland, R. M. 1976. The family social system and child deviance: A comparison of deviant and non-deviant families. Unpublished dissertation, University of Teneessee, Knoxville.

Bijou, S. W., and Baer, D. M. 1965. Child Development. Vol. 1. A Systematic and Empirical Theory. Appleton-Century-Crofts, New York.

Cronbach, L. J., Gleser, G. C., Nanda, H., and Rajaratnam, N. 1972. The Dependability of Behavioral Measurements: Theory of Generalizability for Scores and Profiles. John Wiley and Sons, Inc., New York.

DelFini, L. F., Bernal, M. C. and Rosen, P. M. 1976. Comparison of deviant and normal boys in home settings. In E. J. Mash, L. A. Hamerlynck, and L. C. Handy (eds.), Behavior Modification and Families, pp. 228–248. Brunner/Mazel, New York.

Hoffman, L. 1971. Deviation amplifying processes in natural groups. In J. Haley (ed.), Changing Families: A Family Therapy Reader, pp. 285–311. Grume and Stratton, New York.

Huse, E. F. 1975. Organization, Development and Change. West Publishing Company, St. Paul, Minn.

Jones, R. R., Reid, J. B., and Patterson, G. R. 1974. Naturalistic observation in clinical assessment. In P. McReynolds (ed.), Advances in Psychological Assessment. Vol. 3. Jossey-Bass, San Francisco.

Kara, A. 1975. The operant conditioning model in relation to response class phenomena. Unpublished dissertation, University of Tennessee, Knoxville.

Kazdin, A. E. 1973. The effect of vicarious reinforcement on attentive behavior in the classroom. J. Appl. Behav. Anal. 6:71–78.

Lobitz, G. K., and Johnson, S. M. 1974. Normal versus deviant children: A multi-method comparison. Paper presented at the Sixth Annual Banff International Conference on Behavior Modification.

Madsen, C., Becker, W., and Thomas, D. 1968. Rules, praise and ignoring: Elements of elementary classroom control. J. Appl. Behav. Anal. 1:139–150.

Moore, D. R. 1975. Determinants of deviancy: A behavioral comparison of normal and deviant children in multiple settings. Unpublished doctoral dissertation, University of Tennessee, Knoxville.

Morgan, B. J. T., Simpson, M. J. A., Hanby, J. p., and Hall-Craggs, J. 1976. Visualizing interaction and sequential data in animal behavior: Theory and application of cluster analysis methods. Behavior 56:1–43.

O'Leary, K. D., and Kent, R. 1973. Behavior and modification for social action: Research tactics and problems. In L. A. Hamerlynck, L. C. Handy, and E. J. Mash (eds.), Behavior Change: Methodology, Concepts and Practice. pp. 69–96. Research Press, Champaign, Ill.

Patterson, G. R., and Reid, J. B. 1970. Reciprocity and coercion: Two facets of social systems. In C. Neuringer and J. L. Michael (eds.), Behavior Modification in Clinical Psychology, pp. 133–177. Appleton-Century-Crofts, New York.

Risley, T. R. 1968. The effects and side effects of punishing the autistic behaviors of a deviant child. J. Appl. Behav. Anal. 1:21–34.

Sajwaj, T., Twardosz, S., and Burke, M. 1972. Side effects of extinction procedures in a remedial preschool. J. Appl. Behav. Anal. 5:163–175.

Sherman, T., and Cormier, W. H. 1974. An investigation of the influence of student behavior on teacher behavior. J. Appl. Behav. Anal. 7:11–21.

Solomon, R. W., and Wahler, R. G. 1973. Peer reinforcement control of classroom problem behavior. J. Appl. Behav. Anal. 6:49–56.

Wahler, R. G. 1969. Oppositional children: A quest for parental reinforcement control. J. Appl. Behav. Anal. 2:159–170.

Wahler, R. G. 1975. Some structural aspects of deviant child behavior. J. appl. Behav. anal. 8:27–42.

Wahler, R. G. 1976. Generalization Processes in Child Behavior Change. National Institute of Mental Health Grant Proposal.

Wahler, R. G., Berland, R. M., and Leske, G. 1975. Environmental boundaries in behavior modification: Problems in residential treatment of children. Unpublished manuscript, Child Behavior Institute.

Wahler, R. G., and Coe, T. D. 1975. A crisis episode in behavior modification: What not to do in implementing a community program. Paper presented at the Association for the Advancement of Behavior Therapy convention, December, 1975. San Francisco.

Wahler, R. G., House, A. E., and Stambaugh, E. E. 1976. II. Ecological Assessment of Child Problem Behavior: A Clinical Package for Home, School and Institutional Settings. Pergamon Press, New York.

Wahler, R. G., Leske, G., and Berland, R. M. 1977. Phenomenological reports: An empirical model. In B. C. Etzel, J. M. LeBlanc, and D. M. Baer (eds.), New Developments in Behavioral Research: Theory, Method and Application. In Honor of Sidney W. Bijou. Lawrence Erlbaum Associates, Hillsdale, N.J.

Wahler, R. G., and Moore, D. R. 1975. School-home behavior change procedures in a "high-risk community." Paper presented at the Association for the Advancement of Behavior Therapy convention, December, 1975, San Francisco.

Wahler, R. G., and Nordquist, V. M. 1973. Adult discipline as a factor in childhood imitation. J. Abnorm. Child Psych. 1:40–56.

Wahler, R. G., Sperling, K., Thomas, M., Teeter, N., and Luper, H. 1970. The modification of childhood stuttering: Some response-response relationships. J. Exp. Child Psych. 9:411–423.

COMMENT

Ecobehavioral Perspectives: What Helps Depends on Where You're Standing

Emily Herbert-Jackson

The chapters by Warren, Rogers-Warren, and Wahler et al. illustrate the authors' concern and sincere commitments to the continued success of behavioral interventions. Each chapter presents suggestions for consideration by researchers and practitioners as the field of applied behavior analysis moves in the direction of assuming responsibility for solving social problems. The thesis of the comments that follow here is that the usefulness of the particular suggestions made in each chapter will depend significantly on the particular problems addressed by researchers and practitioners. A single perspective will not be appropriate for meeting all needs.

The ecobehavioral perspective advocated by Warren focuses on dimensions of the response: its rate, generalization, durability, and diversity. His suggestions for improving the success of interventions are for the most part limited to steps that may be pursued *after* treatments have been applied. The reaction of the environment to a change is considered carefully. Notable exceptions to this post hoc approach are his suggestions to use normative data to characterize response rates and consumer input in making decisions on response rate criteria. Each of these considerations would best be pursued before treatments are applied.

Following Willems' call, Warren urges applied behavioral analysts to take more measures: measuring for generalization across settings, measuring over time for durability, measuring more behaviors, and measuring consumer satisfaction to detect undesirable side effects. These suggestions are not new (see Baer, Wolf, and Risley, 1968). In fact, they reinforce an existing perspective which may compete with attending to and solving problems that go beyond applications to isolated instances.

Implicit in Warren's recommendations is the assumption that the *problems* with which applied behavior analysts work are isolated behaviors of individuals, often defined as skill deficits, that require training programs or at least rearrangement of contingencies in the narrow sense of the immediate reinforcers. The most common intervention strategy used in this model is to remediate the individual's deficit and hope for main-tenance by a benevolent environment. This perspective has been useful because a substantial portion of applied behavioral research has been conducted in classrooms or institutions (Kazdin, 1975) where behavior analysts have had *limited* responsibility for implementing and maintaining programs but *major* responsibility for treating the special problems of deviant individuals. First, deviant individuals, then their caregivers, were our accessible routes for impacting on social problems. But even within this model, viewing most problems as skill deficits (e.g., "He couldn't do it if his life depended on it") or deficiencies of immediate reinforcers ("It doesn't pay to do it right") is misleading (Mager and Pipe, 1970). Unless the behavioral context is carefully examined *before* intervention, a correct diagnosis of the problem may be missed. Other problems of deviant individuals include: 1) deficient feedback, e.g., "Nobody ever tells me if I do it right or wrong, and I can't tell," 2) attitudes of "It pays to do it wrong," suggesting that the existing consequences need attention, 3) lack of additional prompts in situations where incompatible responses are automatic as in "Whenever this comes up, oops I've done it again," 4) or complaints of "too many interferences," suggesting the need for organiza-tion and management solutions. The strategies proposed by Warren can be expected to improve successes in applied behavior analysis only to the extent that the problem already has been identified correctly and fits into the reeducation model discussed by Wahler. Then what is proposed is basically to take more measures after intervening in order to strengthen the generalizability or external validity (Campbell and Stanley, 1963) of treatments. This may assure more careful application of existing behavioral technology to similar problems, but the model seems incomplete when designing comprehensive programs just because the problems are rarely so circumscribed.

Ann Rogers-Warren's proposals go beyond Warren's by suggesting that success may depend on a more thorough assessment of settings *prior* to interventions. A particular advantage of such assessments is that they may indicate modifications in nonsocial variables, such as organization of activities or physical design, thereby reducing or eliminating the need to manipulate social antecedents or consequences of the response. In order to consider these often overlooked behavioral influences, Rogers-Warren proposed a strategy: identifying target behaviors, evaluating the physical setting, evaluating the contingency environment, and determining setting-imposed limits and facilitations for desired behaviors.

There is certainly value in enumerating these steps for behavior analysts who may not always follow them systematically. And it should be noted that this type of assessment is directed at clarifying the *problem.* Unfortunately, the first step proposed, identifying target behaviors, tends to focus attention on just one set of dependent measures. Of course a change in target behaviors is one criterion for assessing the success of an intervention, but the *critical problem* may well be events remote from those behaviors. For example, while praise may improve a child's sharing with others, insufficient time in the daily class schedule may be devoted to activities where sharing might be promoted. The steps proposed by Rogers-Warren very directly respond to Willem's call for analyzing behavioral contexts, and the intervention strategies that she suggests, e.g., taking advantage of naturally occurring reinforcers, are consistent with an ecological perspective.

Wahler and his colleagues suggest and model quite a different approach which goes beyond a dyadic reeducation model, e.g., parent-child, teacher-pupil, and beyond the operant model of a few responses and their immediate antecedents and consequences. The social systems strategy is primarily an assessment approach focusing on behavioral covariations across levels of analysis. Rather than assessing the behavioral context directly, as proposed by Rogers-Warren, Wahler proposes broadening the scope of analysis to all levels of behavioral covariations: within individuals—across settings and over time, between individuals, and among systems of individuals in the community. On the other hand, Warren's suggestions deal with just the within-individual level of analysis. Wahler goes across behavioral levels but focuses his assessments on social systems rather than the whole of behavioral contexts. By measuring behavioral covariations, he is, of course, picking up the effects of both social and nonsocial variables, but this strategy deemphasizes the nonsocial behavioral setting.

It is important to recognize that the social systems approach developed from this group's experience at attempting to solve problems. Their perspective was a product of finding limited durability or across-setting generalization of treatment outcomes for noninstitutionalized deviant children and their families. The ability to identify deviant and nondeviant individuals and families on the basis of behavioral covariations suggests that the social systems perspective has much potential for leading to successful interventions at the level of the community.

Each of these chapters provides a perspective and recommended procedures to achieve greater success in applied behavioral analysis. As Baer reminds us (Chapter 5 of this volume), the criterion of success will be solutions to problems, whether one takes a "fix-it" or "understand-it" approach to behavior analysis. The usefulness of the proposed recommendations depends very much on the kinds of problems addressed. As the problems addressed go beyond classrooms or institutions where behavior analysts may directly intervene to change immediate antecedents and consequences for an individual, or beyond opportunities to directly influence caregivers, or, as in Wahler's examples, to opportunities to directly influence programs that may influence caregivers and thereby clients, the perspectives needed surely will change.

LITERATURE CITED

Baer, D. M., Wolf, M. M., and Risley, T. R. 1968. Some current dimensions of applied behavior analysis. J. Appl. Behav. Anal. 1:91–97.
Campbell, D. T., and Stanley, J. C. 1963. Experimental and Quasi-experimental Designs for Research. Rand McNally, Chicago.
Kazdin, A. E. 1975. The impact of applied behavior analysis on diverse areas of research. J. Appl. Behav. Anal. 8:213–229.
Mager, R. E., and Pipe, P. 1970. Analyzing Performance Problems or 'You really oughta wanna.' Lear Siegler/Fearen, Belmont, Cal.

OVERVIEW

On Weddings

David Krantz

During many wedding ceremonies, the question is raised, "If any among you can show just cause why this couple may not lawfully be joined, let him now speak or else hereafter forever hold his peace." I recognize that it is not good social form to answer this challenge, but I am afraid that I have some concerns about the proposed wedding between ecological psychology and applied behavior analysis. At times, I wonder whether we are witnessing a marriage, with a sharing between two partners, or an agreed upon rape with applied behavior analysis in the dominating role.

Implicitly, the proposed joining has less the quality of sharing than the form of applied behavior analyst incorporating aspects of the ecological perspective. Before any wedding plans are made, it is important to examine carefully one assumption which is at the core of the proposed wedding. The assumption is: Whatever the differences between the ecologist's and the applied behavior analyst's use of the term "environment," these differences are less important than the points of shared meaning.

This is not a new assumption in the history of psychology. Our field has always been plagued by a multiplicity of languages and theoretical systems. Most often, psychologists have disregarded this "Tower of Babel," unconcernedly pursuing their own perspectives. Occasionally, there are attempts to put some order into this disarray (see Henle, 1957). One dominant strategy has been to argue that beneath the terminological differences between theoretical languages, there really is the same reality being referred to in different ways. Whatever differences exist between the terms, they are not of major significance. Therefore, two language forms can legitimately be reduced to one. This was the assumption behind such noteworthy examples of reduction as Dollard and Miller's (1950) and Whiting and Child's (1953) translation of psychoanalytic concepts into Hullian terms, or Campbell's (1963) translation of Gestalt-Lewinian concepts to Hullian terms.

I believe that this same assumption is involved in wedding ecological and applied behavior analysis perspectives, whereby the applied behavior analysis language and theoretical systems will express and incorporate the meanings associated with the ecologist's notion of "environment."

One major problem with such reduction can be illustrated from the operant conditioners' own literature. In the case of the operant term "conditioned reinforcement" and the Hullian term "secondary reinforcement," these apparently similar concepts seemingly could be reduced. Both terms similarly refer to the situation in which a previously neutral event acquires reinforcing properties. However, such an approach would by-pass more fundamental considerations. As Gollub (1970) points out, there are some essential differences between the two terms:

> ... attempts to prove the validity of one or the other of these formulations have been generally unconvincing. Experiments have established an empirical edifice for each account which, although not fully explaining all the data presented by the other formulation, is too well constructed to permit empirical disproof. A fair assessment of the status quo acknowledges two different, although sometimes overlapping, procedures for establishing conditioned reinforcement.
>
> Proponents of an experimental analysis of behavior usually avoid such questions as "why does a reinforcer reinforce?" Instead they discover and identify reinforcements by their effects ... the compulsion to explain reinforcement in terms of some ultimate biological cause, whether conditioned or unconditioned, is not a cross for the experimental analyst to bear.

What is underlined by this illustration is that the meaning of a theoretical term cannot be disentangled readily from the context of its theoretical system. To say that "conditioned reinforcement" and "secondary reinforcement" refer to the same reality is to view the terms superficially and unfairly out of their defining theoretical contexts, and these contexts are fundamentally different. Similar concerns have been raised about the reduction of Gestalt-Lewinian terms to Hullian concepts (Henle, 1965).

It may be that a similar isolation of terms is happening in the present discussion. The ecological perspective and its notion of "environment" has its roots and theoretical structure based in the Gestalt tradition and in the work of Lewin and Brunswik. Applied behavior analysis, on the other hand, has its bases in the radical behaviorisms of Watson and Skinner. These two different perspectives on psychology have traditionally been in antagonism, although they have tended to deal with different domains of psychology—perception for the Gestalt tradition, learning for the behavioristic tradition. I wonder how the historical ancestry and the differences between each system's assumptive underpinnings could have so miraculously disappeared in the present discussion.

Or take another divergence between ecological and applied behavior analysis strategies. Barker (1965) makes a strong case that ecological psychology must use transducer designs. These designs (as opposed to operator approaches) place the experimenter in a nonstructuring, observing role in the setting being studied. The environment, therefore, is to be described, not manipulated. The environment's units are to be found, not stipulated. The operator methodology, in contrast, is an intrusive one in which settings are changed in line with the experimenter's requirements and expectations. While applied behavior analysts are concerned with behavior in naturalistic settings, they still maintain more of an operator than transducer attitude. They tend to take real-life settings and, through manipulation, create modified environments. This divergence in methodology can lead, as Barker argues, to a lack of applicability and translatability between operator and transducer findings. This issue of methodology is very reminiscent of operant conditioners' concern about the applicability of traditional between-groups research findings to the outcomes of their preferred within-groups studies (Sidman, 1960).

Such issues need not remain in the realm of philosophical analysis. Science provides a method, called the "defining experiment," to determine whether the terms refer to the same thing or to different concepts. In such experiments, a situation is sought which would allow each concept to predict differentially. If no such situation can be found, then the two terms are most likely referring to the same thing. If an appropriate situation is found, then the adequacy of each concept can be determined by its fit with the data. (However, even such defining experiments can be theory-loaded. See Krantz (1969) for an historical case.) One interesting example of this approach is the "distance effect" predictions from the Gestalt as compared to the Hullian tradition (see Hebert and Krantz, 1965) in which different theoretical views were pitted against each other. But such illustrations are few and far between. While such cases may be instructive, they also may represent relatively uninteresting and unimportant arenas of comparison between two theoretical systems that may be virtually nonoverlapping. Also, the two systems may not be sufficiently defined to produce such sharp, one-tailed predictions. I wonder what is the degree of overlap between the applied behavior analyst's and the ecologist's concept of "environment". Would it be the case, if defining situations were established, that no setting can be found that allows for differential prediction? This is the expectation that implied reduction of applied behavior analysis would suggest, but then how would such an outcome be interpreted–same meaning to the ecologist's and the applied behavior analyst's "environment" or nonoverlapping systems?

A premature or superficial joining or reduction of the term "environment" could lead to a weakness of both theoretical perspectives. Such a strategy would diffuse the potential confrontation of systems, which, in their disharmony, could force a clarification and an extension of each. Often, controversy is acromonious and nonproductive (Krantz, 1969), but there are cases (Boring, 1929; Henle, 1973) when such dialogues do illuminate and extend. The putting together of the present systems might provide the applied behavior analysis approach with greater breadth and a larger range of techniques. But such values must be weighed against the disvalues of avoiding potentially important and real issues. The emerging sense of harmony and comfort between the present two perspectives thus may be illusory and ill-timed.

I feel a certain degree of discomfort with my preceding arguments, largely because they may be only partially relevant. The issue of the relation of systems or their relative incommensurability, to use Kuhn's (1962) term, may be more important to the pure scientist than to the technologist. A technologist is primarily concerned with solving immediate problems. He rightfully draws on any method, concept, or tool to accomplish this purpose without concern as to its origins or theoretical underpinnings. The applied behavior analyst projects the image of being a technologist with his concerns about "does it work."

Yet, I am not totally convinced that the applied behavior analyst is desirous or would be totally satisfied with the role of tinkerer/problem-solving technologist. For all the previous discussion of the pragmatics of changing particular target behaviors, there also have been the concerns with generalizability across settings and durability of responses. Such concerns smack more of scientific than technological aspirations. What needs to be clarified is what role the applied behavior analyst wants to assume. The issues of systems relationship obviously become more real if the scientist's role is dominant.

However, even if the technologist role is what is involved, the incommensurability questions are still relevant. The seemingly simple criterion of "does it work" is itself theory loaded. For example, how does one choose and define behavior that will indicate whether the manipulation worked or not? In the present discussion, the applied behavior analyst's use of an operator methodology may lead to a greater dissociation of the target response from other ongoing behaviors and their interactions than would happen had the more transducer-oriented ecologist been consulted in the decision.

I do not want to be perceived as a philosopher-pessimist. I prefer the image of an issue clarifier. Perhaps the proposed wedding between ecological and applied behavior analysis views of the environment can and should occur. But there are too many open, unexamined questions and assumptions in the present discussion for me to feel comfortable in giving my blessings. There is one gift, however, I can extend to the prospective couple—a piece of advice. Beware of the subtle ways that assumptions and theoretical perspectives can intrude and create disharmony among the concepts, methods, and techniques used. It is all too easy to assume that our theoretical system is the right one, because we not only think within it but also never make explicit our own assumptions or those of other systems. Baer's *tour de force* (Chapter 5 of this volume), as a case in point, never makes explicit his assumptive underpinnings in applied behavior analysis. It is these sets of assumptions that allow his diagram to look as it does. A similar diagram, developed from an ecological perspective, probably would look very different.

By way of concluding, I feel that the proposed wedding of ecological psychology and applied behavior analysis could benefit from some premarital counseling to determine if the partners are compatible and if there is any real benefit to their union. Marriage is a holy and sacred institution that should not be entered into lightly.

LITERATURE CITED

Barker, R. G. 1965. Explorations in ecological psychology. Amer. Psychologist 20:1–14.

Boring, E. G. 1929. The psychology of controversy. Psych. Rev. 36:97–121.

Campbell, D. T. 1963. Social attitudes and other acquired behavioral dispositions. *In* S. Kuch (ed.), Psychology, a Study of a Science. Vol. 6. McGraw-Hill, New York.

Dollard, J. and Miller, N. 1950. Personality and Psychotherapy. McGraw-Hill, New York.

Gollub, L. R. 1970. Information on conditioned reinforcement: A review of Hendry's conditioned reinforcement. J. Exp. Anal. of Behav. 14:361–372.

Hebert, J., and Krantz, D. L. 1965. Transposition: A re-evaluation. Psych. Bull. 63:244–257.

Henle, M. 1957. Some problems of eclecticism. Psych. Rev. 64:296–305.

Henle, M. 1965. On gestalt psychology. *In* B. Wolman (ed.), Scientific psychology. Basic Books, New York.

Henle, M. 1973. On controvery and its reolution. *In* M. Henle, J. Jaynes, and J. Sullivan (eds.), Historical Conceptions of Psychology. Springer, New York.

Krantz, D. L. 1969. The Baldwin-Tichner controversy. *In* D. Krantz (ed.), Schools of Psychology. Appleton-Century-Crofts, New York.

Kuhn, T. 1962. The Structure of Scientific Revolutions. University of Chicago Press, Chicago.

Sidman, M. 1960. Tactics of Scientific Research. Basic Books, New York.

Whiting, J., and Child, I. 1953. Child Training and Personality. Yale University Press, New Haven.

Index

Noncompliance, 4
Nonexperimental techniques, 73
Noninteraction (SOC), 223
Nonlaboratory setting, 198
Nonmanipulative examination, 69
Nonmetaphorical organisms, 102
Nonphenomenal attempt, 116
Nonreligious settings, 145
Nonsocial toy play, 219
Nonspeech deviant behaviors, 18
Normative data, 180
Nuclear weapons, 127
Number of persons observed, 53
Nursery schools, 134, 144

Object play (SOC), 223
Objectivity, 20, 116
Observational methodology, 161
Occupancy time, 143
On-task behavior, 204
One-time contacts, 135
Open architecture schools, 144
Open assessment, 189
Open environment design, in infant
    day care, 152
Open-field tests, 54
Open programs, 144
Operant conditioning, 7, 16, 86
Operator methodology, 235
Opposition (SOC), 223
Oppositional behavior, 85
Oppositional children, 79, 219
Optimizing intervention strategies,
    207
Ora and Reisinger Regional
    Intervention Program, 128
Oral reading rate in hard-of-hearing
    children, 177
Ordered sequences, of actions, 138
Oregon Research Institute, 218
Organ systems, 47
Organism-behavior-environment
    systems, 10
Organization
    social, 68
    in terms of levels, 45
Organizational-behavioral systems,
    14

Organizational variables, 152
Orthogonal set, 191
Overpopulation, 104

Paired-associate memorization, 104
Pandemic condition, 127
Paradigm, 116
Paranoid schizophrenics, delusional
    speech, 186
Paraprofessionals, 88, 151
Parent-child interactions, 213
Passive aggression, 115
Paternalism, 128
Path analysis, 169
Patient behavior displays, 46
Pattern learning, 53
Pediatric ward activity program,
    151
Peer-administered reinforcement,
    205
Peer-established rules, 157
Peer interactions, 84
Peers, 7
Penicillin, 35
Person, and environments, 133
Person-centered analysis, 4
Person-environment systems, 167
Personality traits, 66
Pharmaceutics, 16
Phenomenal analysis, 119
Phenylketonuria, 78
Physical aggression, 4
Physical impacts, 138
Physical milieu, 66
Physical variables, 204
Piggybacking, 23
Placebo outcomes, 63
Planned change, 197
Plant ecology, 65
Play, effect of toy storage, 156
Pluralism, 73
Polarity, 117
Positive behavior correlation, 4
Positive-negative polarity, 117
Posterior fontanel, 48
Post-hospital adjustment, 55
Post-treatment follow-up checks,
    184